The Anglo-Saxons
Synthesis and Achievement

The Anglo-Saxons

Synthesis and Achievement

Edited by
J. Douglas Woods and David A.E. Pelteret

Wilfrid Laurier University Press

Canadian Cataloguing in Publication Data

Main entry under title:

The Anglo-Saxons : synthesis and achievement

Includes bibliographical references.
ISBN 0-88920-166-8

1. Civilization, Anglo-Saxon − Addresses, essays, lectures. 2. England − Civilization − To 1066 − Addresses, essays, lectures. I. Woods, J. Douglas (Jon Douglas), 1942-   II. Pelteret, David Anthony Edgell, 1944-

DA152.2.A53 1985   942.01   C85-098569-2

Copyright © 1985

WILFRID LAURIER UNIVERSITY PRESS
Waterloo, Ontario, Canada   N2L 3C5

85 86 87 88 4 3 2 1

Cover design by David Antscherl

The cover illustration is reproduced from the *Book of Durrow*, fol. 192v, by courtesy of The Board of Trinity College, Dublin. (See chaps. 6 and 8.)

No part of this book may be stored in a retrieval system, translated or reproduced in any form, by print, photoprint, microfilm, microfiche, or any other means, without written permission from the publisher.

Printed in Canada

This book is dedicated to
the memory of
Angus Cameron
and
Colin Chase
"boccræftige weras"

Contents

Preface ix

Abbreviations xi

    Introduction
       David A. E. Pelteret 1

1 The Bayeux Tapestry: History or Propaganda?
       Shirley A. Brown 11

2 The Boundaries of Old English Literature
       Angus Cameron 27

3 *Beowulf*, Bede, and St. Oswine: The Hero's Pride in Old English Hagiography
       Colin Chase 37

4 Domestic Peace and Public Order in Anglo-Saxon Law
       Rebecca V. Colman 49

5 Two Early Anglo-Saxon Holy Men: Oswald and Cuthbert
       John Corbett 63

6 The Celtic Church in Anglo-Saxon Times
       Claude Evans 77

7 Anglo-Saxon Use of the Apocryphal Gospel
       Antonette di Paolo Healey 93

8	The Image of the Worm: Some Literary Implications of Serpentine Decoration *Andrew J. G. Patenall*	105
9	Slavery in Anglo-Saxon England *David A. E. Pelteret*	117
10	Germanic Warrior Terms in Old Saxon *J. Douglas Woods*	135
	Bibliographical Essay *David A. E. Pelteret*	151
Index		171

Preface

The papers in this volume were originally delivered as lectures at a colloquium entitled The Anglo-Saxons and Their Neighbours held at Scarborough College in the University of Toronto in January and February of 1979. All the lectures have subsequently been revised for publication. Present at the colloquium were specialists in the period, other students and faculty of the University, and interested members of the non-university community. The editors hope that this volume will attract a similarly diverse audience. To assist those who have no special knowledge about the Anglo-Saxons, but who would like to be better informed about the topics covered in this book, a brief Bibliographical Essay has been provided.

The editors would like to thank Scarborough College, which sponsored the colloquium, and Professor Michael Gervers, who not merely initiated and organized the gathering, but also encouraged the contributors to turn their verbal presentations into written form. Thanks should also go to Mr. Paul Ellison and Ms. Migs Reynolds of the University of Exeter Computer Unit, to Mr. Bob Blackburn and Ms. Shirly Manimalethu of the University of Toronto Computer Service, and to Mrs. Elaine Nascimento and Mrs. Clara DeAbreu of New College, University of Toronto, for considerable help with the word processing of this text.

This book has been published with the help of a grant from the Canadian Federation for the Humanities, using funds provided by the Social Sciences and Humanities Research Council of Canada.

J. Douglas Woods
David A. E. Pelteret

Abbreviations

AASS	Joannes Bollandus and Godefridus Henscherius (eds.). *Acta Sanctorum....* New ed. Ed. by Joannes Carnandet. 69 vols. Paris, Brussels, and Rome, 1863.
ASE	*Anglo-Saxon England.*
ASPR	Anglo-Saxon Poetic Records.
BAR	British Archaeological Reports.
Bede, *HE*	Bertram Colgrave and Roger A. B. Mynors (eds. and trans.). *Bede's Ecclesiastical History of the English People.* Oxford Medieval Texts. Oxford, 1969.
BL	British Library.
EETS, OS	Early English Text Society, Original Series.
EETS, SS	Early English Text Society, Supplementary Series
EHD I	Dorothy Whitelock (ed. and trans.). *English Historical Documents* ca. *550-1042.* English Historical Documents 1. 2nd ed. London and New York, 1979.
EHD II	David C. Douglas and George W. Greenaway (eds. and trans.). *English Historical Documents 1042-1189.* English Historical Documents 2. 2nd ed. London and New York, 1981.
EHR	*English Historical Review.*
Haddan and Stubbs, *Councils*	Arthur Haddan and William Stubbs (eds.). *Councils and Ecclesiastical Documents Relating to Great Britain and Ireland, Edited after Spelman and Wilkins.* 3 vols. Oxford, 1869-78.

Liebermann, *Gesetze*	Felix Liebermann (ed.). *Die Gesetze der Angelsachsen*. 3 vols. Halle, 1903-16.
MGH	Monumenta Germaniae historica.
PBA	*Proceedings of the British Academy*.
PRIA	*Proceedings of the Royal Irish Academy*.
PRSAI	*Proceedings of the Royal Society of Antiquaries of Ireland*.
Stenton, *ASE*	Frank M. Stenton. *Anglo-Saxon England*. Oxford History of England 2. 3rd ed. Oxford, 1971.
TOES	Toronto Old English Series.

Introduction

David A. E. Pelteret

Modern Western culture is deeply indebted to the Anglo-Saxons, for they preserved much learning from the Ancient world and helped disseminate it through Europe.[1] In the process, they developed a rich and complex culture. Yet many today perceive theirs as a barbarous age, a few "brief" centuries when "nothing happened." The scholarly world is in some measure at fault here. There has been a tendency to concentrate on the reign of King Alfred, a few poetic literary works such as *Beowulf*, and the dramatic metallurgical artistry of the Sutton Hoo treasure. We are all, of course, to some degree in thrall to the culture of our age, and it is natural to respond most sympathetically to aspects of another culture that are nearest to our own. Yet we devalue the past if we do not seek to break these cultural shackles by perceiving another era on its own terms. In the papers that follow, all the authors have attempted to do just this so as to deepen our understanding of the Anglo-Saxons and their accomplishments.

1 See Max L. W. Laistner, *Thought and Letters in Western Europe A.D. 500 to 900*, rev. ed. (London, 1957); Wilhelm Levison, *England and the Continent in the Eighth Century* (Oxford, 1946).

In the first paper in this collection, Shirley Brown examines the Bayeux Tapestry, a work of art that records the end of the Anglo-Saxon era. We have long been aware, particularly through the work of Marxist art critics, that works of art should not be taken at their face value; consciously or unconsciously, art frequently embodies an ideology.[2] The Bayeux Tapestry is ostensibly a valuable primary source of information on the events surrounding the momentous year 1066, though it is clear from the borders of the Tapestry with their Aesopian references that it has an ideational structure more complex than the simple depiction of historical events.[3] Professor Brown brings to the Tapestry both the eye of the art critic, notably in her observations on the spatial dimensions of the work, and of the historian, in her elucidation of the relationships between place and person (e.g., Harold and Bosham, Harold and Stigand). Her analysis prevents us from seeing the Tapestry as a neutral record of historical facts. Instead, we are forced to "read" it in a different way; the surface events portrayed retreat in importance in the face of a political case that is being argued. This perspective is frustrating for the historian of *événements*, yet I sense we are thereby moving closer to the intention of the artist(s) who produced this still enigmatic, but fascinating, work of art.

Students of literature have been drawn to the Anglo-Saxons because of their writings in the vernacular, unique both in scope and volume for their time in Western Europe. But as E. G. Stanley recently wrote of the Anglo-Saxons, "They did not design their writings to be read as literature; they lacked the concept *literature* and so they could not know that what they wrote might be read as literature by later ages, even when they themselves may have known that some of their writings were well written."[4] It is modern scholarship that has given birth to the "corpus of Old English literature." An examination of the scholarship, however, shows that a rather deformed and stunted body has been created.[5] What Angus Cameron essentially argues in his article is that we need to transform our aesthetic. Too long have we limited our studies to a few, mainly poetic, works, which we have then proceeded to assess in terms of contemporary canons of taste. Professor Cameron suggests that we need to give serious attention to such works

2 See, for example, John Berger, et al., *Ways of Seeing* (Harmondsworth, 1972).
3 Hélène Chefneux, "Les Fables dans la Tapisserie de Bayeux," *Romania* 60 (1934), 1-35, 153-94; Léon Herrmann, *Les Fables de la Broderie de Bayeux*, Collection Latomus 69 (Brussels, 1964).
4 Eric G. Stanley, "The Scholarly Recovery of the Significance of Anglo-Saxon Records in Prose and Verse: A New Bibliography," *ASE* 9 (1981), 235.
5 Stanley B. Greenfield and Fred C. Robinson, *A Bibliography of Publications on Old English Literature to the End of 1972*, using the collections of E. E. Ericson (Toronto and Buffalo, 1980) lists about 3675 books and articles that have been published on poetry as opposed to about 1412 on prose, as Stanley (loc. cit.) points out, even though poetry forms less than ten per cent of the extant body of written material.

as the laws and charters, which customarily have been considered to be outside the purview of the literary critic. When one reflects on his arguments, one recognizes that the willingness to view as literature what has hitherto been regarded as devoid of literary merit carries with it several concomitants. These include being prepared to discard, if necessary, certain aesthetic demands (e.g., the requirement for organic unity),[6] and more particularly, being willing to steep oneself in the writings deemed important to that age, such as patristic and apocryphal literature, saints' lives, and poetry written in the Hiberno-Latin tradition. The process implies re-education, for even classicists tend to be poorly read in these fields. Anglo-Saxon scholars have started to undertake this sometimes arduous task, and in the process have discovered that Anglo-Saxon writings can be richly allusive.[7]

Colin Chase's article exemplifies the advantages that are to be gained from enlarging our literary horizons. He has examined the *Vita Oswini*, a work that has been overlooked by literary critics and has been generally shunned by historians, dubious of the reliability of such a late compilation, and shown that it is a revealing primary document that discloses a major conflict in the values of the age in which it was written. His paper is illuminating as much in its implications as in its main thesis.[8] It impresses on one that saints' Lives form one of the most important genres of medieval literature, providing potential source material for scholars working in a number of disciplines.[9] Because a Life is late and betrays the fact that the author drew on little or no source material contemporary with his subject does not mean that it is devoid of interest—indeed it can take us to the centre of the intellectual and emotional conflicts of a period.

In order to develop the parallels that exist between the *Vita Oswini* and *Beowulf*, Professor Chase employs the insights gained by the French scholar, Georges Dumézil, from his extensive studies on the mythology and social structure of the peoples speaking the Indo-European languages. Though his work has been known for some time to Icelandic scholars working in the British academic tradition,[10]

6 The views of Arthur K. Moore, "Medieval English Literature and the Question of Unity," *Modern Philology* 65 (1967-68), 285-300, are interesting in this regard.
7 As illustrated in the writings of James E. Cross and Milton McC. Gatch on homiletic literature. See, for example, James E. Cross, "The Literate Anglo-Saxon—on Sources and Disseminations," *PBA* 58 (1972), 67-100 and separately, and Milton. McC. Gatch, *Preaching and Theology in Anglo-Saxon England: Ælfric and Wulfstan* (Toronto and Buffalo, 1977). The latter work has an extensive bibliography.
8 The usefulness of his approach for the dating of Beowulf, for instance, is shown in his paper, "Saints' Lives, Royal Lives, and the Dating of *Beowulf*," in Colin Chase (ed.), *The Dating of Beowulf*, TOES 6 (Toronto and Buffalo, 1981), 161-71.
9 For references, see the Bibliographical Essay below, p. 155.
10 Gabriel Turville-Petre reviewed a number of Dumézil's works in an article in *Saga-Book* 14 (1953-57), 131-34, and in 1964 made several favourable references to his

Dumézil's writings have only started to become widely known in the English-speaking world through the translations of some of his major studies in the last decade.[11] His conclusions are controversial, and a number of mythographers and cultural anthropologists do not find his views acceptable.[12] Whatever the final scholarly judgment on Dumézil's *œuvre*, his findings can nonetheless be provocative of ideas if applied to Anglo-Saxon society as Professor Chase has done.

Since the publication of Felix Liebermann's monumental *Gesetze der Angelsachsen*, completed over sixty-five years ago,[13] much of the work on Anglo-Saxon law has been devoted to the attribution of codes to an author, examining the relationships between secular and ecclesiastical legislation, and providing accurate translations and new editions.[14] Apart from Goebel's *Felony and Misdemeanor*,[15] it is only in the last two decades that a few scholars have returned to the legal sources with the intention of understanding Anglo-Saxon law as a dynamic force within the society.[16] Rebecca Colman ably illustrates the social impact of law in her study of *hamsocn*. In addition to using the well-tried nineteenth-century comparative method, whereby laws from other Germanic tribes are used as a means of mutual illumination, she also enlarges our understanding of *hamsocn* by employing an anthropological perspective. Through examining the physical realities of

writings in what is now the standard work in English on Norse religion, his *Myth and Religion of the North: The Religion of Ancient Scandinavia* (London).

11 Georges Dumézil, *Archaic Roman Religion*, trans. by Philip Krapp, 2 vols. (Chicago, 1970); *The Destiny of the Warrior*, trans. by Alf Hiltebeitel (Chicago, 1970); *The Destiny of a King*, trans. by Alf Hiltebeitel (Chicago, 1973); *From Myth to Fiction: The Saga of Hadingus*, trans. by Derek Coltman (Chicago, 1973); *Gods of the Ancient Northmen*, ed. by Einar Haugen, Publications of the UCLA Center for the Study of Comparative Folklore and Mythology 3 (Berkeley, 1973); *Camillus: A Study of Indo-European Religion as Roman History*, ed. by Udo Strutynski and trans. by Annette Aronowicz, et al. (Berkeley, 1980).

12 See, for example, Geoffrey S. Kirk, *Myth: Its Meaning and Functions in Ancient and Other Cultures*, Sather Classical Lectures 40 (Berkeley, 1970), 210. His work has been more positively appraised by Covington S. Littleton in *The New Comparative Mythology: An Anthropological Assessment of the Theories of Georges Dumézil*, 3rd ed. (Berkeley, 1980). Littleton drew the attention of English-speaking scholars to Dumézil's work in his first edition in 1966. See also Gerald J. Larson (ed.), *Myth in Indo-European Antiquity*, Publications of the UCSB Institute of Religious Studies (Berkeley, 1974).

13 Liebermann, *Gesetze*.

14 For references, see the Bibliographical Essay below, pp. 155-57.

15 Julius Goebel, *Felony and Misdemeanor: A Study in the History of English Criminal Procedure*, Vol. 1 (New York, 1937; rptd. with an introduction by Edward Peters, Philadelphia, 1976).

16 See, for example, Eric John, *Land Tenure in Early England: A Discussion of Some Problems* and *Orbis Britanniae and Other Studies*, Studies in Early English History 1 and 4 (Leicester, 1960 and 1966); Michael M. Sheehan, *The Will in Medieval England*, Pontifical Institute of Mediaeval Studies, Studies and Texts 6 (Toronto, 1963); Thomas M. Charles-Edwards, "Kinship, Status and the Origins of the Hide," *Past and Present*, No. 56 (1972), 3-33.

early English settlement, Professor Colman helps us to understand how one form of anti-social behaviour, that of felonious entry into a homestead causing terror to its occupants, could flourish in that early period. We thus are able to understand how, through coping with that form of anti-social behaviour, rudimentary law takes shape. Anglo-Saxon law is thereby seen to have a vitality that we might not initially perceive when our eyes first run down the succession of numbered clauses in the printed editions of the codes.

The impact that such rudimentary law had on Anglo-Saxon society remains controversial. In contrast, there can be no doubt about the significance of the Christian Church in shaping the society. "The Christian Church" is, however, an umbrella term that demands further definition. As it stands the phrase implies an impersonal and monolithic institution. John Corbett shows that the Church certainly was not an impersonal institution and Claude Evans that it was not monolithic.

John Corbett stresses that Christianity was not a religion that arrived after the Anglo-Saxons did, but that it preceded these invaders and was firmly rooted in England in a form that was shaped by the social practices and values of the late Antique world. In the Christianity of this time, when the Western Roman Empire was at its nadir, the Holy Man was a central figure. By drawing on the insights of Peter Brown, Professor Corbett has moved, like Colin Chase, outside the field of Anglo-Saxon scholarship. Professor Peter Brown's sensitive analyses of the societies of late Antiquity have highlighted and defined the role of the Holy Man.[17] Professor Corbett suggests that there was a degree of continuity of Romano-British Christianity into the Anglo-Saxon period in the importance accorded certain Holy Men. Early Anglo-Saxon saints should thus not be seen as *sui generis* but as individuals who performed a social role and provoked a social response similar to the great Holy Men of Roman Gaul.

Claude Evans examines Christianity from an institutional perspective. She concentrates on Christianity as it was practised by the peoples who geographically surrounded the Anglo-Saxons: the Celts.[18] Their Christianity took a somewhat different institutional form from that which took root after the Roman mission to England under Augustine in A.D. 597. Because our primary source on the early history of these two forms of Christianity in England is Bede, a historian with compelling powers of synthesis who had a particular axe to grind, there is a natural tendency to disregard the importance to Anglo-Saxon culture of the Celtic Church. This Church tends to be generally regarded as distinguished by an unusual tonsure and an antiquated way of cal-

17 See the works cited by John Corbett below, p. 66, n. 8.
18 For background references on the Celts and the Celtic Church, see the Bibliographical Essay below, pp. 160-64.

culating Easter. As an institution, it is felt to have largely disintegrated with the Synod of Whitby, thereafter leaving little impact on England. Claude Evans's paper reminds us that this view is both simplistic and inaccurate. The Celtic Church was in some respects better suited to the non-urban country that England had become after the departure of the Romans. Moreover, it continued to flourish on the periphery of England for some centuries after Whitby. There is thus no reason to believe that its traditions and practices ceased to influence the Anglo-Saxon Church after the seventh century. Cornwall and Brittany were, after all, closer geographically than Rome, and the Celtic Church possessed a powerful ascetic and artistic tradition that for some reason seemed to strike a particular resonance with the Anglo-Saxons. Why these traditions should have appealed to the Anglo-Saxons is not altogether clear and deserves further consideration. In keeping with the subtitle of this book, Dr. Evans emphasizes in her paper that Anglo-Saxon culture was the synthesis of several traditions, not just Germanic and Mediterranean, but also Celtic.

Two other traditions are investigated (in quite different ways) by Antonette Healey and Andrew Patenall. Dr. Healey examines the place of apocryphal writings, drawn largely from Mediterranean and Near Eastern sources, in early English literature. Hers is a valuable contribution towards the monumental task of encompassing the literary horizons of the Anglo-Saxon world. Though most of these writings are unlikely to have been read by the average medievalist, they provided the impulse for much literature, art,[19] and scholarship in the Middle Ages. Until we become familiar with these works, we shall miss many of the allusions, and hence the complexity of thought, contained in the literature of the Anglo-Saxon period.[20] Dr. Healey's paper enlarges our understanding of the Anglo-Saxon Church and its doctrines by showing that some of these apocryphal writings had apparent canonical, or near-canonical, status. Her approach has interesting implications for our knowledge of how Christianity was perceived in Anglo-Saxon England, particularly when we remember that there are also canonical writings that were then unknown. Her paper shows, furthermore, that certain themes which were to undergo dramatic, literary, and iconographical development in the High Middle Ages, such as the Harrowing of Hell, were already well known in the Anglo-Saxon period.[21]

19 For instance, the ox and the ass in the Christmas manger scene so well known to everyone find no mention in the canonical gospels; they were imported into medieval iconography from the *Pseudo-Matthew*.
20 For example, Archbishop Wulfstan II of York made use of the work of the ninth-century monk Abbo of St. Germain-des-Prés, most of whose homiliary remains unpublished. See Gatch, *Preaching and Theology*, 109 and 238 n. 17. On Abbo, see Joseph R. Strayer (ed.), *Dictionary of the Middle Ages* (New York, 1982), I, 53, s.v. *Abbo (Adbo) of St. Germain-des-Prés*.
21 On the Harrowing of Hell, see Rosemary Woolf, *The English Mystery Plays* (London,

The Germanic traditions of the Anglo-Saxons are drawn upon by Andrew Patenall in his analysis of the literary implications of serpentine decoration. His paper illustrates a truth that medievalists are slowly rediscovering, after a long period when the study of human experience has been fractured into a number of "disciplines" with their own methodologies and intellectual traditions. He implicitly argues that in the realm of aesthetics, mankind has not compartmentalized perceptions into completely separate modes such as "Art" and "Literature."[22] These modes have always been in some measure interrelated. We intuitively concede a unity of aesthetic perception, for instance, when we apply the word "Baroque" to both architecture and music, or "Romantic" to both music and literature. In the Middle Ages, in particular, there was no clear division between the verbal and the visual. When a text was copied, art could be embodied in the very written form of the words, especially the illuminated initials, or be placed adjacent to them in margins or facing pages.[23] The compositional structure of a manuscript page could be reproduced in tapestry or fresco. This reproduction is best illustrated in works dating several centuries after the Anglo-Saxon period,[24] but the Bayeux Tapestry,[25] among other examples,[26] shows that this approach was not alien to the earlier Middle Ages. Professor Patenall adopts the aesthetic principles that have arisen from the study of Anglo-Saxon illumination and metalwork, and applies them to a poem hitherto deemed "diffuse," i.e.,

1972), Chapter 12, and the notes, which supply references to its iconographical developments.

22 See Frederick P. Pickering, *Literature and Art in the Middle Ages* (London, 1970). The relationship between Art and Literature in the Renaissance has long been studied.

23 A fine example from the Anglo-Saxon world is the Lindisfarne Gospels. See Thomas D. Kendrick, et al. (eds.), *Evangelia Quattuor Codex Lindisfarnensis*, 2 vols. (Olten-Lausanne, 1956-60); and Janet Backhouse, *The Lindisfarne Gospels* (Oxford, 1981).

24 On tapestries, see Gerardina T. van Ysselsteyn, *Tapestry: The Most Expensive Industry of the XVth and XVIth Centuries; A Renewed Research into Technic* [sic], *Origin and Iconography* (The Hague and Brussels, 1969); on murals, see Ernest W. Tristram, *English Wall Painting of the Fourteenth Century* (London, 1955), Plate 1. That the idea of linking art and writing in a medium other than parchment was familiar to the Anglo-Saxons is proved by the Frank's Casket (runes and pictorial representation on bone) and the Ruthwell Cross (runes and an iconographical programme on stone).

25 This is a combination of pictures and verbal descriptions. See Frank M. Stenton, et al., *The Bayeux Tapestry: A Comprehensive Survey*, 2nd ed. (London, 1965); Charles H. Gibbs-Smith, *The Bayeux Tapestry* (London, 1973); and Shirley A. Brown's essay in this volume.

26 A fresco originally thought to date from the thirteenth century has now been convincingly attributed to the Anglo-Saxon period through its stylistic resemblances to the Winchester School of manuscript illumination. See R. Gem and P. Tudor-Craig, "A 'Winchester School' Wall-Painting at Nether Wallop, Hampshire," *ASE* 9 (1981), 115-36.

rambling and poorly controlled. His examination of *The Phoenix* from this perspective shows that the poem has, on the contrary, a complex syntactic and imagistic structure. His critique indicates by implication that the inadequacies seen in the poem exist in the minds of critics who have given insufficient credit to the complexity of the Anglo-Saxon literary imagination.

That the social structure of the Anglo-Saxons was no less complex than their intellectual world can be seen in their wide range of social terminology.[27] The shifting use of some of this terminology proves that the structure of the society was far from static.[28] Unfortunately, we lack information in such highly relevant areas as demography, and as a consequence, our social analysis is impeded.[29] Furthermore, we often wish to ask questions of the society that the Anglo-Saxons did not ask of themselves. One such set of questions revolves around the existence of slavery in England. No free Anglo-Saxon thought the matter worthy of discussion, and no slave gave written expression to his views on his status. Nevertheless, there is a fairly substantial body of documentation on slaves and slavery. That the Anglo-Saxons did not find the matter interesting points to a major difference between them and us, who have frequently brought passion and ideology to bear in the examination of this institution.[30] David Pelteret's paper attempts to eschew ideology and instead seeks to use the extant evidence to answer several obvious and straightforward questions about Anglo-Saxon slavery. This study aims at contributing towards the still-incomplete descriptive analysis of all the social groups within Anglo-Saxon England.[31]

The final paper in this collection employs techniques that until the last few years would not have been practical to employ. The whole corpus of Old English has been placed in the computer and a concordance of the language has been generated and printed on microfiche.[32]

27 This is best exemplified by Domesday Book, which was compiled in 1086, but which frequently uses Anglo-Saxon terminology. For editions of and publications on this great survey, see the Bibliographical Essay below, pp. 167-69.
28 See, for example, Henry Loyn, "Gesiths and Thegns in Anglo-Saxon England from the Seventh to the Tenth Century," *EHR* 70 (1955), 529-49.
29 The standard work on English demography in the Middle Ages is Josiah C. Russell, *British Medieval Population* (Albuquerque, New Mex., 1948), but many scholars feel that at our current state of knowledge, demographic analysis for the Anglo-Saxon period falls into the realm of divination.
30 See Moses I. Finley, *Ancient Slavery and Modern Ideology* (New York, 1980).
31 Though most of the major groups from the period have now received comment from scholars (for references, see the Bibliographical Essay below, pp. 168-69), there are still many minor terms such as *discþegn*, *dreng*, and *butsecarl* that might provide fruitful information about the society. The role of some of the important classes, such as the *ceorlas*, could also profitably be subjected to a fresh examination.
32 Richard L. Venezky and Antonette di P. Healey, *A Microfiche Concordance to Old English*, Dictionary of Old English Project, University of Toronto, and University of Delaware (1980).

For the first time, it is possible to make linguistic statements based on hard numerical data rather than on impressionistic observations. This is the approach that Douglas Woods employs to analyze the use of Germanic warrior terms in Old Saxon. Since there is a lack of sufficient data from Old Saxon, he employs its British sister, Old English, for comparative purposes. Though his interests are primarily linguistic, his conclusions are of value to both the literary critic and the historian. If used with appropriate controls, as Professor Woods does, the lexico-statistical method could prove to be a technique of service to these three fields of academic study.

The papers in this volume thus explore the richness of the society and culture of Anglo-Saxon England. Possessed themselves of a fairly sophisticated native culture, the Anglo-Saxons could not ignore two radically different cultures with which they came in contact. Yet they did not succumb to them. Instead, over a period of some six centuries, they blended the traditions and practices of the Celtic and Mediterranean worlds with those drawn from their own Germanic roots. From this synthesis, a distinctive society was born whose achievements have helped shape the culture of the West.

1

The Bayeux Tapestry: History or Propaganda?

Shirley A. Brown

The so-called Bayeux Tapestry is actually an embroidery of wool on linen, measuring 231 feet long and nineteen and a half inches high.[1] The Tapestry first came to public attention around 1730 when drawings of its two fragments were published,[2] but it was its first

---

1 There are a number of complete illustrations of the Bayeux Tapestry, the most conveniently available being found in Frank Stenton, et al., *The Bayeux Tapestry: A Comprehensive Survey*, 2nd ed. (London, 1965); and in Simone Bertrand, *La Tapisserie de Bayeux et la manière de vivre au onzième siècle* (La Pierre-qui-Vire, 1966). The Tapestry was deposited in the former Bishop's Palace across from the Cathedral of Notre-Dame in Bayeux in 1913; it has recently been restored and placed in new quarters. For a physical history of the Tapestry, see Simone Bertrand, "The History of the Tapestry," in Stenton, *Bayeux Tapestry*, 88-97.
2 Antoine Lancelot, "Explication d'un monument de Guillaume le Conquérant," *Memoires de littérature tirés des régistres de l'Académie royale des Inscriptions et Belles-Lettres depuis l'année MDCCXVIII jusques et compris l'année MDCCXXV* 6 (1729), 739-55. Also, Bernard de Montfaucon, "Monument d'Harold," *Les monumens de la monarchie françoise* (Paris, 1729-33), Vol. 1, 371-79, and Vol. 2, 1-32. Also, Lancelot, "Suite de l'éxplication d'un monument de Guillaume le Conquérant," *Memoires de littérature tirés des régistres de l'Académie royale des Inscriptions et Belles-Lettres depuis l'année MDCCXXVI jusques et compris l'année MDCCXXX* 8 (1732), 602-68.

exhibition in the Louvre in 1803 which sparked widespread speculation about the Tapestry's use, dating, and interpretation.[3]

Not the least of the problems provided by the Tapestry is the understanding and interpretation of the narrative it presents, and the assessing of its value as a historical document. Because it tells a tale of the events leading up to, and culminating in, the Battle of Hastings of October 1066, an expedition which dramatically altered the course of history in both England and France, a prodigious amount of partisan scholarship has resulted. For many historians, the Bayeux Tapestry is an almost contemporary, and therefore reliable, source of historical information for the years between 1064 and 1066.[4] The weight of art historical evidence which points to an origin of the Tapestry in the latter part of the eleventh century[5] would seem to corroborate this view. As a result, the embroidery has been used to both prove and disprove speculations about actual occurrences and about the relationship between Harold Godwinson and William of Normandy. The tenacity with which historians have retained their reliance on the embroidery as a historical document persists to this day in spite of warnings that the Tapestry's account of events cannot be taken at face value as history.[6]

The detailed recording of events which produce such drastic political and dynastic changes is more commonly found in poetry and historical prose than in the visual arts of the Middle Ages, and the suggestion that the Bayeux Tapestry was meant primarily as a "historical document" must be investigated with care. The Norman Conquest is well documented for an event of the eleventh century, but its several

---

3 For a bibliography of the Tapestry, see Alphonse J. J. Marquet de Vasselot and Roger A. Weigert, *Bibliographie de la Tapisserie, des tapis et de la broderie en France* (Paris, 1935), 298-309; and Otto K. Werckmeister, "The Political Ideology of the Bayeux Tapestry," *Studi Medievali*, 3rd ser., 17 (2) (1976), 589-95. I have compiled a more complete and up-to-date bibliography, which should soon be available.

4 David C. Douglas and George W. Greenaway, *English Historical Documents 1042-1189*, EHD II, 1st ed. (New York, 1953), 217: "It provides, together with the Bayeux Tapestry..., the best contemporary description of the Battle of Hastings," and "The only strictly reliable evidence for the journey [of Harold] and the famous oath is contained in the narrative [of William of Poitiers] and in the Bayeux Tapestry." Also, Richard D. Wissolik, "The Saxon Statement: Code in the Bayeux Tapestry," *Annuale Mediaevale* 19 (1979), 69-97, a very interesting article which seeks to link the Bayeux Tapestry with Eadmer's *Historia Novorum in Anglia* as historical sources for 1064-66. For a cautionary response, see Nicholas P. Brooks and H. E. Walker, "The Authority and Interpretation of the Bayeux Tapestry," *Proceedings of the Battle Conference—1978* (Ipswich, 1979), 34.

5 Francis Wormald, "Style and Design," in Stenton, *Bayeux Tapestry*, 24-36; and Brooks and Walker, "Authority," 13-19.

6 Stenton, "The Historical Background," in Stenton, *Bayeux Tapestry*, 9; and Werckmeister, "Political Ideology," 589: "Thus, the Bayeux Tapestry appears not only questionable as a historical source in the way all contemporary sources lack objectivity, a point that has long been recognized. It appears as a piece of political ideology, made up to serve the interests of a person and his social group."

descriptions are often at variance with each other, and at first estimate, they seem far from satisfactory. As a rule, medieval works of history and biography must be understood as interpretations of events and people which reflect the purpose for which the literary work was intended. Often, the laudatory or critical motivations behind these "historical" accounts are apparent, and in some instances, they clearly overrule accuracy. To suggest that if an event described in one of the contemporary written accounts also appears in the Bayeux Tapestry, then it must have happened as so described, is risky business indeed. As we shall see, there are some very interesting idiosyncrasies in the Tapestry's narrative which lead me to suggest that historical accuracy was definitely not the main purpose of the Bayeux Tapestry.

The first half of the Tapestry presents a visual narrative of the events leading up to the Norman takeover of England. The Tapestry apparently relates how King Edward sent Harold Godwinson on a mission to Normandy, presumably to renew the pledge of the English crown to Duke William.[7] But we are also reminded of the possibility that Harold set out to secure the release of his two kinsmen who were being held as peace security in Normandy.[8] Harold, landing in Ponthieu by error or chance, was taken prisoner by Count Guy; he was quickly rescued on William's orders and taken to the ducal palace at Rouen. We then see Harold accompanying William on a successful expedition against Conan of Brittany, for which the Anglo-Saxon Earl receives arms and armour from the Norman Duke. Afterwards, they journey to Bayeux where Harold swears his famous oath to support William's claims to the English throne. Harold returns to England where King Edward soon dies and is buried in the newly-completed Westminster Abbey. The English thegns offer Harold the crown, and he is installed by Stigand, Archbishop of Canterbury.

At this point, almost half the Tapestry has been surveyed, and a somewhat confused series of events has been given a prominence far beyond its apparent deserts. The next section of the Tapestry shows in detail some of the elaborate preparations of the Norman fleet. The sea-passage to Pevensey is uneventful, and much following space is given to the establishment of a camp at Hastings. Finally, the last third of the Tapestry depicts the actual Battle of Hastings. Some specific events of the day are shown: William exhorts his knights to fight bravely but wisely; Leofwine and Gyrth Godwinson are killed; the Norman rout is turned back by Bishop Odo, William, and Eustace of Boulogne; the Norman rally results in Harold's death, and the English

---

7 This motive is not explicit in the written captions which accompany the illustrations. The reasons for the expedition are left obscure, perhaps because they were apparent to the viewer of the time. The interpretation given above follows the usual explanation of the Norman historians.
8 Wissolik, "Saxon Statement," 69-97.

flee. The Tapestry ends abruptly at that point, and we have no indication of how much longer it initially was.

At first, it seems odd that the Battle of Hastings is given such relatively cursory coverage in the Tapestry's narrative, and that the preliminary events merit such detailed telling. It has been suggested that the main purpose of the Tapestry's narrative was to uphold established Norman propaganda, which emphasized William's "lawful" claim to the English throne, based upon Edward's designation and Harold's oath.[9] Thus the first half of the Tapestry established both the legal and moral cause of the Invasion as more important than the fighting itself.[10] In both cases, the war is treated as a "just war," and its atrocities must be downplayed.

But the question still remains: was the Tapestry's goal merely to repeat what had already been established by the history-makers, or was its narrative meant to be more complex than that? Was the originator consciously referring to several different sources for his information, and were deliberate parallels being drawn with other art or literary forms?

With these considerations in mind, it seems reasonable to compare the Tapestry's version of events with the written accounts of the Norman Invasion which were in existence before, or contemporary with, the proposed production date of the embroidery, and thus possibly known by the person who undertook the commission for the Tapestry. For various reasons, I place the Tapestry's creation in the 1080's.[11] This eliminates Eadmer, Ordericus Vitalis, Robert Wace, and William of Malmesbury as direct sources for the Tapestry, although the last three have often been cited in studies of the work. However, these later versions of the Conquest story, which augment the existing eleventh-century accounts, raise the possibility of lost sources and an oral tradition to which the originator of the Tapestry's narrative might have had access.[12]

9 This interpretation, which differs somewhat from the "pure history" suggestion, rightly indicates the propagandistic aspects of many medieval historical writings, whose purpose it was to justify the expansionist tendencies of ambitious rulers such as the Normans.

10 The development of the "moral cause" viewpoint is undertaken by Charles R. Dodwell in "The Bayeux Tapestry and the French Secular Epic," *Burlington Magazine* 108 (1966), 549-60.

11 The date usually suggested by those who feel the Tapestry was meant as a cathedral decoration is before the consecration of Bayeux Cathedral in 1077. Werckmeister, "Political Ideology," 581-89, has suggested it was made between 1082 and 1087. My arguments for the later dating, arrived at independently, are based on the relationship between the Tapestry, Odo of Bayeux, and the *Carmen de Hastingae Proelio*, and will appear in a forthcoming publication.

12 This suggestion must be entertained at least for those places where existing sources are lacking, but must not be used as a necessary substitute for artistic invention. Later accounts of the events might well be using the Bayeux Tapestry's narrative as evidence and not be relying on either a lost source or "inside information."

Principal among the works which were written in the direct context of the Norman Invasion of England, and which still exist, are: the entries in the *Anglo-Saxon Chronicle*;[13] the *Vita Ædwardi Regis*, written in England in 1065-67 on the orders of Queen Edith;[14] the *Carmen de Hastingae Proelio*, a verse description of the Battle of Hastings, probably written in 1067;[15] and the accounts of William of Jumièges of ca. 1071,[16] and William of Poitiers, written between 1071 and 1077.[17]

It has been acknowledged by almost all writers on the Bayeux Tapestry that the narrative it constructs has many correspondences

13 *Anglo-Saxon Chronicle*, trans. by George N. Garmonsway, 2nd ed. (London, 1954).
14 *Vita Ædwardi Regis qui apud Westmonasterium requiescat*, ed. and trans. by Frank Barlow (London, 1962). The *Vita* now exists in one manuscript, BL MS Harley 526, of ca. 1100. It exhibits the hands of that time from Christ Church, Canterbury. Apparently there was a copy at Westminster by 1085, but it does not seem to have been the same manuscript. The extant copy may very well have come from the autograph. See *Vita Ædwardi*, lxxix-lxxxii.
15 *The Carmen de Hastingae Proelio of Guy, Bishop of Amiens*, ed. and trans. by Catherine Morton and Hope Muntz, Oxford Medieval Texts (Oxford, 1972). The *Carmen* is preserved in one manuscript, Bibliothèque Royale de Belgique no. 10615-729, written ca. 1100. It apparently was not copied from the autograph but from an intermediate version. Scholars speculate that the original may have been deposited in a monastery in Liège, or at Saint-Bertin in Saint-Omer, or even at Saint-Riquier. It could easily have been available at one of the teaching centres in northern France to which young clerics were sent for training. It is furthermore notable that Guy of Amiens accompanied Queen Mathilde to England in 1068 for her coronation, so that the poem may very well have been circulated among the royal entourage. See *Carmen*, lix-lxiii. More recently. Ralph H. C. Davis, in "The *Carmen de Hastingae Proelio*," *EHR* 93 (1978), 241-61, argues for a twelfth-century dating. See also Ralph H. C. Davis, L. J. Engels, et al., "The *Carmen de Hastingae Proelio*: A Discussion," *Proceedings of the Battle Conference on Anglo-Norman Studies II—1979* (Ipswich, 1980), 1-20.
16 William of Jumièges (= Gulielmus Gemeticensis), *Gesta Normannorum Ducum*, ed. by Jean Marx, Société de l'Histoire de Normandie (Rouen and Paris, 1914). For a translation of the pertinent section see EHD II, 228-30, No. 3. The story of the Norman Conquest of England is a small part of the history of the Norman Dukes. This tract was exceedingly popular and was copied and revised many times. The autograph is lost, but the work exists now in no fewer than twenty-six pre-fifteenth-century manuscripts, of six different versions. It was revised in the twelfth century by writers as disparate as Ordericus Vitalis, Robert de Torigny, and a monk from Caen. Its wide circulation could easily have made it popular in both Norman England and on the Continent during the late eleventh century. See *Gesta Normannorum Ducum*, xxix-xliii. This work is referred to as William of Jumièges in this essay to distinguish it from William of Poitiers's history.
17 William of Poitiers's *Gesta Guillelmi ducis Normannorum et regis Anglorum* has been edited under the title *Histoire de Guillaume le Conquérant*, ed. and trans. by Raymonde Foreville (Paris, 1952). The earliest and only manuscript containing the *Gesta Guillelmi* is an early seventeenth-century copy by André du Chesne of an exemplar from the collection of Robert Cotton. The Cotton manuscript, which may very well have been the autograph, has disappeared, and quite possibly was destroyed in the disastrous fire which decimated Cotton's library. See *Gesta Guillelmi*, l-liii. For dating, see also Davis, "Carmen," 245 n. 2, where he indicates 1077 as the closest possible date for the writing of this history. William of Poitiers's work will be referred to as either the *Gesta* or the *Gesta Guillelmi* in this essay; all references will be to the edition by Foreville.

with the pertinent sections of the *Gesta Guillelmi* of William of Poitiers. It is true that, at first study, the Tapestry's story seems to follow established Norman propaganda which emphasized William's rightful claim to the English throne. William of Poitiers was chaplain to the Norman duke, and his account of the deeds of the duke-king may quickly have become "official" history. But there is still argument as to whether this means that the Tapestry's narrative designer knew and used the *Gesta* as a source for his story, or whether they both came from a common background of knowledge.[18] For our purposes, we can leave that aspect of the problem aside.

There are many instances of apparent borrowing from the *Gesta Guillelmi* found in the Tapestry's story: the inclusion of Harold's journey to Normandy as Edward's emissary, the Breton campaign against Conan in which Harold participated, the importance attached to Harold's oath-taking, Harold's coronation with Stigand as celebrant, the dispatching of English spies to Normandy after the crowning, the messenger sent to William at Hastings by Rodbert fitzWimarch, and William personally delivering the pre-battle harangue to his troops. Let us look at these correspondences more closely.

The extant contemporary English sources make no mention of a journey to Normandy undertaken by Harold, nor of the designation of William of Normandy as Edward's heir. William of Poitiers (I.41) states that King Edward, feeling he was soon to die, sent Harold to Normandy to reaffirm his designation of William as heir to his throne. He chose Harold because of his riches and power, and also because he believed that an alliance between William and Harold might avert English opposition to the choice. This basic idea is also found in William of Jumièges (VII.13) and the *Carmen de Hastingae Proelio* (vv. 287-96); the latter is probably the earliest reference we have to Harold's journey to Normandy. Although there is no specific indication of the reasons for Harold's journey shown in the Tapestry, it has generally been assumed that the narrative is following the Norman explanation, and this would appear to be supported by the rest of the tale.

One must also seriously consider the more recent suggestion that there is an underlying theme in the depiction of Harold's journey: Eadmer (I.6-7) later wrote that Harold had set out to rescue two kinsmen who were being held as hostages by William.[19] But the additional idea that an Anglo-Saxon code or viewpoint was sneaked into the Tapestry's narrative, beyond the comprehension of its presumably Norman patrons,[20] I find unnecessary. If the Tapestry's story was not meant to be unmitigated Norman propaganda, then the addition of the

---

18 For the latest opinion on this problem, see Brooks and Walker, "Authority," 5 and n. 17.
19 Wissolik, "Saxon Statement," 69-97.
20 Wissolik, "Saxon Statement," 71-72.

secondary plot, the hostage story, found in the Anglo-Saxon accounts, becomes less awkward. It need not necessarily be at odds with the Tapestry's generally Norman character.

Only the Tapestry indicates Bosham specifically as the port from which Harold and his retinue sailed. Bosham commanded the harbour of Chichester and was one of the more important sailing ports on the Channel. It was a rich area, and in 1064 Harold owned the manor as well as the manor church, which is probably indicated in the Tapestry. During the 1050's, Harold's father, Earl Godwin, had acquired the manor and church, reportedly by unscrupulous means and trickery; it was from Bosham that he and his family fled when they were driven into exile by Edward. It was at the end of this exile that the two hostages, Wulfnoth and Hakon, were sent to Normandy. Are we to find an allusion to the hostages in the inclusion of Bosham? Perhaps, but it is equally likely that we have here a moral hint, in the inclusion of Harold's devotions at Bosham, of his perfidious nature and the hypocrisy of his faith. His father had rebelled against King Edward and then taken what was not rightly his, namely the Bosham estate, and the son was to continue the family tradition, and seize the English crown.

The episode between Harold and Guy of Ponthieu is found only in William of Jumièges and William of Poitiers; the Tapestry seems to follow the latter's story closely. The *Gesta* (I.41) relates how Harold was rescued from that barbaric group by threats and money and delivered by Guy personally to William at the border castle of Eu; William then brought Harold to his chief city, Rouen, where he lavished great hospitality on him, for he was pleased to have such an illustrious mediator with the English. The Tapestry follows this story rather closely, without mentioning specific locations, either Eu or Rouen, but it is assumed that the designation of the arcaded building as "palatium suum" is a reference to the ducal palace at Rouen.

William of Poitiers (I.44-45) and the Bayeux Tapestry are the only two extant sources that give information about the clash between Duke William and Conan of Brittany, but they differ substantially in their versions of the events. According to the *Gesta Guillelmi*, William undertook a campaign into Brittany to relieve Riwallon, Lord of Dol, who was under siege by Conan, the dissident Count of Brittany, who refused to give allegiance to his rightful lord, William. There is agreement between the embroidery and the *Gesta* that Harold and his retinue accompanied the Normans into Brittany. Harold's heroism in rescuing the Norman soldiers from the sand at the treacherous crossing of the Couesnon near Mont-Saint-Michel is attested to only in the Tapestry.

When the Norman knights, strangely without armour, arrive at the besieged town of Dol, Conan is seen, in the Tapestry, sliding down a rope from the fortifications and escaping. According to William of Poitiers, Conan was outside the town, and not within, when the Normans arrived; he fled into the countryside with William in pursuit. The embroidery shows the Normans riding past Rennes with its motte-and-bailey castle, and finally catching up with the Bretons at Dinan, which is attacked by fully-armoured knights, and its palisade burned. Conan is forced by the odds to surrender the town's keys. This finale to the expedition is at complete variance with William of Poitiers, who claims that Conan, having met with Geoffrey of Anjou, fled beyond William's reach, and a pitched battle never occurred. (See plates 1 and 2.)

— Special permission of the Bibliothèque Municipale, Bayeux

Plate 1.   The Normans attack Dol and Conan flees.

The Bayeux Tapestry's version of these events obviously serves to render William greater glory than does the literary account. But which account gives us the clues as to what "really happened"? If the Tapestry were meant to indicate actual events, how do we explain the inconsistency with William of Poitiers? Surely if William the Conqueror had been ultimately successful in defeating Conan in battle, this would have appeared as such in the *Gesta*, written during the 1070's, and within the court circle itself. The subjugation of Conan, as shown in the Tapestry, on the other hand, furnishes the viewers with a good example of how Duke William could easily subdue a rebellious vassal, and was perhaps a warning to future errant subjects, and a foretaste of what was to happen to Harold. As such, it is more essential to the Tapestry's story than to history.

William of Poitiers mentions only one settlement by name, Dol, where Riwallon was ensconced. The Tapestry furnishes the route of the chase by adding Mont-Saint-Michel, Rennes, and Dinan to the list of place-names. Mont-Saint-Michel was a very popular pilgrimage spot in Normandy and was under ducal patronage; it was from this monastery that the monks came to settle in the Abbey of Saint-Vigor which Bishop Odo of Bayeux founded just outside his episcopal city. The inclusion of the island sanctuary in the Tapestry is probably a reference to both popular piety and to a patron.

– Special permission of the Bibliothèque Municipale, Bayeux

Plate 2.   Conan surrenders the keys of Dinan.

The next sequence of events depicted in the Tapestry—Breton campaign, bestowal of arms,[21] and oath-taking—are all mentioned fully by William of Poitiers (I.42), but interestingly enough, in reverse order. The Tapestry order allows the oath-taking to become the culmination of Harold's stay in Normandy, and it is the last thing he does before he sails back to England. It provides the first real climax of events in the embroidery's narrative and is a turning point in the tale.

Several times, the *Carmen de Hastingae Proelio* (vv. 233-34; 239-40; 297-300) mentions a pact of allegiance between Harold and William, but the oaths are never explained and each time Guy of Amiens indicates that the agreement between the two leaders was private. William of Poitiers is the first source to give specific details about the oaths[22] which he also indicates as taking place at Bonneville-sur-

---

21 Werckmeister, "Political Ideology," 563-79, forwards a lengthy and legalistic interpretation of the arms-giving scene as an indication of the legal relationship between Harold and William. The complex exposition of political ideology seems out of character with the Bayeux Tapestry's narrative, which I prefer to see as more straightforward.
22 Only the *Gesta* details the overtly preposterous terms of the oath, which are all to the Norman's benefit: Harold would represent William in Edward's court and do all he

Touques. The Tapestry places the ceremony at Bayeux, presumably out of deference to Bishop Odo, the probable patron of the Tapestry,[23] but this still leaves us with the necessity of deciding which source is most "reliable." The oath-taking is shown in the Tapestry as a formal ceremony rather than a private agreement. William presides, seated, holding his sword of office erect while Harold swears his oath upon two objects, which are either portable altars or reliquaries. This indication of formality gives greater importance to the action and increases the inevitability of the consequences when the oath is broken. (See plates 3 and 4.)

– Special permission of the Bibliothèque Municipale, Bayeux

Plate 3. The Normans and Harold come to Bayeux.

could to ensure William's accession; and he would place and support garrisons in castles about England for William's use, especially at Dover, at his own expense. In return, William confirmed Harold in all the lands he currently held in England, with all his dignities. It is then stated that Harold swore to these terms freely, after having paid ceremonial homage to the Duke and having become his vassal.

23 Odo's patronage has long been accepted as probable on the grounds of the emphasis given in the Tapestry's narrative to his important contribution to the Norman victory, and because of the reference to Bayeux in the oath scene. Odo's patronage will be dealt with in my forthcoming publication.

– Special permission of the Bibliothèque Municipale, Bayeux
Plate 4. Harold's oath.

The Norman sources, William of Jumièges (VII.13) and William of Poitiers (II.1), state that Harold, supported by English "partisans," immediately upon King Edward's death seized the throne, and that he was crowned with undue haste on the same day as the funeral. The Tapestry seems to follow closely the *Gesta*'s description. The two men who offer Harold the crown while pointing back to the deathbed scene have been interpreted as representing the Witan.[24] However, there would have been little time for an election to take place between Edward's death and the coronation if it were held the same day as the funeral. They may perhaps be better seen as the English "partisans" who upheld Harold's claim to the throne. Supporting this interpretation is the deliberate presence of Archbishop Stigand at the coronation, which agrees with the *Gesta*. Later English sources, such as Florence of Worcester, Ingulph of Croyland, and the Anonymous Chronicler of York, state that Harold was crowned by Ældred of York, obviously to circumvent the difficulties of Stigand's irregular succession.[25] Existing English sources contemporary with the event do not specify which prelate presided at the ceremony. The scenes here appear to correspond with Norman ideology, as outlined by William of Poitiers, with

---

24 Charles H. Gibbs-Smith, *The Bayeux Tapestry* (London, 1973), fig. 26.
25 Stigand, a close associate of Earl Godwin, Harold's father, became Archbishop of Canterbury in 1052, after Robert of Jumièges was driven out of England. He was repeatedly excommunicated by a series of popes before and after receiving the pallium from Benedict X in 1058, and finally removed in 1070 when Lanfranc was given the position.

the purpose, not of denying that Harold was an anointed king, but of showing that his status was iniquitous. (See plates 5 and 6.)

– Special permission of the Bibliothèque Municipale, Bayeux

Plate 5. The death of King Edward.

– Special permission of the Bibliothèque Municipale, Bayeux

Plate 6. The crowning of Harold as King of England.

As mentioned earlier, the first half of the Tapestry sets up the moral cause for the Norman takeover of England. William had been designated as heir to the throne and had received oaths of support from Harold Godwinson, the most powerful of the English nobles. When

Harold defies his freely-given oath and is crowned King of England by a usurper Archbishop of Canterbury, the course of history is set. William must invade England to secure what is rightly his! With this statement clearly made, the emphasis in the Tapestry's narrative turns to a reaffirmation of the important personal role played in the sequence of events by William's half-brother, Odo of Bayeux. The attention given Odo would seem to indicate that he had more than a passing interest in the production of the Tapestry.

The second half of the Tapestry's story appears to be similar to accounts other than William of Poitiers's *Gesta*, but there are still a few scenes where a careful reading of this history would seem to help us understand what is being represented in the Tapestry.

Immediately following the coronation and comet tableau, a man is shown speaking to Harold. It has been assumed that this conversation is connected with the preceding comet scene, and that this omen is the subject of the discussion, with the future invasion foretold by the ghostly ships in the border beneath.[26] But it would make better sense if this episode and the sailing to Normandy in the next scene were viewed as a sequence. William of Jumièges (VII.13) tells us that Duke William sent a messenger to Harold after the coronation, urging him to honour the Norman claim to the throne of England. William of Poitiers (II.41) on the other hand, relates how Harold sent spies to Normandy and that one of them was captured and brought before William. The man speaking to Harold may very well be the messenger sent to Harold by William, who, according to William of Jumièges, threatens invasion if the crown is not relinquished. The more likely possibility is that this is a member of the English spying team, receiving last minute instructions before heading off to the Continent. The adjacent scene shows a ship landing in Normandy, and this is almost certainly the ship delivering the spy. Since there is no greeting party at the landing, it probably is not the return of the Norman messenger, and it is distinctly labelled as an English ship.[27]

After the landing at Pevensey and the hurried construction of a fortified camp at Hastings, the Tapestry shows how news is brought to William about Harold. Both the *Carmen de Hastingae Proelio* (vv. 195-276) and the *Gesta* (II.10-12) indicate that there was an exchange of clerical envoys by the two sides; but the messenger in the

---

26 Dodwell, "Bayeux Tapestry," 559.
27 The fact that the man speaking to Harold wears the "Anglo-Saxon" haircut while the man wading with the boat's anchor sports the shaved nape of the "Norman" style should not be emphasized. The haircut distinction in the Tapestry breaks down by this point, and it is misleading to allow it to determine interpretation. Notice the very next scene where the order to build ships is given by a Duke William with a full head of "Anglo-Saxon" hair! It is only the clerical haircut which seems to be consistent in its use.

Tapestry does not appear to be a monk. The depiction here is probably based on William of Poitiers, who further states that first there arrived at Hastings a messenger from a Norman living in England, named Rodbert (presumably Rodbert fitzWimarch). Rodbert's man, according to the *Gesta*, brought news of Harold's victory at Stamford Bridge and warned William to be cautious. Rodbert is described as a relative of the Duke,[28] and he was made an official in the new establishment after the Conquest.

Just before the first encounter of the French and the English forces, Duke William is shown exhorting his soldiers to "prepare themselves manfully and wisely for the battle against the English." This corresponds with both the *Carmen* (vv. 314-34) and the *Gesta* (II.15), but is closer to William of Poitiers's version, since the Duke addresses his troops himself. In the *Carmen* the elaborate speech is put into the mouth of a monk who has just returned from the English camp.

From the above observations, it can be seen that there are many instances of close correspondence between the narratives found in the Bayeux Tapestry and in the *Gesta Guillelmi*. But it can also be seen that there are some surprising discrepancies, such as the outcome of the Breton campaign, the sequence of events leading up to Harold's oath-taking, and the location of that ceremony. In the main, the Tapestry's story corresponds with the Norman propaganda approach as espoused by William of Jumièges and even more by William of Poitiers, but it is a selective correspondence which follows the character, and not necessarily the letter, of the histories.

The balance of the Tapestry, which shows the actual fighting at Hastings, is closer to other descriptions of the battle. Of particular and crucial interest is the relationship of the Tapestry narrative to that found in the *Carmen de Hastingae Proelio*.[29] Most of the battle scenes correspond with the description of the fighting in the poem, and the depiction of the deaths of Harold and his housecarls appears to be a direct borrowing. The inclusion of the Count of Boulogne as a close companion-at-arms of Duke William also seems to indicate a knowledge of Guy of Amiens's poem. The *Vita Aedwardi* (II, f. 55-57) definitely furnished the scene for the death of King Edward, including the detail of the people present, their physical placement, and emotional reactions. (See plate 5.)

If the person responsible for the Tapestry's narrative deliberately chose many of his events from the stock of literary descriptions of the Norman Invasion, and decided to produce a piece of selective Norman

---

28 *Gesta*, 170 n. 1.
29 See my forthcoming publication. For a new and alternative interpretation, see David Bernstein, "The Blinding of Harold and the Meaning of the Bayeux Tapestry," *Proceedings of the Battle Conference on Anglo-Norman Studies IV—1982* (Woodbridge, 1983), pp. 40-64.

propaganda, he was equally aware of other literary forms. The inclusion of several Aesopian fables in the borders of the Tapestry[30] and similarities of technique found between the embroidery's narrative and the late eleventh-century *chanson-de-geste*[31] must lead to a serious reassessment of the Bayeux Tapestry and its place in a larger literary context.

Because the Tapestry has sometimes been regarded as a unique object whose purpose was to present "historical truth," it has generally been studied in isolation, and the truly eclectic character of its narrative has been missed. Because the series of events depicted appears to be partly a deliberate choice taken from a variety of sources, and partly its own story, one must not use the Bayeux Tapestry images as corroborating evidence to determine what actually happened between 1064 and 1066.

A "true" historical source it may not be, but the Tapestry's narrative certainly does fall into the category of propaganda. The story illustrated in the embroidery is long and presents a complex series of events and relationships. It is a story shaped by a purpose, a purpose which was determined by the circumstances of its commissioning and use. I see that part of the character of the narrative was a deliberate and obvious recalling of the range of literary material then current describing the same events. We must also not overlook the entertainment value inherent in the illustration of a popular and still topical story. The author of the Tapestry's narrative, whom I see as akin to a "librettist," was obviously a well-read person, probably a cleric, who was familiar with the literature of the mid- and late-eleventh century in Normandy and England. The commission to assemble the programme for the Bayeux Tapestry was an opportune way to express his wide knowledge and perhaps to reflect the learning, real or otherwise, of the patron's circle. In doing so, he produced a great, and truly eclectic, work of "artistic propaganda."

30 Hélène Chefneux, "Les Fables dans la Tapisserie de Bayeux," *Romania* 60 (1934), 1-35, 153-94; also Léon Herrmann, *Les fables antiques de la broderie de Bayeux*, Collection Latomus 69 (Brussels, 1964); and Dodwell, "Bayeux Tapestry," 559.
31 See my "The Bayeux Tapestry and the *Song of Roland*," *Olifant* 6 (1978-79), 339-50.

2

The Boundaries of Old English Literature

Angus Cameron

Recently, I have been thinking about problems of Old English literary history, and have been summing up my thoughts on this literature of a millenium ago which I have studied for the past fourteen years and from which I have read texts or at least citations almost every day. In the course of my work on the Dictionary of Old English, I have listed and looked at most of the surviving texts at one time or another, and this forced inclusiveness has given me a different view of Old English literature. I would like to sketch for you the boundaries of what I have seen.

I decided first of all to compare my views with those of the recent historians of Old English literature, because I wanted to see how they described their work and how they characterized their subject. I began with Stanley Greenfield, whose *Critical History of Old English Literature* appeared in 1965 and is, in my opinion, the best book of its kind. Greenfield gives 162 pages to the poetry and sixty-four to the prose. He describes the tasks of the literary historian as follows:

> Some of the problems facing the writer of a history of Old English literature have been implied in the foregoing paragraphs: the necessity of filling in historical background; of determining how much culture is "literary"

or important for literary understanding; of assessing the role as "Old English" of Latin writings by those of Anglo-Saxon stock; of explaining certain linguistic features; and so on. More properly the domain of the literary historian is commentary on poetic and prose styles, on genres and traditions, on metrics and prosody, as well as assessment of individual works and authors. Complicating the task are chronological problems with the poetry (the major surviving manuscripts all date from around A.D. 1000), the anonymity of authors, and the like. For these reasons the first part of this book is devoted to the prose literature, mingling Latin and vernacular works as chronology and genre demand. Social and cultural history may thus less obtrusively lend their authority to the literary picture. Poetic tradition obviously flourished first: Ingeld had precedence over Christ in time, at any rate, in the Anglo-Teutonic mind, and Old English poetic style existed prior to a vernacular prose; but we can trace the development of the prose with greater precision. One final advantage accrues to this organization: the account of the poetry comes as a proper climax.[1]

Greenfield proceeds to do all these things and his account is reasonable, as far as it goes. He concludes:

This critical history has, I hope, presented convincing evidence of the stature of our earliest English literary heritage and of its continuity with the literature following the Norman Conquest. In its special fusion of Christian and pagan materials and attitudes, it nevertheless reveals its peculiar individuality as a body of literature within the larger continuum; it also, in that fusion, abides Alcuin's question, with which I began. But as individual pieces of prose and poetry, a goodly portion of Old English literature, as I have tried to show, still out-tops knowledge, serene in its immutable and imperishable beauty.[2]

My second literary historian is C. L. Wrenn, who published his *Study of Old English Literature* near the end of his life in 1967, although he must have formed many of the ideas in it a good thirty years before. Wrenn defines his subject early in his preface:

The term "literature" is here understood as covering the whole body of surviving writings of the Anglo-Saxon period. But since a good deal of this can only be of technical interest to the linguistic or historical scholar, the main emphasis throughout will be on "literature" in the more restricted sense, implying those writings which are recognized as having permanent "literary" value for such things as the evocation of beauty or other primarily aesthetic appeal.[3]

Wrenn is always searching for "literary merit" or "poetic power" in a text, and if he doesn't perceive them, his commentary is very brief. He characterizes Old English poetry as follows:

Four general features of Old English culture, and therefore of its poetry, may be broadly listed as remarked in the preceding chapter:

[1] Stanley B. Greenfield, *A Critical History of Old English Literature* (New York, 1965), 3-4.
[2] Greenfield, *Critical History*, 230.
[3] Charles L. Wrenn, *A Study of Old English Literature* (London, 1967), vii-viii.

(a) a love of ordered ceremony and ornament;
(b) a genius in the conservation of tradition;
(c) gnomic moralizing; and
(d) a remarkable power of adaptive assimilation.[4]

Wrenn's characterization is very unlike the one I would make, and is based, I suspect, on his reading of *Beowulf* together with the texts in Sweet's *Anglo-Saxon Reader*. He makes Old English literature sound as if it were all written by Polonius, and you can just imagine him warming to the strains of "Neither a borrower nor a lender be."

Wrenn devotes 120 pages to poetry and sixty-six to prose in his book, and defends his partiality this way:

> It is, so to speak, a law of nature that the oral making of verse arises early in the history of a people's culture, whereas prose can only develop in a relatively maturing state of civilization when the art of writing, as distinct from oral tradition, has begun to serve utilitarian and didactic purposes. Religion, magic, the natural rhythms of work and of the seasons, all ask for poetry and song or chant from virile human beings in a natural state of living; while the writing of prose normally comes much later as the result of deliberate and conscious effort. It follows, therefore, that it is in their poems that men develop most fully and naturally the inner and individual qualities of their language, and that aesthetic excellences, if found at all, are to be sought in the verse rather than the prose of an early stage of literature. For these and similar reasons, then, verse rather than prose must receive the first and more considerable attention of the student of Old English literature.[5]

My preference at this point would have been to turn to Kenneth Sisam's *Studies in the History of Old English Literature*[6] gathered in 1953, but Sisam, with characteristic reticence, never sets out what he is attempting to do in broad terms. Therefore, my third literary historian is George K. Anderson, who published his *The Literature of the Anglo-Saxons* in 1949. Anderson describes his subject in this way:

> The term "Old English Literature" (or "Anglo-Saxon Literature") should cover all written remains, surviving as well as conjectural, composed in England from the time of the coming of the Angles and Saxons through, let us say, the first generation after the Battle of Hastings; more specifically, it should include everything from the runic literature—nearly all of which has been lost—to the entries in *The Anglo-Saxon Chronicle* dating from about the time of the death of William the Conqueror, though hard and fast dates, in determining the boundaries between Old and Middle English, are both futile and meaningless. This literature, as we have traced it, comprises a miscellaneous narrative type exemplified in the various kinds of epic poetry; a reflective sort of lyric, or "elegiac" verse; didactic poetry in many forms; a few personal poems; a large *corpus* of monitory prose, consisting of saints' lives, expositions of theological matters, homilies, and instructive dialogues; several translations from foreign

---

4 Wrenn, *Study*, 18.
5 Wrenn, *Study*, 35.
6 Kenneth Sisam, *Studies in the History of Old English Literature* (Oxford, 1953).

writings, including some biblical translations and paraphrases; some works on grammar, geography, astronomy, and some mixed natural lore; a large amount of medical and pharmaceutical material; and the usual stones and pebbles of early literature, such as glosses, inscriptions on monuments, and runes. In other words, nearly every kind of recognizable literary type is somehow represented. The most striking exceptions are the drama and the novel, however this latter type is to be defined.[7]

On the last page of his book, he gives the following amazing characterization of his subject.

> Whatever posterity decides to do about this corner of English literature cultivated a thousand years ago, one thing is still certain, and that is that Old English literature needs no apology. It is not difficult to be condescending, even contemptuous, in our judgement of it. In some measure this judgement will depend upon what the individual reader may be seeking. Old English literature is the expression of a people which has not yet found itself. Most of us would agree on that. It therefore presents none of the far-reaching problems of modern industrial and mechanical life. It is Church-ridden. It ignores women to what seems to us an intolerable degree. Its structure is all too often weak; it repeats itself; its subject-matter is limited; it lacks sensuousness and brilliance; it has little esthetic appeal. So much for its liabilities. But consider closely its origins. One has no right to expect the impossible. This literature, with all its deficiencies, has a fierce masculinity, a stern moral fiber ingrained on simple but rigorous ethical principles, and a stout-hearted pessimism tinged at least upon the surface with Christian hope. Virility, sturdiness, and insight—this is the trinity from which all abiding literature must spring. For the rest, Old English literature has rude and direct power, a muffled kind of romantic eloquence, and a naïve but instinctive ability to put its hand upon eternal truths.[8]

After all this, what apology can there be?

All three literary historians describe their subject in ways very different from each other and very different from the way I would. Yet, when I look over the history of Old English scholarship I should not have been surprised, for scholars in every century since the revival of Anglo-Saxon studies have quarried the surviving manuscripts and come up with their own interests. In the sixteenth century, the antiquaries around Archbishop Parker edited the Laws and the West Saxon Gospels. In the seventeenth century, their successors produced editions of the Old English *Psalter*, Bede, Boethius, the Old Testament translations, the *Anglo-Saxon Chronicle*, and the Cædmon manuscript of poetry. In the eighteenth century, when interest was much less, the only new texts to appear were one homily by Ælfric, *The Battle of Maldon*, the Old English translation of Orosius, and King Alfred's Will.[9] In the nineteenth century, the antiquaries were replaced by his-

---

7 George K. Anderson, *The Literature of the Anglo-Saxons*, rev. ed. (London, 1966), 404-5.
8 Anderson, *Literature*, 411.
9 A good account of this early work is found in Eleanor N. Adams, *Old English Schol-*

torians and philologists who presented the texts which reflected their own interests. The narrowness of these interests can be illustrated by a comment of Henry Sweet in the introduction to his edition of King Alfred's translation of Gregory the Great's *Pastoral Care*: "In fact, I look upon a translation to a text like this, which is of exclusively philological interest, as so much waste paper...."[10] This remark is made of the translation of a book which is one of the cornerstones of Christian culture in the Dark Ages.

Anderson's, Wrenn's, and Greenfield's summaries, then, reflect their own scholarly interests and the work which had been done in Old English literature up to the time they wrote. Most scholars interested in textual and critical work had concentrated on the poetry, and specifically the poetry which Wrenn's four criteria reflect so clearly.

Between their work and mine came the work of Neil Ker; his *Catalogue of Manuscripts containing Anglo-Saxon*[11] appeared in 1957. Now this antedates the books of Wrenn and Greenfield, and while both mention Ker in their bibliographies, they have not had the time to absorb his information or think about its implications.

Ker's *Catalogue* is, in my opinion, the most important contribution which has ever been made to the study of Old English literature. While it is invaluable to palaeographers and codicologists, it is far more than its title implies. In its prefatory material and its indexes, as well as in its entries for the manuscripts, it gives for the first time a clear survey of what Old English literature has survived and what it is about.

Although much time and speculation has been expended on the "lost literature of Anglo-Saxon England," the hundreds of epics like *Beowulf* which might have perished during the Middle Ages and in the dissolution of the monastic libraries in the sixteenth century, I prefer to to spend my time on the texts at hand. From the evidence of medieval library catalogues, they seem quite representative of what was produced.

Ker lists over 400 manuscripts containing Old English; of these, he considers 189 to be major manuscripts.[12] In addition, he lists another thirty-nine manuscripts written on the Continent which contain Old English materials (mostly glosses) which are germanized to varying degrees. In the twenty years since the *Catalogue* appeared, he has turned up fifteen new manuscripts (only one of which can be termed major) and additional leaves to six already known manuscripts.[13] To

---

arship in England from 1566-1800, Yale Studies in English 55 (New Haven, 1917); see also Owen Manning (ed. and trans.), *The Will of King Alfred* (Oxford, 1788).
10 Henry Sweet (ed.), *King Alfred's West-Saxon Version of Gregory's Pastoral Care*, EETS, OS 45, 50 (London, 1871; rptd. 1958), ix.
11 Neil R. Ker, *Catalogue of Manuscripts containing Anglo-Saxon* (Oxford, 1957).
12 Ker, *Catalogue*, xv.
13 Neil R. Ker, "A Supplement to *Catalogue of Manuscripts containing Anglo-Saxon*," *ASE* 5 (1976), 121-31.

these can be added the materials which Ker does not list, the charters, often surviving in cartularies from the later Middle Ages,[14] and the 113 inscriptions in runes and in the Latin alphabet.[15]

Altogether, these sources give us a corpus of just over three million running words of text. Not all of these can be considered as literature. I would draw a distinction between continuous and discontinuous text and consider the former as literature. The latter, including interlinear glosses and glossaries are really aids to the study of literature, and Latin literature at that. If we remove these glosses and glossaries, we have 2,300,000 running words of text. You might be surprised to know that the poetry makes up only eight and a half per cent of this total, while the prose makes up the other ninety-one and a half per cent.

Although Anderson would consider anything from Hengest and Horsa on, surviving or not, as Old English literature, vernacular texts first appear in the eighth century and continue to be written until the twelfth. Ker finds that a date around 1200 is the natural end to the period. It is marked by a change in writing style as well as a shift in subject matter in vernacular texts. Many of the earliest texts are glosses and glossaries, and I suppose that our oldest literary texts are the Northumbrian copies of *Cædmon's Hymn* in the Leningrad and Moore Bede manuscripts,[16] dated around 750 or slightly earlier. One of Ker's greatest services is that he has dated all the manuscripts for us. Of the 189 major manuscripts, two are from the eighth century, six from the ninth, twenty-one from the tenth, 133 from the eleventh and twenty-seven from the twelfth.[17] Old English literature, as we have it, starts with the reign of King Alfred, but is largely a product of the late tenth and eleventh centuries, of the Benedictine revival and its aftereffects.

Ker has also identified the work of twenty-seven different scriptoria from the Anglo-Saxon period,[18] and more will doubtless be recognized as the work of comparing hands in vernacular and Latin manuscripts goes on. The most important scriptoria whose work has survived were those of the Winchester houses, Exeter, Worcester, Abingdon, and the two Canterbury houses, Christ Church and St. Augustine's.

While we know a great deal more than we did about the dating and localizing of manuscripts, the chronology of the texts themselves is far

14 Peter H. Sawyer, *Anglo-Saxon Charters: An Annotated List and Bibliography*, Royal Historical Society Guides and Handbooks 8 (London, 1968).
15 Elisabeth Okasha, *Hand-List of Anglo-Saxon Non-Runic Inscriptions* (Cambridge, 1971).
16 Dorothy Whitelock (ed.), *Sweet's Anglo-Saxon Reader in Prose and Verse*, 15th ed. (Oxford, 1967), 181-82.
17 Ker, *Catalogue*, xv-xix.
18 Ker, *Catalogue*, lvi-lx.

more difficult to establish. Here the prose texts give us the most help. Some of the early manuscripts of the works of Ælfric and Wulfstan date from the authors' own lifetimes, and may indeed contain additions and corrections in their own hands.[19] At the other limit, we know that a gap of nearly two centuries must lie between the twelfth-century manuscript of the English *Soliloquies of St. Augustine* and its composition by King Alfred.[20] The dating of the poetry is the most difficult of all. The four manuscripts which contain most of the poetry all date from the late tenth and early eleventh centuries, but nineteenth- and twentieth-century scholars, impelled by the desire to have pre-Christian texts and relics of the Heroic Age, have offered dates as early as the sixth century for poems like *Beowulf* and *Widsith*. Chronologies based on linguisitic criteria are now largely discredited and need to be thought anew if they are to be used.[21]

So far, I have spoken about the physical manifestations of Old English literature; now I would like to discuss the contents of the manuscripts. The tools of literary criticism, textual criticism, and literary history can be applied to all that has survived if we as scholars only see their appropriateness. The recent developments in interdisciplinary studies have opened up many new texts to us. We now can see how images from patristic writings can be traced in vernacular prose and poetry and can appreciate the art with which they have been used. In the laws and charters, we find the ultimate home of the literary formula. I wonder what would have been the result if Francis Peabody Magoun, Jr. had hit upon the writs of Edward the Confessor rather than *Beowulf* in his search for oral formulaic evidence.

In looking at the poetry, I think it is very important to distinguish between oral and written traditions, and not to assume that they are one and the same thing. While we know that there was an oral tradition of English poetry from Bede and other historians, we can only speculate on its attributes. While the written poetry has a metre common to poetry in all the Germanic languages, this does not necessarily mean that its other conventions are the same as those of the old oral traditions. To put the problem in an example, I have no way of knowing whether our text of *Cædmon's Hymn* represents Cædmon's original song or an Old English poet's response to Bede's Latin paraphrase.

19 Norman Eliason and Peter Clemoes, *Ælfric's First Series of Catholic Homilies (British Museum Royal 7 c. xii, fols. 4-218)*, Early English Manuscripts in Facsimile 13 (Copenhagen, 1966); and Neil R. Ker, "The Handwriting of Archbishop Wulfstan," in Peter Clemoes and Kathleen Hughes (eds.), *England before the Conquest: Studies in Primary Sources Presented to Dorothy Whitelock* (Cambridge, 1971), 315-31.
20 Thomas A. Carnicelli (ed.), *King Alfred's Version of St. Augustine's* Soliloquies (Cambridge, Mass., 1969).
21 Ashley Crandall Amos, *Linguistic Means of Determining the Dates of Old English Literary Texts*, Medieval Academy Books No. 90 (Cambridge, Mass., 1980).

My mild reproach to the earlier literary historians is that they have given a great deal of time to a small number of texts and have merely catalogued or ignored the rest. The poetry has been better treated than the prose, but here again, the concentration has been on a few poems whose texts have certainly benefitted from it, and show, by comparison with the neglected texts, just what can be done.

Pride of place in the study of the poetry has always been given to the heroic poems, and *Beowulf*[22] is certainly a rich and beautiful text which repays rereading however often the scholar comes back to it. The historical poems from the *Anglo-Saxon Chronicle*[23] and *The Battle of Maldon*[24] have always had readers, as have some of the philosophical lyrics or wisdom poems of the Exeter Book.[25] I, myself, would put more emphasis on the extraordinary religious lyrics and meditative poems. The power of the *Dream of the Rood* and of the *Advent Lyrics* in the Exeter Book has been recognized, but there are many other poems whose less obvious beauties await study. More work can be done on the saints' lives, the biblical paraphrases, and the translations of the *Metres of Boethius*. Finally, among the shorter poems, besides the well-known riddles and maxims, there are also charms and mnemonic pieces, hymns, liturgical poems, and dedications to be studied.

In the study of Old English prose, we have made great advances in the past twenty years. Most of the texts are now in print, or will be shortly. The works of Ælfric[26] (to whom we ascribe no less than 197 separate texts) have received gratifying attention at the hands of editors and commentators, as have the works assigned to Archbishop Wulfstan of York.[27] Besides these, we have the anonymous homilies, sermons, saints' lives, and narrative pieces (156 texts in all), the *Anglo-Saxon Chronicle*, the Alfredian translations, the biblical translations, the rules for monks and canons, the laws, the penitentials, the computus texts, the medical texts, the charters (375 of them in English plus the bounds for another 600), and a host of shorter texts including a lapidary, a translation of *Alexander's Letter to Aristotle*, prognostics of various kinds including several tracts on the interpretation of

---

22 Frederick Klaeber (ed.), *Beowulf and The Fight at Finnsburg*, 3rd ed., with 1st and 2nd supplements (Boston, 1950).
23 Elliott Van K. Dobbie (ed.), *The Anglo-Saxon Minor Poems*, ASPR 6 (New York, 1942), 16-26.
24 Eric V. Gordon (ed.), *The Battle of Maldon*, Methuen's Old English Library (London, 1937).
25 George P. Krapp and Elliott Van K. Dobbie (eds.), *The Exeter Book*, ASPR 3 (New York, 1936).
26 Peter Clemoes, "The Chronology of Ælfric's Works," in Peter Clemoes (ed.), *The Anglo-Saxons: Studies in Some Aspects of Their History and Culture presented to Bruce Dickins* (London, 1959), 212-47.
27 Dorothy Bethurum (ed.), *The Homilies of Wulfstan* (Oxford, 1957).

dreams, a set of signs to be used in monasteries during periods of silence, and notes on the ages of the world, the dimensions of the world, and the number of bones and veins in the human body.[28] All of these texts await further study, and if the literary critic, the textual critic, the historian, the liturgist, the palaeographer, the codicologist, the historians of medicine and of science, the art historian, and the anthropologist can co-operate, then we will all benefit from them.

All of these texts have to be set in the context of the contemporary Anglo-Latin literature which has survived in larger quantities than the vernacular and has been less studied. In the past, literary historians of the vernacular have used Anglo-Latin literature to fill in the gaps in their narrative, but much more than this needs to be done. The two literatures clearly meet at certain points, for instance in the rules for monks and canons which always come in bilingual texts. The relationship between the two and how they come in contact needs to be studied carefully for their mutual benefit.

In concluding this tour of the boundaries of Old English literature, I think I owe it to my predecessors to try to give you my characterization of the subject. I do so, knowing that it may sound quaint in ten or twenty years' time.

Old English literature is firmly within the mainstream of the Western European tradition. Its remains are perfectly understandable in the context of contemporary Latin evidence and consistent with the development of the later vernacular literatures in England, France, and Germany.

It flourishes for a very short time. Virtually nothing survives from before the reign of King Alfred, and although texts are copied into the twelfth century, there is understandably no new impetus after the Norman Conquest of 1066. It is also a literature of southern England. The north plays virtually no part in it as it has survived.

It is a literature sponsored and preserved by the Church. Without the Church, we would have very little or nothing from this period because all the manuscripts which have survived were copied in monastic and cathedral scriptoria and were kept and used in their schools and libraries. That so much was written in English is due partly to the scholars of the Benedictine reform who promoted vernacular texts as a step towards the learning of Latin. I find nothing in this literature of the tension between pagan and Christian values which strikes Greenfield so forcibly. I think that, by the tenth century, people knew exactly where Ingeld fitted in the scheme of things. The astonishing development of his Celtic cousin Arthur in the next few centuries shows that.

---

28 For these minor texts, see Angus Cameron, "A List of Old English Texts," in Roberta Frank and Angus Cameron (eds.), *A Plan for the Dictionary of Old English*, TOES 2 (Toronto, 1973), 25-306.

Old English literature is above all a literature of things useful for men to know, to think on, and remember; translations from the Bible, the great cycles of homilies, narrative texts salted with maxims, laws, documents dealing with bequests, medical recipes, and, failing these, charms. As well as being instructive, it had, and has, moments of great beauty for the ear and eye, intricate imagery, and strong narrative passages. It is in no sense a primitive literature, and after a thousand years, its texts are still rich and rewarding for students to think upon.[29]

[29] For a recent survey of Old English literature, similar in tone to this, but much more detailed, see Eric G. Stanley, "The Scholarly Recovery of the Significance of Anglo-Saxon Records in Prose and Verse: A New Bibliography," *ASE* 9 (1981), 223-62.

3

Beowulf, Bede, and St. Oswine: The Hero's Pride in Old English Hagiography[1]

Colin Chase

In Book Three of his *Historia Ecclesiastica Gentis Anglorum*, Bede devotes most of one chapter (chapter 14) to the character and rule of Oswine, king of Deira until 651. The tone and emphasis which Bede adopts differ in some notable ways from his habitual style:

> In the first part of his reign, Oswy had a companion in royal power named Oswine, who was of King Edwin's line, a son of Osric whom we mentioned before and a man of outstanding piety and religion, beloved of everyone. He remained over the province of Deira in the greatest possible prosperity for seven years. But the man who was ruling over the other, northern, part of Northumbria, that is, the province of Bernicia, could not remain at peace with him; rather, after the points of contention grew between them, he put him to a very sad death. For when both of them had gotten an army together against one another, and Oswine saw that he would not be able to fight against Oswy, because he had a great many allies, he thought it more sensible to give up the idea of fighting for the present and to await a better chance. So, he disbanded the army he had gathered and commanded everyone to go individually to their homes from the place called *Wilfaresdun*, which is about ten miles northwest of the

---

[1] Much of the material in this essay has been summarized for a different purpose in my "Saints' Lives, Royal Lives, and the Date of *Beowulf*," in Colin Chase (ed.), *The Dating of Beowulf*, TOES 6 (Toronto, 1981), 161-71.

town of Catterick; and he himself went away with only one of his most loyal soldiers, named Tondhere, to hide in the home of his thane Hunwald, whom he also felt certain was entirely loyal to him. *Sed heu! pro dolor! longe aliter erat!*; for betrayed by that same thane, he was killed by Oswy through the agency of his reeve, named Æðelwine, in a murder detestable to everyone. This occurred on the twentieth of August, in the ninth year of his reign, at a place called Gilling, where afterwards a monastery was built in reparation for this crime, in which prayers were daily to be offered for the salvation of both kings, the one murdered and the one who ordered the murder.[2]

"*Sed heu! pro dolor! longe aliter erat!*" This phrase has a strange ring for Bede. Though Bertram Colgrave translates it, "But alas, it was quite otherwise," the original seems less restrained. In Old English the equivalent would have been more like "ac hilahi, afæstla sarlic," to translate the first phrase, and the parallel in *Beowulf* to the latter part would be "Ne wæs þæt þa gen" (734) or "Him seo wen geleah" (2323). Almost every chapter in Bede's history deals with someone's death, and yet to my recollection, nowhere else is he driven to interjection, a facet of language not in harmony with the usual moderation and control of his restrained style. In fact, one of the chief ways in which a sense of the divinely ordered nature of the universe suffuses Bede's work is in his ability to impose a rounded phrase or polished period on incidents which might otherwise be personal tragedies or national catastrophes. Abbess Hild dies after a long and painful illness: "In the midst of her words of encouragement she happily saw the approach of death; or rather, to use the language of the Lord, she passed from death to life," (IV.23) or Britain, along with the rest of the Empire, undergoes the

2 "Habuit autem Osuiu primis regni sui temporibus consortem regiae dignitatis, uocabulo Osuini, de stirpe regis Eduini, hoc est filium Ostrici, de quo supra rettulimus, uirum eximiae pietatis et religionis, qui prouinciae Derorum septem annis in maxima omnium rerum affluentia, et ipse amabilis omnibus, praefuit. Sed nec cum eo ille qui ceteram Transhumbranae gentis partem ab aquilone, id est Berniciorum prouinciam, regebat, habere pacem potuit; quin potius, ingrauescentibus causis dissensionum, miserrima hunc caede peremit. Siquidem congregato contra inuicem exercitu, cum uideret se Osuini cum illo, qui plures habebat auxiliarios, non posse bello confligere, ratus est utilius tunc demissa intentione bellandi seruare se ad tempora meliora. Remisit ergo exercitum quem congregauerat, ac singulos domum redire praecepit a loco qui uocatur Uilfaresdun, id est Mons Uilfari, et est a uico Catactone x ferme milibus passuum contra solstitialem occasum secretus; diuertitque ipse cum uno tantum milite sibi fidissimo, nomine Tondheri, celandus in domum comitis Hunualdi, quem etiam ipsum sibi amicissimum autumabat. Sed heu! pro dolor! longe aliter erat; nam ab eodem comite proditum eum Osuiu cum praefato ipsius milite per praefectum suum Ediluinum detestanda omnibus morte interfecit. Quod factum est die tertia decima kalendarum Septembrium, anno regni eius nono, in loco qui dicitur Ingetlingum; ubi postmodum castigandi huius facinoris gratia monasterium constructum est, in quo pro utriusque regis, et occisi uidelicet et eius qui occidere iussit, animae redemtione cotidie Domino preces offerri deberent." The text is that of Roger A. B. Mynors (Oxford, 1969), 256. [Latin translations by Colin Chase. Old English translations supplied posthumously by Andrew Patenall. – Eds.]

terrible persecution of Diocletian: "At that time the greatest glory of a devoted profession of faith in God also elevated Britain" (I.6). Such phrases run, like a major key, through the whole work, rendering the conventional artifice of declamatory rhetoric unnecessary.

This contrast between our small phrase and the tone of the whole work makes Bede's momentary outburst very interesting. He seems to recognize that this material needs to be treated differently from what he has ordinarily encountered. One can rejoice with the martyrs in achieving a much-desired reward, and one can point to the justice in the violent deaths of apostate kings, such as Osric and Eanfrith, Oswine's father and uncle (III.1), but to describe without passion the deliberate betrayal of a king by his trusted thane is quite another matter.

And yet, though the phrase disturbs the calm of Bede's habitual attitude momentarily, nothing else in the passage or in the rest of the chapter builds on the effect. In fact, there appears to be a consciously controlled effort to inhibit any close or sustained identification with the king's outraged innocence or any indulgence in the emotions appropriate to such identification. Principally, this is accomplished through the structure of the narrative.

First, immediately after the bare facts of Oswine's betrayal and death are narrated, we are told of the monastery built at Gilling in reparation for the crime, where prayers are to be offered constantly for both Oswine and Oswy. Before we have had time to dwell on the enormity of Oswy's and Hunwald's crime, we learn of an ultimate equilibrium established in the spiritual order.

Second, in a passage more than twice as long as the one which details Oswine's betrayal and death, Bede tells a story to exemplify the deep humility which characterized the king. The curious thing about this story is that, while the ostensible theme is Oswine's humility, at least to modern sensibilities, the tale seems a much more striking description of Bishop Aidan's detachment, for this is the well-remembered incident when the bishop gave to a beggar the horse with which Oswine had supplied him. The point to be made is that in the structure of the narrative, the story of Aidan's horse functions as a transition between a brief focus on the reign and fate of Oswine and a more sustained concern with the character of Aidan, for the three succeeding chapters are taken up exclusively with miracles worked through St. Aidan during his life. Again, the structure of the narrative averts attention from the outrageous deed done to Oswine.

Finally, the next time Oswine's slayer, King Oswy, appears in Bede's *History*, he is conforming to a far different role. In chapter 22, we are told that "at the instance of King Oswy, the East Saxons accepted the faith they had once rejected, at the time of Mellitus's expulsion" (III.22), and again in chapter 24, far from being the villain of the piece, under the pressure of the pagan King Penda's vicious attacks, Oswy turns "to God's mercy for help," vows to build monasteries and to consecrate his daughter to God, and defeats an army thirty times larger than his because, in Bede's phrase, he trusts in Christ as his leader. From villain, Oswy has become hero and saint of Bede's account.

One important effect of this treatment of the story of Oswine and Oswy is to prepare the reader for the role which Oswy was to play in the critical decision coming out of the synod of Whitby, a decision so central to the larger theme of Bede's work. Another effect, however, less important to Bede's overall concern, but more germane to my purpose, is to distract attention from the sort of questions and emotions that would inevitably have arisen from a fuller, more direct treatment of Oswine's story, at least if our usual description of early Anglo-Saxon culture is at all accurate. One might think, for example, of the story told in the *Anglo-Saxon Chronicle* under the year 755 and describing events climaxing in 786. One might contrast the sort of motivation that drove the swineherd in that story to push his *seax* into the deposed King Sygebryht's flesh, apparently a considerable time after Sygebryht's slaying of Cumbran. One might remember the attitude of the followers of the story's protagonists, Cynewulf and Cyneheard, their unwillingness to accept any kind of terms, and the fierce determination to avenge their lord which drove Cynewulf's men to ride to Merton through the early morning. One might recall the numerous parallel tales evoked by names such as Finn and Hnæf, Frodo and Ingeld, Ongentheow and Hæthcyn, Byrhtnoth and Byrhtwold. All this is commonplace in Anglo-Saxon studies and yet reflects an emphasis strangely missing from Bede's story of the murder of Oswine. Where is the revenge motive? What has happened to the idea that lord and thane are in competition to prove their valour on the battlefield? Where have Oswine's followers gone once he is dead? Were it not for Bede's momentary passionate exclamation, "Sed heu! pro dolor! longe aliter erat!" we would wonder if he belonged to the same culture.

In a recently published paper based on his 1973 Cornell lecture, Patrick Wormald noted similar differences between Bede's treatment of English history and the content of Anglo-Saxon vernacular poetry.[3] Identifying a "vast zone of silence"[4] separating Bede's world from Beowulf's, Wormald argues that *Beowulf* may legitimately serve to

---

3 Patrick Wormald, "Bede, 'Beowulf' and the Conversion of the Anglo-Saxon Aristocracy," in Robert T. Farrell (ed.), *Bede and Anglo-Saxon England: Papers in Honour of the 1300th Anniversary of the Birth of Bede, Given at Cornell University in 1973 and 1974*, BAR 46 (Oxford, 1978), 32-95.
4 Ibid., 36. The phrase is adapted from Arnaldo Momigliano, "Pagan and Christian Historiography in the Fourth Century A.D.," in Arnaldo Momigliano (ed.), *The Conflict between Paganism and Christianity in the Fourth Century* (Oxford, 1963), 96.

make up for this lack, since its author was in touch with values and attitudes apparently unimportant to Bede. Possibly, in Wormald's view, this was because he was an oblate to Monkwearmouth-Jarrow at the age of seven and had never had sustained contact with the aristocratic warrior class of his time. Though I am dubious about the methodology, since most of the explicitly heroic literary remains from Anglo-Saxon England are either late, like *The Battle of Maldon*, or of disputed date, like *Beowulf*, my intent in this discussion is to investigate the same "zone of silence" which appears to separate Anglo-Saxon history from the Old English epic, with a view not to filling out Bede's picture but to understanding *Beowulf*.

Though Oswine appears to have excited as little attention in the time immediately following his death as he excites in our own day, apparently in the years just before and after the Conquest, a cult arose on his behalf, owing first to the invention of his body in the ill-fated rule of Tostig as Earl of Northumbria (1055-65), and then, most probably, to the efforts of Ealdwine of Winchcombe and Reinfrid, the Norman knight turned monk, who joined together in a mission to the north to revive the ancient piety both had discovered in Bede.[5] Directly or indirectly, this activity must lie behind the desire to write a more extensive account of Oswine's life than could be found in Bede, a desire which bore fruit in an account surviving today in the Cotton manuscript Julius A. x. Though edited by James Raine in 1838, this anonymous *Vita Oswini* has attracted little attention either from historians or literary critics, probably because it adds neither information nor elegance to Bede's account.

For my purposes, however, what it does add is more important than either. The anonymous *Life* includes everything found in Bede's account, most of which is lifted verbatim and acknowledged with unusual care, but is more than six times longer. Much of the additional material is simply the kind of prolix rhetorical expansion illustrative of the difference in style and temper between Bede and his age and the tastes of the late eleventh and early twelfth centuries. But a large proportion of it reflects just the kind of emphasis missing in Bede but so strong in Anglo-Saxon heroic literature such as *Beowulf*.

For example, early in the story, when the author is telling about the death of Oswine's father, Osric, at the hands of Cædwalla and about the prince's ten-year exile among the West-Saxons, he feels he has to explain that "his relatives and followers took the blessed Oswine away because he was too young, and the tenderness of his years and his lack of means did not permit him to avenge the death of his fath-

---

5 For Ealdwine and Reinfrid see, for example, Stenton, *ASE*, 677-80. The invention is established in the *Miracula* of St. Oswine appearing in BL MS Cotton Julius A. x., ff. 10-43 (see especially f. 15r) and edited by James Raine, *Miscellanea Biographica*, Publications of the Surtees Society 8 (1838), 1-59.

er."[6] In a saint's life, such a detail is a little surprising and can serve as an early warning signal that it is dangerous to impose our own ethical system or our own reading of the Gospel even on a work explicitly identified with Christianity, though in the light of Dorothy Whitelock's massive evidence illustrating revenge as a positive value throughout the Anglo-Saxon period, few of us should need such a warning.[7]

A second detail, less important, perhaps, but still worth noting, occurs when the author comes to describe, in general terms, a two-year period during which Oswy first attempts to subvert Oswine's rule to himself and then despairs of the attempt: "When, therefore, he saw that the dragon's craft was doing him no good, he put on the ferocity of the roaring lion."[8] The only point to be made from this is that the *Vita Oswini* shares an imaginative context which includes Sigurd, Beowulf, St. George, and their respective dragons.

The most extensive expansions of Bede's work occur in the final section of the *Vita Oswini*, describing events leading up to the king's death. In Bede's account, Oswine's decision to turn from the fight against Oswy is dealt with in two sentences: "When Oswine saw that he would be unable to compete with Oswy, who had a large number of allies, he thought it would be more sensible to give up the idea of fighting at that time and to wait for a better chance. He therefore disbanded the army and sent his soldiers each to their own homes." For the author of the *Vita Oswini*, the motivation is not clear or explicit enough. He therefore both describes Oswine's motivation for us and gives him a speech in which he explains to his men why he has decided to avoid the fight against Oswy:

> The renowned and divinely favoured King Oswine, knowing that every law and right allow the meeting of force with force, and surrounded by his own troops, went to meet him [Oswy] at a place called *Wilfaresdun*. But King Oswine, the holiest of men, though he was aware that all his followers were not only willing to fight the enemy, but even prepared to lay down their lives for their king, began to reflect on the cold-blooded evil to which this crisis had given rise and that he alone was the reason for the commission of so much manslaughter, near and far, and becoming sincerely concerned rather to spare his men than himself, addresses them in the following words:
>
> "O faithful thanes and valiant soldiers, I am very grateful to you for your service to me in war and for your honour, and I give you thanks for your good will toward me. But far be it from me that you should meet the

---

6 "Tuleruntque beatum Oswinum propinqui et fautores eius quia infra annos erat et etatis imbecillitas et facultatis tenuitas patris mortem uindicare non permittebat et cum eo apud occiduos saxones per decennium exularunt," BL MS Cotton Julius A. x., f. 3r. Raine, *Miscellanea*, 2. The Latin text is taken from my transcription of a photocopy of the manuscript.

7 Dorothy Whitelock, *The Audience of Beowulf* (Oxford, 1951), 13-18.

8 "Cum igitur draconis insidias nichil sibi prodesse persensit, leonis rugientis feritatem induit," BL MS Cotton Julius A. x., f. 7r; Raine, *Miscellanea*, 7.

hazard of war only for my sake, after you made me your king at a time when I was a poor exile. I prefer to return to exile with a few of my followers, as I did once, or even by myself. In fact, I would prefer to die than that so many fine men should be endangered for my sake. For that is a cruel and disloyal man who would try to destroy many for his sake when he is unable to avert the judgment of God."[9]

The point the author is so anxious, perhaps too anxious, to make is that Oswine turns from the fight neither because of the treachery of his followers nor out of personal fear, but because he is concerned for the lives of his men. This is the reverse of the kind of heroic abandon Hamlet envies in Fortinbras, who sends to their deaths

> twenty-thousand men
> That for a fantasy and trick of fame
> Go to their graves like beds, fight for a plot
> Whereon the numbers cannot try the cause.
>
> IV.iv.60-63

This interpretation of the motives of King Oswine is interesting because it stands as a sort of literary commentary on Bede's work, for I think we can reasonably take it that the material added by the anonymous author would have been considered by Bede to be implicit in his original. The nature of the speech just quoted is doubly interesting because it relates so directly to current discussion of the central theme of *Beowulf*. In two separate, but related, studies of 1965 and 1967, John Leyerle described the "major theme of *Beowulf*" as a "fatal contradiction at the core of heroic society. The hero follows a code that exalts indomitable will and valour in the individual, but society requires a king who acts for the common good. . . ."[10] Though certainly not contemporary with *Beowulf*—however uncertain the date of composition of that poem is—the evidence of this speech does come from a cultural context demonstrably similar to, and modelled upon, that from which

9 "Praeclarus itaque Deoque acceptus Rex Oswinus, sciens quod uim ui repellere omnes leges omniaque iura permittent, suorum circumdatus acie, loco qui Wilfaresdun dicitur ei obuius uenit. Sanctissimus autem Rex Oswinus, uidens suos cum aduersariis unanimiter uolentes non solum contendere uerum etiam pro suo rege paratus occumbere, uoluens in animo discriminis horrendum facinus seque solum homicidii hinc inde passim committendi in causa esse, suis potius quam sibi parcendo pie consulens, sic eos alloquitur:
   'Congratulor, quidem, o fidissimi principes et strenuissimi milites, uestre militie et probitati, et gratias ago bone erga me uestre uoluntati. Sed absit a me ut mei solius causa belli discrimen periculose quidem omnes incurratis, qui me quamquam iure dominum, pauperem tamen et exulem, regem uobis constituistis. Malo itaque, sicut hactenus, ubi ubi cum paucis uel solus exulare. Immo potius diligo mori, quam uos tot et tales mei solius causa contingat quoquomodo periclitari. Impius, enim, et inhumanus est, qui cum Dei iudicio nullo modo possit auertere, plures sui causa conatur euertere,'" BL MS Cotton Julius A. x, f. 7r; Raine, *Miscellanea*, 8.
10 "Beowulf the Hero and the King," *Medium Ævum* 34 (1965), 89; "The Interlace Structure of *Beowulf*," *University of Toronto Quarterly* 37 (1967), 8-9.

Beowulf arose. To that extent, it supports the notion that a conflict between the demands of the heroic code and the responsibilities of kingship would have been meaningful within that cultural context, and supports it perhaps more convincingly than the witness of St. Thomas Aquinas, the only author cited in Leyerle's articles who treats precisely this aspect of the issue.[11] If the author of the *Vita Oswini* ever did have an opportunity to turn the leaves of Cotton Vitellius A. xv, one feels sure that some of the darker implications of Beowulf's decision to fight the dragon alone would not have been lost on him.

In fact, the response of Oswine's men to his proposal that they disperse sounds remarkably like an inverted version of Wiglaf's speech to Beowulf's retainers, a version in which the retainers try desperately to avoid the sort of final judgment with which Wiglaf charges his comrades. Accordingly, Oswine is addressed in these terms:

> O remarkable king, O king worthy of the name of king, we beg you to be kind to us, though we are unworthy. Was there some time when we proved cowards or disgraces to our families, or did you find us too slow somewhere in going to battle? In fact, many a time we passed unscathed through the enemy lines. So we want you to let us fight against the enemy in this battle that is approaching, and to take the auspices of these evil times with iron, on the point of the sword. If things should go badly for us in the fight, it is better that we die in battle than that we become a byword for cowardice in the songs of the people, as deserters of our lord.[12]

These men would agree entirely with Wiglaf's judgment:

> Nu sceal sincþego ond swyrdgifu,
> eall eðelwyn eowrum cynne,
> lufen alicgean; londrihtes mot

[11] That such a conflict would have been meaningful at an earlier date in the Anglo-Saxon period is also clear from Alcuin's citation of a situation for debate in his popular *Disputatio de Rhetorica et de Virtutibus* 13: "Conparatio est, cum aliud aliquod factum rectum aut utile contenditur, quod ut fieret, illud quod arguitur dicitur esse commissum, ut in illo exemplo, quod paulo ante posuimus. Cum dux Romanus ab hostibus obsideretur, nec ullo pacto evadere potuit nisi pacaret ut hostibus arma daret: armis datis milites conservavit, sed post accusatur maiestatis. Intentio est 'non oportuit arma relinquere': depulsio est oportuit: quaestio est 'oportueritne': ratio est: 'milites enim omnes perissent, si hoc non fecissem': infirmatio est 'non ideo fecisti.' Ex quibus iudicatio est, perissentne, et ideone fecisset. Conparatio, an melius esset ad hanc turpissimam conditionem venire, vel milites perire." Wilbur S. Howell (ed. and trans.), *The Rhetoric of Alcuin and Charlemagne*, Princeton Studies in English 23 (Princeton, 1941), 82 and 84. This evidence establishes the existence of this line of thought in Anglo-Saxon legal and ethical tradition, but is less helpful than the *Vita Oswini* for illuminating the narrative concerns of works of a more literary character.

[12] "O rex insignis, o regis nomine dignus, nobis indignus, petimus, esto benignus. Numquid nos ignauos aut degeneres aliquando repperisti, an apparuimus alicubi in conflictu bellico tardiores? Hostium profecto cuneos securi persepe penetrauimus. Liceat ergo nobis cum hostibus instantis certaminis inire conflictum, et in ore gladii peruersae aetatis rimari uiscera ferro. Si fortasse nobis in pugna sinistre cesserit, melius est nobis mori in bello quam apud uulgus domini desertores in prouerbio cantitari," BL MS Cotton Julius A. x., f. 7v; Raine, *Miscellanea*, 8.

> þære mægburge monna æghwylc
> idel hweorfan, syððan æðelingas
> feorran gefricgean fleam eowerne,
> domleasan dæd.
>
> 2884-90a

[Now to your people shall the granting of treasure, the gifts of swords, the joys of home cease; each man of your kin shall wander destitute of land-rights when princes far and near learn of your flight, that inglorious deed.]

Such a fate, say Oswine's soldiers to their reluctant captain, would be worse than death: "Deað bið sella / eorla gehwylcum þonne edwitlif!" ["For any earl death is better than a life of ignominy"] (2890b-91).

But, of course, the author of the *Vita* is not free to change the main outline of the story, and the king remains firm. He assures his men that they have always been brave and unflagging in battle, but goes on to say that since Oswy pursues him and not them, "it is expedient that one man die for the nation rather than that a nation of so great size be destroyed for the sake of one man, especially when I know that a complete reward has been laid aside for me,"[13] this last a reference to bishop Aidan's prediction that the king would die a martyr's death.

Still, in spite of the unwavering front Oswine puts up before his men, as he concludes his speech and turns anxiously to prayer, we see that the issue is not nearly so clear to him as he pretends:

> Father of mercies, and God of all consolation, grant that under the pressure of such great distress I may choose the better way. For if I fight this battle, I appear in your eyes guilty of shedding blood. If I flee I stain my own honour and my family name. Fleeing, I displease men. Fighting I displease you.[14]

In this speech, which comes at the climax of the *Vita Oswini*, just as the king is to go off to meet his death, the central issue of the story is fixed in an unresolved conflict of opposed, and equally imperative, value systems. In Leyerle's description, these value systems involve the contradictory requirements of the heroic code and the responsibilities of royal office, and correspond, respectively, to Georges Dumézil's military ethic and ethic of sovereignty, two of the three fundamental ethical systems according to which any society may be described.[15] The fact that in the *Vita Oswini* this conflict is perceived

---

13 "'Expedit ergo ut unus moriatur pro populo' (John 11, 50) quam ut populus tantae multitudinis deleatur pro uno, presertim cum mihi scierim mercedem plenam esse repositam," BL MS Cotton Julius A. x., ff. 7v-8r; Raine, *Miscellanea*, 8.
14 "Pater misericordiarum et totius consolationis Deus... da mihi in tantae angustiae instantia meliorem eligere uiam. Quia si bello conflixero, fundendi sanguinis coram te reus appareo. Si fugam iniero et propriae dignitati et parentum nobilitati degener appareo. Et hominibus fugiens displiceo et tibi dimicans," BL MS Cotton Julius A. x., f. 8r; Raine, *Miscellanea*, 9.
15 Dumézil's system is elaborated in *The Destiny of the Warrior*, trans. by Alf Hil-

but left unresolved is important. The fact that nowhere is Oswine's desire to protect his name, shun disgrace, and gain glory on the battlefield equated with pride is even more important. In this explicitly religious context, in which the hagiographer had every reason to depict what his hero chose not to do as evil, and what he chose to do as unalloyed good, it apparently never occurs to him to suggest that the impulse to fight against impossible odds was born of the sort of pride against which Hrothgar warns the young Beowulf.

While the *Vita Oswini* does support the identification of a conflict in *Beowulf* between the heroic code and royal responsibility, it does not support the further conclusion, espoused by John Leyerle, Margaret Goldsmith, John Halverson, James Smith, and others, that the hero is himself infected with the pride or avarice of which Hrothgar speaks.[16] In the *Vita Oswini*, an ethic of sovereignty and a heroic, military ethic not only coexist, but the tension arising from their coexistence creates the martyr-king's dilemma. Those who argue for Beowulf's moral failure do so, in my view, by subjecting the heroic code of which he is a perfect exemplar to the judgment of another value system, e.g., an ethic of sovereignty (Leyerle) or an ethic springing from Christian-monastic culture (Goldsmith). What the *Vita Oswini* helps us to do is to see that such value systems can exist in the same culture and in the same person, where they can, and will, produce dilemmas and tensions, but that one need not be invoked as a norm by which the other must be judged. Neither Oswine nor his author conclude that the generous spirit which makes the king's men want so much to fight his enemies is wrong or not to be admired, or that in determining to break off the fight, the king is resisting the blandishments of pride or cupidity. At the same time, the form of the story and its outcome tell us that the king's concern for the life and safety of those who follow him is also an inescapable imperative.

Though Hrothgar does warn Beowulf against pride and avarice in the famous and extensive "sermon" before his friend's departure for home (1700-84), the hero clearly avoids the trap against which he is warned. In graphic terms, the old king had depicted the growth of pride as if it were a fatal disease or poisonous wound:

Wunað he on wiste; no hine wiht dweleð
adl ne yldo, ne him inwitsorh

tebeitel (Chicago, 1970); *Archaic Roman Religion*, trans. by Philip Krapp, 2 vols. (Chicago, 1970); *Gods of the Ancient Northmen*, ed. by Einar Haugen, Publications of the UCLA Center for the Study of Comparative Folklore and Mythology 3 (Berkeley and Los Angeles, 1973).

16 Leyerle, see n. 10 above; Margaret Goldsmith, *The Mode and Meaning of 'Beowulf'* (London, 1970); John Halverson, "The World of *Beowulf*," *English Literary History* 36 (1969), 593-608; James Smith, "*Beowulf*—I," *English* 25 (1976), 203-29 and "*Beowulf*—II," *English* 26 (1977), 3-22 (written ca. 1957, ed. by Martin Dodsworth).

on sefan sweorceð...
oð þæt him on innan oferhygda dæl
weaxeð ond wridað; ...
þinceð him to lytel, þæt he longe heold
gytsað gromhydig, nallas on gylp seleð
fætte beagas...

1735-37, 1740-41, 1748-50

[He lives in prosperity; to him comes no wit of sickness or of age, nor does any care darken his mind... until his share of pride grows and flourishes within him... that which he has long had, meanly hoarded, seems to him too little.]

Presumptuous pride stifles generosity and leads to avarice, which prevents him from sharing with his followers, but Beowulf does not lapse into presumption and avarice. Rather, in his old age, he goes out to meet a deadly threat against his people and in his dying moments exults over the dragon's treasure, not for himself, but "þæs ðe ic moste minum leodum / ær swyltdæge swylc gestrynan" ["that I might bestow such (a treasure) on my people before my death-day"] (2797-98). In his dying moment, Beowulf has become, not like the Heremod against whom Hrothgar warned him, but like Sigemund, who had slain another dragon and "elne gegongen, / þæt he beahhordes brucan moste" ["valiantly prevailed, so that he might enjoy the treasure-hoard"] (893-94).

But the poem does not end with Beowulf's death. We hear from the messenger what the people are to expect as a result of his death: the renewed warfare of Franks and Frisians and Swedes (2911 ff., 2922 ff.); a life of violence, poverty, and frequent exile; and we hear from the poet what is to be the eventual destiny of the gold, buried in the funeral monument "þær hit nu gen lifað / eldum swa unnyt, swa hi(t æro)r wæs" ["... where it lies yet, as useless to men now as it was in times past"] (3167-68). Beowulf's courage and generosity are to yield a harvest of bitterness and suffering. As with Oedipus, and as with Hamlet, the tragic effect lies precisely in the gap between intention and result, "between the idea and the reality." What the poem as a whole does is what John Leyerle begins by saying it does: it points to "the fatal contradiction at the core of heroic society," but that contradiction is not the soft, moral flaw of Hrothgar's sermon, but the harsh and unrecognized error in judgment which confuses a heroic military ethic with an ethic of sovereignty. In Aristotelian terms, *Beowulf* ends in a tragic reversal unattended by discovery, peripety without recognition. This is the kind of irony that overshadows the final lines of *Beowulf*. Neither the hero, nor Wiglaf, nor the messenger, nor anyone realizes "the fatal contradiction at the core of heroic society." Their silence is not simply poetic reticence or obscurantism, but the fact that they never understand why the courage and generosity of their leader has led so inevitably to violence, suffering, poverty, and exile. Structural juxtaposition has itself revealed the profound irony of Beowulf's story, an irony which finally transcends the political strategies of warring nations and the doctrinal differences of opposed creeds, in much the same way that Albany's speech at the end of *Lear* transcends the rivalries which trigger the action of that play:

> The weight of this sad time we must obey,
> Speak what we feel, not what we ought to say.
> The oldest hath borne most: we that are young
> Shall never see so much, nor live so long.

4

Domestic Peace and Public Order in Anglo-Saxon Law*

Rebecca V. Colman

In our society, the concept of personal safety has long been intertwined with assumptions about the role of the state. For most of us, unarmed citizens that we are, the state is seen as a forceful protector whose first duty it is to provide law and order. But when the security of our streets and the safety of our homes can no longer be taken for granted, people find themselves questioning those assumptions. And so it is of some interest to look back to the early days of English history when public authority was minimal, and self-reliant communities looked to their own defense, while slowly and painfully they learned to build together that greater security which, singly, no one of them could have achieved.

The thread of our story winds back through legal records to that period of English history before the Norman Conquest, from which little has come down to us in descriptive writing. Old English literature has so far yielded little to the probings of legal historians; but rich seams of information were discovered in the nineteenth century in the early law codes of Western Europe, once scholars like Wilda, Heinrich

---

* I would like to thank Father Michael Sheehan, Pontifical Institute of Mediaeval Studies, Toronto, for many fruitful discussions on this and other aspects of early law.

Brunner, Maitland, and Maine, to name only a few, learned to unlock their secrets by comparative and interdisciplinary study. It was these scholars, bred in an era of nationalistic scholarship, with every major country competitively publishing its own *monumenta* in extravagant folio editions, who demonstrated that their own fragmented and enigmatic source materials made most sense when grouped with similar materials from other countries within the broad West European-Scandinavian legal tradition. Such is the case with the materials from which this paper is fashioned. By focussing on a particularly significant crime of violence against the homestead, known in England as *hamsocn*, and familiar, under other similar names, to all West European and Scandinavian countries in the early Middle Ages,[1] we shall be able to see to what extent security could be achieved in disordered times. We shall also see how, in combating this and other threats to domestic peace, the communal need for public order fostered political integration. And, finally, the principles which emerged to guide people in their centuries-long struggle to contain the crime are still apposite today, and indeed, are fundamental to most legal systems.

Like other legal terms dating from proto-literate times, *hamsocn* presents problems of interpretation and meaning we cannot hope to solve in narrowly legalistic terms. Definitions are lacking in early law codes, and references are so sparse as almost to defy serious attention. Any attempt to deduce a specific meaning, or to isolate a characteristic feature, has to contend with the changing circumstances of four or five centuries and with a variety of local traditions which affect the definition and treatment of what nevertheless emerges as a widely recognizable crime throughout Western Europe. As for court records, on which one would normally rely for quantitative evidence, they come late and have to be interpreted within a social context radically different from that surrounding the earliest appearances of the word. Holdsworth considers *hamsocn* already obsolescent by the time court rolls begin to be useful to us: "Bracton and the rolls of the king's court... still [mid-thirteenth century] tell us of old customs and archaic words...

---

1 *Heimsuchung* (Germany), *hemsoken* (Sweden), *husfrithbrøthe* (Jutland). Since this paper was delivered, parts of it have appeared in the author's "Hamsocn: Its Meaning and Significance in Early English Law," *American Journal of Legal History* 25 (1981), 95-110, where more detailed discussions of terms may be found. *Hamsocn* has generally been considered a Scandinavian loan-word, although Erik Björkman, *Scandinavian Loan-Words in Middle English* (Halle, 1900), 12, admitted that such "as a rule... cannot be proved to be so." Liebermann, *Gesetze* II, 504, s.v. *Heimsuchung*, 1. EHD I, 428, n. 3. Johannes C. H. R. Steenstrup, *Normannerne*, 4 vols. (Copenhagen, 1876-82), IV, 348, while granting the possibility of Nordic origin for *hamsocn*, thought *socn* "incontestably an Anglo-Saxon word" (*er ubestrideligt et angelsaksisk Ord*). One might add that the developed sense would be seeking out someone in order to attack him. Cf. Gothic *sôkjan* as 'dispute': Joseph Wright, *Grammar of the Gothic Language*, 2nd ed. with a Supplement to the Grammar by Olive L. Sayce (Oxford, 1954), 344.

[like] hamsoken...."[2] Yet the charge was to be pleaded in courts for centuries to come (it survived as a capital offense in Scotland until 1887),[3] and in spite of the obvious attenuation of the crime, sufficient vitality remains in the ancient phrases used by plaintiffs for us to glimpse something of its earlier character.

King Edmund's *Code Concerning the Blood Feud* (A.D. 939x46), where *hamsocn* first appears in surviving records, simply states that anyone committing it or *mundbryce* (the breach of a special, known peace, in this case, probably the king's, but cf. Alfred, fn. 18) would "forfeit all that he owns," and "it would be for the king to decide" whether or not he should preserve his life. This tells us very little about the crime except that it was a royal plea and, therefore, a serious offense, as the penalty also indicates; but scholars, drawing on the contemporary and richer European evidence, have felt justified in filling in the probable detail. W. E. Wilda, who pioneered comparative studies incorporating previously neglected Norse material, demonstrated a widespread concurrence of felonies, such as arson, rape, kidnapping, beating, and murder (in the most seriously regarded cases of *Heimsuchung*, murder drawing the heaviest penalties), and he included Edmund's *hamsocn* in this category. And Felix Liebermann, arguing from the context of Edmund's clause, also thought that manslaughter, *Totschlag*, was the aggravating factor in that case.[4] Half a century after Edmund, the *De Institutis Lundonie*, dated by Liebermann A.D. 991x1002, further emphasized the seriousness of the crime by declaring that anyone killed in the act would be devoid of right to *wergild* (life price), *iaceat in ungildam œkere*, an injunction repeated in the subsequent Laws of Cnut (II.62.1), and reiterated, with modification, over two hundred years later, ca. 1250x58, in the pages of Bracton: "where one defends himself against *hamsocn* ... and the intruder is slain, he will be free of liability if he who killed could defend himself in no other way."[5]

The earliest definition of the crime occurs a century after the *De Institutis Lundonie*, in the so-called *Leges Henrici Primi*, ca. 1114x18, a private digest of Anglo-Saxon laws and customs with fragments culled from other codes. Here, *hamsocn* is translated into Latin, *invasio domus* ('attack on a home'), and variously described as armed attack

---

2 William S. Holdsworth, *A History of English Law*, 4th ed. (London, 1936), II, 258.
3 John L. Wark (ed.), *Encyclopaedia of the Laws of Scotland*, 16 vols. (Edinburgh, 1926-35), V, 116-17.
4 EHD I, 428, No. 38; Wilhelm E. Wilda, *Das Strafrecht der Germanen*, Geschichte des deutschen Strafrechts 1 (Halle, 1842, rptd. Aalen, 1960), 957-58; Liebermann, *Gesetze* III, 128, n. 2.
5 Agnes J. Robertson (ed. and trans.), *The Laws of the Kings of England from Edmund to Henry I* (Cambridge, 1925), 75; Liebermann, *Gesetze* I, 234, 235; EHD I, 464, No. 49; Samuel E. Thorne (trans.), *Bracton on the Laws and Customs of England*, 4 vols. (Cambridge, Mass., 1968-77), II, 408.

with a raiding party, *cum haraido*; pursuing someone while hurling stones, shooting arrows, or delivering blows in some other way; premeditated invasion of a house by day or night and there attacking one's enemy; and finally, chasing someone in flight into a mill or sheepfold or into another house during the course of a struggle. These phrases read like *disjecta membra* of half-forgotten codes mingled, perhaps, with familiar case histories. We have first, a probable borrowing from the Frankish laws, *Lex Ribuaria* 64 (Liebermann derived *haraidum* from the Ripuarian *hariraida*), and further on, what seems to be a mere fragment of Alfred's intricate regulations controlling legitimate blood feud. The reference to missiles, though reminiscent of Langobardian and Bavarian law as Brunner pointed out, could also have been prompted by common enough experience; and extending the *locus* of the crime to include mills and sheepfolds reminds one of the extension of *husfrithbrøthe*, the equivalent crime in Danish law, to include "assaulting someone in a twig barn, a ship, or a churchyard"; both could have resulted from unrecorded case histories. Inadequate though they are, these details from the *Leges Henrici Primi* enable us to place the English offense within the genre of similar Continental and Scandinavian crimes of violence.[6]

We get no further until the end of the next century. In the reign of John, we find it listed, but not defined, among the grave crimes dealt with by the *Grant Lai* of the city of London, and Bracton, in his brief reference to it under "Crown Pleas," leaves it simply as *invasio domus contra pacem* ('attack on a home against the peace'). Britton, writing later in the thirteenth century, merely lists it twice, once among the Articles of the Justices in Eyre and once among items for the sheriff's *tourn*. But the *Mirror of Justices*, written, Maitland thought, in the last quarter of the thirteenth century, and which relied heavily on Bracton in most matters, provides the first coherent description of the crime, clearly linking it with personal assault:

> Hamsoken by ancient ordinance is mortal sin, for by law everyone who is inlaw is to have peace in his house. This sin is committed not only by breaking a house but also by the felonious assault of enemies in time of peace on those who are in their own houses with the intention of reposing therein in peace. The aforesaid assault must be made with intent to kill, rob, or beat those within the house. And albeit such sinners do not accomplish their intent, if nevertheless they in any way break in door, window or outhouse or the like by their assault in order to enter feloniously, they are guilty of this crime. Into this sin fall those who feloniously and forcibly enter into another's house and do therein any violence against the peace, though they make no breaking; and that whether by day

---

6 L. J. Downer (ed. and trans.), *Leges Henrici Primi* (Oxford, 1972), clause 80.10, 11, 11a-c; Liebermann, *Gesetze* I, 597, n. i; *Laws of Alfred* 42, in EHD I, 415, No. 33; Steenstrup, *Normannerne* IV, 353.

or by night. Likewise those who disseise folk by casting them out of their dwellings and out of their peaceable possessions wrongfully.[7]

When court rolls begin to appear in useful quantities from the thirteenth and fourteenth centuries, it is possible to see what *hamsocn* might have meant in personal terms, although informative references are few, particularly at the village level, and by then we are far away from the time and circumstances of the term's initial emergence into historical records. Nevertheless, certain significant features can be deduced, the most important being the association of alarm and terror with the offense. One dishonest plaintiff, whose lost cause is recorded in the Crown Pleas of 1201, clearly hoped to profit from this aspect of the crime when he falsely described the accused in the customary form of words as coming "wickedly by night" and breaking his "gates and fences and house doors in hamsoken" and stealing his fowls(!), adding that he himself would have been killed had he not fled. There is a certain jingle-like quality to the phrases used in these pleas, echoes of the ancient terminology of the codes, with their reference to *vis* ('violence') and *fortia* ('force'). A typical entry reads: "wickedly and in the king's peace he came with armed hand and with his force, and broke his houses in hamsoken, and in felony robbed him...." Similarly in the records of the City of Norwich, we read of a cordwainer making hamsoken one night, *vi et armis* ('by force and arms'), upon two Dutchmen whom he threatened to beat and kill; and a certain Hervey de Edgmere "by force and arms with a drawn knife... made hamsoken on Oliver Rounkyn... and at the same hour and place... with the said drawn knife on Margaret Diggard and Thomas her son, and beat her and tore her clothes and cast her in the mud, and took and carried away one mark... and he threatened to kill them."[8] The full meaning of the old phrases, however, has gone, since we have no evidence of overwhelming force, such as the old *vis per collecta hominum* ('gang force'), being used against an unsuspecting home-dweller. Nevertheless, the association of terror with the crime lingered on. Overriding importance was still attached to this aspect of *hamsocn* in modern Scottish law, where physical injury was not necessarily required for a conviction, the emphasis being on "the alarm and terror attending the assault in the whole circumstances of the case and especially the colour

7 Mary Bateson, "A London Municipal Collection of the Reign of John, Part II," *EHR* 17 (1902), 707-30; Thorne, *Bracton* II, 408; Francis M. Nichols (ed. and trans.), *Britton: The French Text Carefully Revised, With an English Translation* (Oxford, 1865), 70, 148; Frederic W. Maitland (ed.), *The Mirror of Justices*, Publications of the Selden Society 7 (London, 1893), 28.
8 Frederic W. Maitland (ed.), *Select Pleas of the Crown Vol. I: A.D. 1200-1225*, Publications of the Selden Society 1 (London, 1887), 26, 43; William Hudson (ed.), *Leet Jurisdiction in the City of Norwich during the XIIIth and XIVth Centuries*, Publications of the Selden Society 5 (1892), 64, 66-67.

of the ultimate and meditated wrong."⁹ Few juries would fail to take such considerations into account today, and it is this feature, perhaps above all, which can help us to understand the full significance of the crime in the earlier years of its prevalence.

Attacks on a man's home have always been considered heinous, but the penalty for *hamsocn* which, as we have seen, could extend to loss of life and all possessions often seems disproportionate to the offense, lifting it out of the category of punishment and into that of ritual purgation. This also happened, we learn from Bracton, in certain cases of rape, where not only the ravisher but mute witnesses, such as his horse, his hound, and his hawk, all suffered mutilation.¹⁰ It is interesting to note in this connection that in eighteenth-century Scotland the legal procedure for *hamsocn* was specifically associated with the procedure in cases of rape.¹¹ Such communal determination to "wipe out all memory of an offence by destroying not only the criminal, but also his property," in Holdsworth's words, raises questions of the deepest historical and philosophical interest;¹² yet most commentators on this aspect of the crime have not gone beyond the notion of sacredness. "The sanctity of the house seems to have been due to the religious origin of the house-peace," was Mary Bateson's tautologous explanation for the forbearance of borough law towards the homes of burgesses; and Sir William Blackstone, most famous of English jurists, concluding a reference to "the ancient law of *hamesecken*," cited Cicero: *quid enim sanctius, quid omni religione munitius, quam domus uniusque civium?* ('for what is more holy, what more fortified by every religious precept, than the home of each citizen?').¹³ It is particularly apposite today, when domestic peace is no longer inviolate, and the notion of sacredness no longer impresses, to ask what were the histor-

9 See n. 3.
10 "By the Law of the Romans, the Franks and the English, even his horse shall to his ignominy be put to shame upon its scrotum and its tail, which shall be cut off as close as possible to the buttocks. If he has a dog with him, a greyhound or some other, it shall be put to shame in the same way; if a hawk, let it lose its beak, its claws and its tail." Thorne, *Bracton* II, 418.
11 "This crime may be followit, persewit, and punisht as the crime of ravishing women." James Balfour, *Practicks: or, A System of the More Ancient Law of Scotland* (Edinburgh, 1754), 541.
12 Holdsworth, *History* II, 46.
13 William Blackstone, *Commentaries on the Laws of England* (New York, 1966), IV, 223; cf. Wilda, *Strafrecht*, 241. Concern for the sacred bounds of the home is eloquently expressed in the German *Weistümer: so melden wir auch das ein ieder mann mit fridt soll sein in seinem haus, als wer es mit einem faden umbfangen oder umbhangen, so soll niemant mit gefahr darein laufen, als von alters herkumen ist,* which may be freely translated: 'We also pronounce that, as has been the case from time immemorial, every man should be able to dwell in peace in his own house as though an inviolable thread were drawn or hung around it,' Georg Winter (ed.), in *Österreichische Weisthümer* 8 (Vienna, Leipzig, 1896), 4.

ical circumstances which then caused, and may again cause, men to feel so deeply and apparently universally about this matter?

The most useful survey of Continental European, English, and Scandinavian sources is still the pioneer work of W. E. Wilda (see note 4). He shows that, despite the uneven quality of the records, certain major features of *Heimsuchung* emerge from the mosaic of localized practices. The worst form of assault was the work of organized gangs, variously termed *contubernia, turpha, collecta hominum, secta, herireita*, or *haraidum*, who deliberately set out to attack individual homes or whole villages, pillaging, setting fire, and forcibly abducting women. The codes roughly differentiate between more and less serious versions of the crime, either in terms of the numbers of men involved (in Bavarian law, *herireita*, a major attack, defined as involving 42 men or more, carried the heaviest fines), or according to the nature of the attack, or both. In the *Lex Salica*, for example, 62 1/2 shillings was the fine for an attack (*si quis villam alienam adsallierit*) but 200 shillings if in such an attack "doorways were broken, dogs killed, men wounded and goods carried away in a cart." If murder occurred, three times the usual wergild had to be paid.[14]

Where fences had been breached, gateways and doors smashed, supporting poles or beams pulled down, and watchdogs killed, malicious intent of a very different order from petty house burglary was presumed, since the marauders, by attacking obvious strong points to handicap resisting victims and possibly facilitate their own escape, were evidently prepared to stop at nothing. The numbers of men involved might range from as few as the five or six mentioned in Lombard and Danish law, to the size of a small army, although there is evidence that single individuals were capable of such harassment. We get an unusual glimpse of the life and times of such freebooters in the biography of the eighth-century English saint, Guthlac, whose early career was devoted to armed raiding.[15] Such acts of terror were called *harizuht* in Frankish law, and *heerwerk* in Danish law—literally 'army operations'—since they differed little, if at all, from the harrying of hostile armies. Their common distinguishing features were their multiplicity of violent crimes, one often leading to another, and the terrifying nature of the preliminary assault.

Evidence of such thuggery, which was understandably treated as, in Wilda's phrase, *der schwerste Hausfriedensbruch* ('the worst breach

---

14 Ernest von Schwind (ed.), *Lex Baiwariorum*, MGH, Leges I, V.2 (Hanover, 1926), 331 (English translation by Theodore J. Rivers, *The Laws of the Alamans and Bavarians* [Philadelphia, 1977], 133). Karl A. Eckhardt (ed.), *Lex Salica*, MGH, Leges I, IV.2 (Hanover, 1969), 58-59, 202-203. Further illustrations in Wilda, *Strafrecht*, 952-53; and Heinrich Brunner, *Deutsche Rechtsgeschichte*, 2nd ed., 2 vols. (Munich, Leipzig, 1906-28), II, 841-45, Section 141.

15 Wilda, *Strafrecht*, 955-56; Bertram Colgrave, *Felix's Life of Saint Guthlac* (Cambridge, 1956).

of house peace') by all codes, can be found in the laws of the West Saxon King Ine, who ruled from 688 to 726, three centuries before the word *hamsocn* appears in England. Clause 13.1 reads: "We call up to seven men thieves, from seven to thirty-five a gang (*hloth*); above that it is an army (*here*)." And the fines were very severe: in the case of a *hloth*, an oath of twenty-four *ceorls* was required to clear a suspect, or the equivalent fine of 120 shillings had to be paid; in the case of an army-sized raid, those accused of participation, if they failed to clear themselves by an equivalent oath, had to pay the value of their wergild, a huge sum for any class. Complicity was one thing, but to have killed on such a raid was virtually inexpiable, to judge from codes which are explicit on the point. For ordinary killing, as in the heat of an affray, the single appropriate wergeld was heavy enough burden; we know from Alfred's laws that a minor unpaid portion, one third, necessitated the slayer's exile; but in raiding cases, there were heavy additional fines as well. In some Continental codes, there were multiple wergilds to pay. These were three-fold in the Salic and Ripuarian laws, and nine-fold in the Alemannic, sums which, in the majority of cases, must have been unpayable even if a man surrendered all he had and added his life value as well, which indeed, was what Edmund's code demanded of those convicted of *hamsocn*.[16] Reading the codes leaves one with a strong impression that some penalties were expected to be unpayable, just as outlawry was originally a veiled form of capital punishment. Occasionally the pretence breaks down, as in Cnut's laws, where the more heinous variety of *hamsocn* known as *husbryce* under the Danish king, together with other felonies, was simply declared *botless* and the culprit had to face the terrors of expulsion from his community with possible death on sight thereafter. Milder forms of breaking and entering, of course, are recorded side by side with the more serious. Ine's law quoted above, for example, equated "thieving" with the smallest-sized gang, but even petty thieves were severely dealt with if caught in the act (killing them was no crime), and persistent thieving ranked among the most heinous crimes in the codes. This is understandable.

At the simpler levels of economic and technological development, such as prevailed over much of Western Europe for some centuries after the migrations, large-scale production and storage systems were unknown, and a village or isolated homestead would contain within its

---

16 *Laws of Ine* 13.1, 14, 15, in EHD I, 400, No. 32. Ceorls were free men with 200-shilling wergilds. *Laws of Alfred* 30, in EHD I, 413, No. 33; Eckhardt (ed.), *Lex Salica*, 202; Joseph Balon, *Traité de Droit Salique*, Ius Medii Aevi 3, 4 vols. (Namur, 1965), II, 437-41; Franz Beyerle and Rudolf Buchner (eds.), *Lex Ribuaria* 67, MGH, Leges I, III.2 (Hanover, 1954), 118; Karl Lehmann (ed.), *Leges Alamannorum* XLIV, 2, MGH, Leges I, V.1 (Hanover, 1888), 105; Rivers, *Laws*, 82; II Edmund 6, in EHD I, 428, No. 38.

confines subsistence for its occupants from one harvest to the next. Persistent internal thieving could not, therefore, be tolerated, and a single raid from a marauding band of the kind mentioned in Ine's laws could reduce a community to beggary. Worse still, if an armed gang of the sort described in the *Lex Salica* (clause 74) established itself in a fortified position in order to prey more effectively, the locality could become denuded of settlements. Archaeologist Malcolm Todd has suggested that the sudden demise of once prosperous communities, like Vallhagar in sixth-century Gotland, is "best explained as the result of insecurity bred of war or incessant raidings"; and a more recent parallel may be found in the remote northern Transvaal, where the Venda people reacted to the ceaseless marauding of Zulu and Swazi by reducing the size of their fields and allowing their production levels to fall. And there are well-known robber-infested areas across the world today where no community can flourish and travellers venture at their peril. The dangers of unchecked marauding are well known to sophisticated societies too. Roman law took cognizance of it in the *Lex Julia de vi publica*, the Emperor Constantine's commentary on the latter presaging the barbarian codes' concern to shield victims of assault who killed in self-defense:

> If any person shall invade another's farm with violence he shall suffer capital punishment. If anyone should be killed, whether on the part of the person who attempted to employ violence or by the person who repulsed the injury, punishment shall be inflicted on the one who intended to eject the possessor by force.[17]

Hamsocn was, and under other names always has been, a crime of particular significance where law and order are either at a rudimentary stage or breaking down, as in some of our cities today, conditions of law categorized by H. L. A. Hart as "embryological" and "pathological" respectively, and which can be comprehended only in terms of their political context. Settling, cultivating, and building all depend on the degree of security available, but achieving that security was a hazardous and patchwork affair. In the early Middle Ages, the "king's peace," which in theory extended irrespective of place over particular people and cases (*hamsocn*, as we have seen, was a royal plea), must

---

17 Balon, *Traité* I, 203; Malcolm Todd, *Everyday Life of the Barbarians: Goths, Franks and Vandals* (London and New York, 1972), 56; Frank M. Stenton observed that "much warfare has escaped the notice of historians," *ASE* 471; N. J. van Warmelo and W. M. D. Phophi, *Venda Law, Part 5: Property*, Republic of South Africa, Department of Bantu Administration and Development, Ethnological Publications 50 (Pretoria, 1967), 1111; Theodore Mommsen (ed.), *Theodosiani Libri xvi cum constitutionibus sirmondianis* (Berlin, 1905, reprinted 1962), 453 (English translation by Clyde Pharr, *The Theodosian Code and Novels and the Sirmondian Constitutions*, Corpus of Roman Law 1 [Princeton, 1952], 234); cf. *Edictum Theodorici Regis* XVI, in Johannes Baviera (ed.), *Fontes Iuris Romani Antejustiniani*, 2nd ed., 3 vols. (Florence, 1941-43), II, 687.

in practice seldom have reached beyond the effective area of the royal presence, even being reduced at times to the circumference of the royal residence. We have a fragment from the tenth century which reads: "Thus far shall be the king's *grith* (peace), from his burh-gate where he is dwelling, on its four sides; that is III miles, and III furlongs, and III acres breadth, and IX feet and IX palms and IX barleycorns," and depending on the strength of the king's position, his protection must often have extended no further, otherwise such a passage would not have been necessary in the laws. Security must, therefore, have depended of necessity on the exertions of other powerful men, ealdormen and bishops, for example, whose establishments could provide shelter, if needed, and whose premises were protected by appropriately heavier fines for breaking and entering (*burgbryce*) than applied in the case of a commoner's compound.[18] But the peace of the peasant's homestead, on which ultimately everyone's prosperity depended, could only have been assured in the first instance by the aggressive alertness of the peasant community, whose defensive attitudes are reflected in the well-known hostility of tribal law towards strangers. Physical structures could provide little or no protection, and where marauders were able to attack with impunity, whether they came from outside or inside the community,[19] people might be forced to flee their homes permanently, with all that entailed of immediate loss and long-term damage to productivity.

In such conditions, the overt use of terror can be an effective weapon in the lawbreaker's hands. No intruder wanted to risk being cut down by an occupant who had the advantage of supporting beams or door frame to fight from, and so the throwing of stones or shooting of arrows at the house, which were familiar features of *Heim-*

---

18 Herbert L. A. Hart, *The Concept of Law* (Oxford, 1961), 114-20. Translation of the tenth-century fragment is by Benjamin Thorpe (ed. and trans.), *Ancient Laws and Institutes of England*, Publications of the Record Commissioners 28 (London, 1840), 224-25; Liebermann, *Gesetze* I, 390; cf. *Leges Henrici Primi* 16, 1. Clause 40 of Alfred's Laws reads: "Forcible entry (*burgbryce*) into the king's residence shall be 120 shillings; into the archbishop's, 90 shillings; another bishop's or an ealdorman's, 60 shillings; into that of a man of a twelve-hundred wergild, 30 shillings; into that of a man of a six-hundred wergild, 15 shillings; forcible entry into a *ceorl*'s enclosure, five shillings," EHD I, 414-15, No. 33. Cf. the role of noble households in medieval Spain: Eugen Wohlhaupter, "Das Privatrecht der Fueros de Aragon," *Zeitschrift der Savigny-Stiftung für Rechtsgeschichte, Germanistische Abteilung* 62 (1942), 101-102.

19 Personal enmity must often have led to such raids; for example, the *Leges Alamannorum* XLIV (n. 16 above), describes one of the parties after a fight gathering a group to wreak vengeance on the other. Cf. item 35: *ob ainer veindschaft hiet und braücht leüt in das dorf*, Winter, *Weisthümer*. (I am indebted to Dr. Karl Helleiner for this reference.) A more serious communal danger, however, is the destructive parasitism of insatiable marauders. But whatever its cause, violence, because it is contagious, has to be restrained, even righteous violence, *propter atrocitatem delicti*, as in the case discussed by Gaius, where one evicts an unlawful possessor of one's property: *Gai Institutionum Commentarii Quattuor* IV.155, in Baviera, *Fontes* II, 185.

suchung/hamsocn, should perhaps be interpreted as attempts to frighten people out before worse befell them. It is easy to see how those particular actions became definitive of the crime, as in the *Leges Henrici Primi* (see above). Brunner thought "the spirit of the old law" required a demonstration of hostile intent (*musste die feindselige Absicht zu typischem Ausdrucke sein*), such as the encirclement *hostili manu* ('by a hostile gang') of Bavarian, Frisian, and Anglo-Warnian law.[20] If intimidation failed, the thieves, or avengers, as the case might be, could set fires and operate all the more easily in the ensuing confusion. It is conceivable that Cnut's "*husbryce* and burning and theft and obvious murder" was no haphazard list but a succession of felonious acts which must often have occurred, and have been expected to occur, together. Hence the association of terror with *hamsocn*, terror of the sort which only systematic and institutionalized development of law and order could hope to eradicate.

But this was a slow and difficult process. In Edmund's time, *hamsocn* was, perhaps, a new name for the old crime of marauding which flourished as rankly in the unsettled conditions of the tenth as of the sixth and seventh centuries. By the twelfth and thirteenth centuries, however, we are in a very different world from the exposed agricultural communities of earlier times. We can begin to see not only the emergence of a centralized monarchical state ready to provide at least minimal order through its itinerant justices, but also, at the local level, new urban communities able to look to their own defense. Increased security, the growing affluence of urbanized Europe, developing administrative and judicial machinery, the diversity of town life with its concomitant diversity of crime, all conspired to reduce the dimensions of *hamsocn*. There was simply less scope for those "razzias ... commises par de fortes bandes de pillards armés" ('raids ... perpetrated by violent gangs of armed plunderers')[21] which earlier terrified the countryside, and the measure of the community's victory may be seen in its assertion of the principle of the inviolability of domestic peace. Medieval English towns generally refused to allow officers to enter the houses of burgesses to arrest, attach or distrain,[22] and it is only in recent times with our increasingly sophisticated techniques of surveillance that the legal safeguards of personal privacy have begun to be eroded.

Before leaving the crime of *hamsocn*, it is interesting to see how it gradually fades from the historical picture. As already noted, the cry of

20 Brunner, *Rechtsgeschichte*, 843. Such terror tactics were also employed during the Mau Mau crisis in Kenya in the 1950's.
21 Balon, *Traité* I, 204.
22 Mary Bateson (ed.), *Borough Customs*, 2 vols., Publications of the Selden Society 18, 21 (1904, 1906), II, XXV. In London, the accused could not be "attached except in mid-street and mid-way and not in a house or under a penthouse," ibid. I, 103.

terror begins to sound rather hollow in some of the cases recorded in the court rolls of the thirteenth century. In others, mere fragments of the once complex crime appear under the old name. For example, simple breaches of the village peace, carrying fines of four or five pence, are listed as *hamsokens* in the manorial court rolls of the later Middle Ages. The action of the woman Sarah, who took a stone and broke the lock on the cottage she had lost as a result of marrying a man from the homage of another lord, is described as an act of *hamsoken* in 1290. Another example of the erosion of meaning is to be found in a case recorded in 1275 of personal assault and name-calling which took place in a bakehouse rented for the St. Ives fair—very different circumstances from those traditionally associated with *hamsocn* and long considered essential to the proper laying of that charge. In eighteenth-century Scotland, it was still "statute" that "gif ony man will accuse ane uther of Hamsucken, it is necessary that he alledge that he assail-zeit him in his awin proper house, quhair he has his winning, rising and lying day and nicht...," but in the changing circumstances of the later Middle Ages in other areas, the more serious surviving features of the crime, the ruthless, not always furtive, seizure of property, endangering, and possibly encompassing, loss of life or limb, gradually ceased to be referred to as *hamsocn*. W. S. Holdsworth thought that Britton's (thirteenth-century) "crime of burglary" probably represented "the older hamsoken," burglars being defined by Britton as "all those who feloniously in time of peace, break churches, or the houses of others, or the walls or gates of our cities or boroughs... the punishment for such felons [being] death."[23] Burglary was not yet defined as a nighttime offense, but it is indicative of the growing security of the later Middle Ages that it had become so by the sixteenth century, stealth proving more practicable in the changed circumstances than alarm-raising terror tactics.

Sir Henry Maine, in his *Ancient Law*, saw in the family the origins of an ordered state; in the history of *hamsocn*, we can see the territorial and personal implications of that theory, as well as something of the long struggle towards the larger security. It is first of all in the areas of individual homesteads, in all their variety of strengths and sizes, that we must expect to find the origins of law and order and beginnings, therefore, of communal security. There are obvious biological reasons why the home should be as secure a place as possible, and why, therefore, people should feel particularly exposed when attacked in their family dwelling. Yet, as we have seen from a variety of evidence, in the

23 Frederic W. Maitland (ed.), *Select Pleas in Manorial Courts*, Publications of the Selden Society 2 (1888), 98, 143; Balfour, *Practicks*, 541; Nichols, *Britton*, 36. (The medieval Latin for burglar, *burglator*, first appears about 1250. It combines Anglo-Saxon *burg* [*burgbryce* was the old term for forced entry, see n. 18 above] with Latin *latro*, a mercenary soldier or robber.)

formative stages of English and other societies neither the physical structures nor, in some cases, the human resources of small communities were sufficient on their own to provide the necessary protection. This had to depend on the growth of larger power. From its first appearance in our records, *hamsocn* was a royal plea, and in the long run it was royal power that provided the public order which ensured personal security. But the struggle was a long one and depended in the first instance, then as now, on the alertness of the local community.

In recounting history, one tends to simplify and rationalize, but there is less self-conscious formulation in customary law than we are used to, and distinctions between what is permitted and what is forbidden grow naturally from a certain way of life, the law often stating what is practicable rather than what is desirable. In the case of illegal entry into homesteads, for example, it was evidently as hazardous to intrude into a strange compound then as in similar societies today; and no sympathy, much less compensation, would be wasted on individuals who got themselves killed while wandering in a strange courtyard at night-time, *in curte aliena noctis tempore* (*Edictus Rothari* No. 32, 33, 34), just as, to quote a modern African example, "no Ibo would come into Tivland at night unescorted unless he were mad or trying to steal"; and Bracton's statement that "no one [is to] receive a stranger into his house . . . except in broad daylight" probably reflects prudent practice as well as stating legal regulation.[24] We are dealing, in other words, with a stage in our legal and social history when rudimentary political and legal arrangements surface slowly, in the wake of communal reactions to often bitter experience. In the case of *hamsocn*, we are dealing with one of the more fundamental aspects of that experience since it concerned the basic security of the home; and the history of the crime not only demonstrates the way in which rules of social intercourse evolve, but also how the sacredness of the home became an established concept.

24 Paul Bohannan, *Justice and Judgement among the Tiv* (Oxford, 1957), 136; Thorne, *Bracton* II, 387.

5

Two Early Anglo-Saxon Holy Men: Oswald and Cuthbert

John Corbett

The history of the Church in Britain during the early Anglo-Saxon period is obscure and controversial. The paucity and uncertainty of our sources makes it difficult to assess the relative importance in that history of Romano-British, Celtic, and Germanic elements. We must make assumptions regarding the roles of these different elements; such assumptions, in turn, condition our whole understanding of early Anglo-Saxon history and especially our understanding of the place in that history of the great English Holy Men who are my immediate concern. Caution seems called for, and an open mind.

It is a matter of record that the Church was firmly established in Britain long before the invasions—sufficiently so to have produced its own distinctive heresy. It seems unnecessary to question the historicity of St. Alban; casual allusions in the church fathers attest to the presence of the faith in Britain even before his time. Pelagius's heresy cannot be excused as a consequence of heathen ignorance or barbarism; it reflects a position on the central theological issue of the Western church—God's grace and man's free will—which had deep roots in Roman social history, as I would suspect, and certainly a wide appeal throughout the Latin empire.¹ The doctrinal perversity of the British may have given God good reason to contemplate their extinction, as Bede would certainly believe.² Instead, in his mercy, God sent St. Germanus from Gaul for their correction. The miraculous cures which Germanus worked and his close association with St. Alban left the British church on a firm and orthodox foundation after his second visit in the 440's—just before Vortigern allegedly summoned the Saxons. We may well suppose that in the following 150 years, the British suffered considerable chastisement at the hands of the barbarians— whether Picts and Scots, or Saxons. But it is not necessary to assume that the British church was extinguished. Bede's prejudice, probably widely shared by his colleagues, may have led him to underestimate the strength and significance of the British church, despite the evidence to the contrary which he himself reports.³ The subsequent importance of the Celtic church, and of the "Celtic" and "Roman" missions to Britain, have perhaps contributed to the distortion begun by the English prejudices of Bede and his like. Surely we need not suppose that the Anglo-Saxon church was a creation almost *ex nihilo*; that its traditions were new, or at least without a substantial British component.⁴

Should we come to believe that the Anglo-Saxon church was something new and distinct in British history, we will face certain embarrassing difficulties. What are the cultural roots of the great Anglo-Saxon Holy Men who came to prominence so soon after the Saxon Conquest? Various origins have been suggested. "Cuthbert belongs to the Celtic rather than to the Roman tradition . . . ; in spite of his dying attacks upon the Celtic 'heretics' he lived and died after the manner of the typical Irish monk."⁵ Alternatively, Anglo-Saxon saints

---

1 See Peter Brown, "Pelagius and his Supporters: Aims and Environment" and "The Patrons of Pelagius: The Roman Aristocracy between East and West," in Peter Brown, *Religion and Society in the Age of St. Augustine* (London, 1972), 183-226.
2 See Bede, *HE*, I.10, 38-39; II.19, 198-203; cf. I.17-21, 54-67, for the intervention of St. Germanus.
3 Compare Bede's remarks on "the godless Cædwalla" in Bede, *HE*, II.20, 202-05; III.1, 12-15.
4 The major new study by Charles Thomas, *Christianity in Roman Britain to AD 500* (London, 1981), appeared after the present paper was written, and its arguments cannot be examined in detail here. Suffice it to note that, after an exhaustive review of the evidence and modern scholarship, Thomas presents a subtle and convincing case for the survival of the Romano-British Church (see his conclusions, summarized in Chap. 15). He accepts the historicity of the early traditions in Bede concerning St. Ninian (see Chap. 11, "St. Ninian, and Christianity in Southern Scotland," especially p. 294 for his conclusion), a matter of some concern in this paper (see n. 16 and the text there), while unnecessarily rejecting Bede's reports of early dedications to St. Martin at Whithorn and Canterbury (see pp. 280-81 for Whithorn and pp. 170-72 for Canterbury), on which see below nn. 16-19 and the text there.
5 See Bertram Colgrave (ed. and trans.), *Two Lives of St. Cuthbert* (Cambridge, 1940), 5; cf. pp. 11-12, where Colgrave refers to the influence of Continental hagiography, especially Sulpicius Severus's work on St. Martin. This is a theme which deserves to

modelled themselves on the traditional heroes of their Germanic culture, so well known to us from *Beowulf*. (In other words, the historical saints are manifestations in Christian guise of a pre-Christian social form; their literary reflection is much influenced by the traditional heroic types of Anglo-Saxon literature.) These views are attractive and probably not without merit. It is natural to compare Anglo-Saxon saints to Germanic heroes or to their Celtic forerunners; many models may have, to some extent, influenced Anglo-Saxon views of the Holy Man. But we must not ignore the larger social context: ancient Northumbria was very much part of the Christian Roman world.[6] Literary stereotypes of saints or heroes must be carefully distinguished from the actual social and religious practices upon which such stereotypes were based and which they influenced in their turn. Even if we choose to emphasize the literary antecedents of Anglo-Saxon hagiography, it is a matter of fact, as Colgrave and others have long realized, that the actual surviving literary lives of the Anglo-Saxon Saints (in Latin, at least) show signs of the dominant influence of late Roman hagiography. The *Lives of St. Cuthbert*, that written by the anonymous monk of Lindisfarne and that written subsequently by Bede, show clearly that their authors were familiar with such important hagiographical works as Evagrius's Latin version of the *Life of St. Antony*, Possidius's biography of St. Augustine, Sulpicius Severus's *Life of St. Martin*, the *Acta Silvestri*, and the *Dialogues of Pope Gregory*, to mention only some of the more important.[7] Here again we are dealing with verbal similarities attesting to literary influences on the authors of the *Lives of Cuthbert*. This evidence may allow us to draw conclusions about the social origins and contexts of the practices to which these *Lives* attest, as well as the specifically literary conclusions which are of predominant importance to many scholars.

But there are dangers here. Unless we deliberately and carefully investigate the social history of the Holy Man in the late Ancient World, verbal similarities and literary influences may obscure more important social influences and structural similarities which do not

be examined in greater detail. For the view which follows on the Germanic origins of models of sainthood in the Anglo-Saxon period, see Clinton Albertson, *Anglo-Saxon Saints and Heroes* (New York, 1967), 1-28, especially pp. 25ff.

6 Peter Brown, "Eastern and Western Christendom in Late Antiquity: A Parting of the Ways," in *Society and the Holy in Late Antiquity* (Berkeley and Los Angeles, 1982), 166-95. Brown is here much concerned to emphasize the essential unity of the Mediterranean world in late Antiquity and the unity of late Ancient Christian culture, a *koiné*, as he calls it, "which, by the end of this period had already spilled far from the shores of the Mediterranean, to the Nestorian hagiography of Sassanian Iran and the Celtic holy men of Northumbria" (ibid., 179).

7 Bertram Colgrave, *Two Lives of St. Cuthbert*, especially the "Introduction," and Index s.vv. "Martin, St.," "Sulpicius Severus," "Gregory of Tours," and "Gregory I the Great."

happen to betray themselves to the philologist through specific phrases or common literary themes. In their studies of early Anglo-Saxon saints' lives, some scholars have tended to emphasize traditional Anglo-Saxon social and literary forms (as Albertson); others have drawn attention to the influence of Latin hagiography (as Colgrave). In these approaches, perhaps too much stress has been placed on literature, literary history, and the "history of ideas," and rather too little on popular belief and practice. The social context of the Roman world, and the social function of the Holy Man within that context, have been unduly neglected.

Dangers must also be acknowledged in the approach which I am proposing; our argument may well be circular. Even if we begin with the intention of reconstructing popular belief and social practice as they relate to Anglo-Saxon Holy Men, deliberately expanding our enquiry beyond the rather narrow bounds of hagiography, it must be admitted that we will still be largely dependent on information derived from the lives of saints. This danger must be acknowledged because it cannot be avoided completely. The only course open to us is to examine our evidence very carefully, distinguishing by means of internal analysis, if possible, hagiographic commonplaces from first-hand reports, and supplementing the hagiographic tradition with whatever external evidence comes to hand. This is a subtle procedure, but I believe that it can lead to positive results. We must also avoid the dangers implicit in a shallow scepticism regarding the commonplaces so often found in the lives of saints. For if one author can be influenced in recounting the deeds of some much admired Holy Man by what he has read in other similar lives and also by his own expectations and those of his audience, nonetheless it remains true that a saint's behaviour must often have conformed to stereotypes. One saint's deeds and his social role may well have resembled closely those of his predecessors. Indeed, this is what I shall attempt to suggest in the cases of Oswald and Cuthbert. Their deeds may have been conditioned by what they knew of the career of St. Martin, and the literary similarity of Bede's *Lives*, for instance, to the *Dialogues* of Pope Gregory may be misleading, obscuring the more important (to my mind) structural similarities in the role and function of Holy Men in late Roman Gaul and Anglo-Saxon Britain.[8] A glance at Bede's accounts of King Oswald and Saint Cuthbert will confirm this impression.

8 There are important similarities to be observed in the social role and function of Holy Men throughout the late Ancient world—and also some striking regional differences, arising from the different ways "in which Christianity adapted itself to its Roman environment" (Brown, "Eastern and Western Christendom," 174). For this whole question, the indispensable introduction is the recent work of Peter Brown, "The Rise and Function of the Holy Man in Late Antiquity," "Eastern and Western Christendom," and "Relics and Social Status in the Age of Gregory of Tours," in *Society and*

An account of Oswald's life and death, and of his cult after death, is to be found in Bede's *Ecclesiastical History* (esp. III.1-13, 212-55; IV.14, 376-81). For Cuthbert, there are two important early lives, the one composed by an anonymous monk at Lindisfarne shortly after his death and the *Life* written by Bede somewhat later (in prose and poetic versions). Bede also incorporates a brief account of Cuthbert's life into his *Ecclesiastical History* (esp. IV.27-32, 430-49). For the present, I shall confine my attention to the account of Cuthbert contained in Bede's *Ecclesiastical History*.

First we shall look at the life of King Oswald. During the whole of Edwin's reign, Oswald and the other sons of Ethelfrid (Edwin's brother-in-law) "lived in exile among the Scots or Picts and received the grace of Baptism," as Bede tells us (*Ecclesiastical History* III.1, 212-15). We could wish to know more about this formative period of Oswald's life. Some plausible speculations come to hand, of which we shall see more in a moment. After Edwin had been killed at Hatfield Chase on October 12th, 633, by the British King Cædwalla, in alliance with the pagan Penda of Mercia, and a brother and cousin had reigned briefly, Oswald came to the throne of Bernicia at the age of thirty. Assembling an army of fellow Christians, who joined him in his prayer for divine aid, he defeated Cædwalla in the great battle at *Denisesburn*. With his own hands, before the battle, Oswald set up a cross at a place called *Hefenfelth*, the 'field of heaven.' "At this spot where the king prayed," so Bede assures us (*Ecclesiastical History* III.2, 214-15), "innumerable miracles of healing are known to have been performed." Here, the brothers of Hexham made an annual pilgrimage on the eve of the anniversary of Oswald's death; and subsequently they built a church around his cross, whose splinters had curative powers. Brother Bothelm's broken arm, for instance, was restored by his faith and some moss from Oswald's cross. As one might imagine from this beginning, Oswald's reign was celebrated as a golden age of faith. The King summoned the famous missionary Aidan to establish Lindisfarne, helped him in his preaching and built churches far and wide. God gave Oswald an earthly kingdom greater than that of his unbelieving ancestors. But even at the height of his power, Oswald was always "wonderfully humble, kindly, and generous to the poor and strangers" (*Ecclesiastical History* III.6, 230-31); many stories were told to illustrate his un-

the Holy in Late Antiquity, 103-52, 166-95, and 222-50 respectively; *The Making of Late Antiquity*, Carl Newell Jackson Lectures (Cambridge, Mass., 1978); and *The Cult of the Saints: Its Rise and Function in Latin Christianity*, The Haskell Lectures on History of Religions, N.S. 2 (Chicago, 1981). It is another question to ask why there should have been so many famous living Holy Men in Britain in our time period, for Brown has noted that the "marked shortage of living holy men" is an "obvious feature" of the world of Gregory of Tours (Brown, "Eastern and Western Christendom," 185). Britain was not Frankish Gaul, however close the two may have been, but this question requires—and deserves—further study in depth.

stinting charity to the poor (see, for example, *Ecclesiastical History* III.6, 230-31, for Oswald's gift of food and silver plate to the poor at Easter dinner with Aidan).

On August 5th, 642 the young King fell in battle at the hands of the pagan Mercians (at Oswestry in Shropshire?). The circumstances of his death, and especially the brutal manner in which Penda fastened his head and arms to a stake on the field of battle, called to mind the early martyrs. It is scarcely surprising that great miracles took place after his death: "sick men and beasts are healed to this day" at the place of his death (so Bede, *Ecclesiastical History* III.9, 242-43), and dust was taken from the ground for a cure. Bede adds a note which we would do wrong to overlook; such cures are not surprising given Oswald's never-failing charity of alms and aid to the sick and needy while he was alive (my paraphrase—see Bede, *Ecclesiastical History* III.9, 242-43). Bede gives several examples of miracles worked by contact with the ground on which Oswald died (*Ecclesiastical History* III.9, 10, 240-45). What is more, on the occasion of the translation of his bones to the Abbey of Bardney at a later point, there were clear signs of divine favour. The water in which his bones were washed gave the ground on which it was poured power to expel devils, a point to which I draw especial attention. Bede gives examples of yet further miracles of exorcism and healing (*Ecclesiastical History* III.11, 12, 244-53).[9] And again, he notes that these miracles are scarcely surprising in view of Oswald's known piety; his dying words became a proverb "God have mercy on their souls, said Oswald as he fell" (*Ecclesiastical History* III.12, 250-51). Oswald's reputation spread far and wide in short order; wondrous acts of power (*virtutes*)[10] were soon reported from Ireland and southern England (*Ecclesiastical History* III.13, 14). Oswald is specifically described as Christ's "faithful servant" (*fidelis famulus* [*Ecclesiastical History* III.13, 254-55]) and "Christ's warrior" (*miles Christi* [*Ecclesiastical History* IV.14, 380-81]). As we shall see, this language is especially significant.

Cuthbert's story seems very different: Cuthbert was no king; for most of his life, he was a monk and hermit. And yet, there are some

---

9 The significance of this exorcism by the relics of St. Oswald is misinterpreted by Wallace-Hadrill in his essay "Bede and Plummer," in John Michael Wallace-Hadrill, *Early Medieval History* (Oxford, 1975), 89; so far from being evidence for "the failure of the traditional method of expelling an evil spirit," this exorcism is quite what any student of Gregory of Tours would expect. It is true that it testifies to the "efficacy of an English saint," as Wallace-Hadrill notes, but we should not interpret this story in the light of national rivalries between English saints and traditional (i.e., "Continental") ways of doing things.

10 The "miracles" or, as I prefer, "deeds of power" worked by saints are regularly described as *virtutes* in the Christian Latin of this period; for an example from Bede on Oswald, see Bede, *HE* III.13, 254-55, *virtutum frequentium operatione claruerit*. For Bede's general use of this term, see Putnam F. Jones, *A Concordance to the Historia Ecclesiastica of Bede* (Cambridge, Mass., 1929), s.v. "virtus."

details worth noting—some points in which he resembles his predecessor Oswald. His career can be briefly recapitulated. Born in 634, he was trained at Melrose Abbey, where he eventually became prior. He did not confine himself to the monastery but preached to the "ordinary folk" far and wide, combating idolatry. He often travelled to squalid, barbarous villages in the inaccessible mountains of northern Northumbria (*Ecclesiastical History* IV.27, 432-35; cf. Bede, *Life*, chap. 9). At every small town where the "English folk" assembled to hear him preach, they confessed their sins and were forgiven. After he had been at Melrose for many years, and had "become renowned for his wonderful deeds of power," *magnis virtutum signis*, Cuthbert was transferred to Lindisfarne where he became prior in 664. Later, while he was a hermit on the isle of Farne, his prayers brought forth a spring from dry ground and a crop from seed sown out of season (*Ecclesiastical History* IV.28, 434-37). From here, he was summoned to be bishop at Lindisfarne but retired to the desert island shortly before his death in 687 (*Ecclesiastical History* IV.28, 29, 434-43). Again, Bede goes to some effort to describe the character and merits of Cuthbert. We might expect Bede to emphasize his grace of contrition, his humility, and his virtues as a teacher: "Like a good teacher, he taught others to do only what he first practised himself" (*Ecclesiastical History* IV.28, 438-39). But we should notice how Cuthbert protected "the people entrusted to him by his constant prayer," and how he regarded as equivalent to prayer the labour of helping the weaker brethren with advice (for he remembered the commandment to love his neighbour as well as God, *Ecclesiastical History* IV.28, 438-39). These are the qualities which characterize a holy patron. After his death, miracles were also worked by Cuthbert's relics, and a special favour was shown to him; after eleven years in the grave, his body was found uncorrupt (*Ecclesiastical History* IV.30, 442-43), a sure sign of sanctity, as readers of Gregory of Tours will recognize.[11] As his life had been marked by many miracles, so his death was honoured. His remains were transferred to a new tomb at Lindisfarne above ground level "so that he might receive the honours due him" (*venerationis gratia*, [*Ecclesiastical History* IV.30, 442-43]). "The miracles of healing which take place at his tomb from time to time," as Bede notes (*Ecclesiastical History* IV.30, 444-45), "bear witness to the holiness of Cuthbert." A few examples of these miracles follow (*Ecclesiastical History* IV.31, 32, 444-49). Especially significant is the case of the devout brother Baduthegn, who was stricken by paralysis (*Ecclesiastical History* IV.31, 444-47). He decided "to visit the tomb of the most reverend father Cuthbert," where he implored God's *mercy* as a *supplicant* on

---

11 For bodies of saints found uncorrupt in their tombs, see Brown, "Relics and Social Status," especially p. 227.

bended knee (*genibus flexis supplex supernam pietatem rogaret*) and prayed for Cuthbert's help (*per eius auxilium* [*Ecclesiastical History* IV.31, 446-47]). The story has a happy outcome: Baduthegn fell into a deep sleep at the tomb and soon awoke completely cured, the reward of his faith, as we would expect. Here we have a fully developed appeal to a saintly patron, a Holy Man who has a special status with God and is known for his care for the poor and afflicted. This social ritual, in its technical language and substance, is Roman and Christian; it will be familiar to anyone who has read Gregory of Tours's account of the wondrous deeds worked by St. Martin or any of his Gallic colleagues.[12]

Certain features in Bede's accounts of Oswald and Cuthbert deserve further attention, suggesting, as they do, some important aspects of their roles as Holy Men. It is noteworthy that both Oswald and Cuthbert sought out and maintained close contact with ordinary people. They both showed great concern to spread the faith, not in any indirect way, but by preaching, teaching, and personal example. Both had a touching concern for the poor, the sick, the possessed, and the afflicted of every sort. (Examples could be multiplied were we to analyze in detail Bede's longer *Life of St. Cuthbert*.) The people returned the care which they received. Here, as elsewhere, the possessed served as sensitive and infallible indicators of the presence of the Holy, for whenever a genuine Holy Man was present, in person or vicariously through his relics, the demons were invariably expelled from the possessed.[13] The poor and needy became the retainers of the Holy Patron, his retinue, the visible measure of his social importance. The sick required his special intercession (*auxilium*) if they were to be cured. While the Holy Man was patron to the people entrusted to him, as we have seen, he was also himself the servant or retainer (*famulus*) of Christ. All these elements and functions we see attested to in Bede's accounts of Oswald and Cuthbert. While alive, these saints re-establish a social consensus around their persons, a consensus which is maintained by their cult as saints after death. Not only do they restore the social order here on earth, but they also serve, alive or dead, as avenues of approach to God. And none of this is at all surprising, for these saints are simply fulfilling the role of the Roman patron as developed and extended by other Christian heroes before them, heroes of whom St. Martin is the prototype in the Western world. There was a ritual of appeal to a patron in the Roman world; there was a technical language in which this ritual was described. Most of the elements of this ritual will be found in one of the cases which we have considered in

12 For further details on this and what follows, see my article, "The Saint as Patron in the Work of Gregory of Tours," *Journal of Medieval History* 7 (1981), 1-13; this theme is discussed at greater length above, p. 66.
13 For the possessed as barometers of the Holy in the world of Gregory of Tours, see Brown, "Relics and Social Status," 237.

detail, the paralyzed Baduthegn's appeal to St. Cuthbert. Other cases drawn from Bede would show more of the same.

It should not be at all surprising to find all this in Anglo-Saxon Northumbria, for we are here dealing not with a culture in isolation, but with a corner of the Roman world, however backwoods and barbarous.[14] A few points should be emphasized. Connections with the Continent were regular, close, and frequent before ca. 450; Britain gave Pelagius to the Roman West, and it responded by despatching St. Germanus on two occasions. Even though these direct contacts were lost, and the Britons received no help when they appealed to Aetius in 446, nonetheless as late as the 490's, Ambrosius Aurelianus could organize a successful defence of Britain against its numerous foes; we should not forget the British victory in the Battle of Badon Hill (A.D. 517).

It is likely that British culture and the British church survived in pockets at least throughout England even in the darkest days of the 500's, as the traditions concerning Gildas attest. The sixth century was the great age of saints in the Welsh church, we are told; and the absence of pagan place names can be adduced as evidence for the relative lightness of the Germanic yoke throughout the north and southwest, and even in Lincolnshire and East Anglia.[15] There are some interesting pieces of evidence concerning the state of the British church in this period; two of the most significant concern St. Martin.

In a digression concerning the evangelization of the Picts, Bede tells us of Bishop Ninian, a Briton who had been trained in Rome. He evangelized the Southern Picts from his episcopal see named after St. Martin and famous for the unusual stonebuilt church which gave its name to the community (*Casa Candida* = *Whithorn*; see *Ecclesiastical History* III.4, 222-23). Another later source tells us that Ninian was a native of North Wales; he had visited St. Martin at Tours, and from him he received masons to build his church.[16] Bede inserts this digres-

---

14 See Brown, "Eastern and Western Christendom," quoted above, n. 6.
15 See Peter H. Blair, *An Introduction to Anglo-Saxon England*, 2nd ed. (Cambridge, 1977), especially p. 124, for the notable absence of place names attesting the worship of heathen gods "particularly the south-western counties, Lincolnshire and East Anglia and the whole country north of Humber." Blair further notes: "Their absence from the south-west and the north can perhaps be attributed to the continuing strength of British Christianity in these areas" (ibid.), but there seems no compelling reason for excluding Lincolnshire and East Anglia in this latter remark. For further discussion of the survival of the Romano-British Church in recent scholarship, see Thomas, *Christianity in Roman Britain* (n. 4 above).
16 For the later traditions concerning Ninian and St. Martin, see Nora K. Chadwick, "St. Ninian: A Preliminary Study of Sources," *Transactions of the Dumfriesshire and Galloway Natural History Society*, 3rd Series, 27 (1948-49), 9-53, especially pp. 21f. and 27f. Chadwick believes that the tradition associating Ninian with St. Martin is an invention of Ailred, in whose *Life of Ninian* it is to be found. But Chadwick has adopted a hypercritical view of the traditions concerning Ninian and St. Martin, in general, and this view has been assessed and refuted in detail by

sion in his account of Oswald and Aidan to explain how the gospel came to southern Scotland. One assumes that in King Oswald's youth (ca. 604-634), St. Martin was well known in the north; presumably, they all had access there to the relatively recent account of St. Martin's wondrous works on which Gregory of Tours was working shortly before his death in 594.[17] This is not so frivolous a supposition as it might seem, for Oswald and Cuthbert seem in many ways to have modelled themselves after Martin, that first typical hero saint of the western Roman world.

We should note, too, another piece of evidence for which we are grateful to Bede—that when Augustine, the apostle of the faith to England, arrived in Canterbury in 597, he found not a city in ruins, beset by the heathens, but a Frankish princess, Bertha, who with the support of her royal family in Francia was working hard to convert her pagan husband, the King of Kent.[18] He found, as well, a Church of St. Martin, apparently founded shortly after Martin's death, ca. 400, and apparently still in use then (as it is now: St. Martin's, Longport).[19] In his new Church of Sts. Peter and Paul, the present cathedral, Augustine incorporated a porch or chapel of St. Martin where the royal family of Kent was buried. There is other evidence of close connections between pagan Anglo-Saxons and Christian Franks well before Augustine's arrival—indeed this evidence is well known, if not always fully appreciated.[20]

P. A. Wilson, "The Cult of St. Martin in the British Isles," *The Innes Review* 19 (1968), 129-43

17 The work of Sulpicius Severus (or of Venantius, which comes to the same thing) would certainly have made St. Martin well known in Northumbria in Bede's time, or even to Cuthbert himself, whether the link between Francia and Northumbria was direct or went by way of Ireland. Wallace-Hadrill has barely noted these possibilities; Willibrord and Wilfrid are mentioned as potential intermediaries in the transmission of the Sulpicius biography ("Bede and Plummer," 91). Of greater interest is the suggested role of St. Ninian's church *Ad Candidam Casam* (loc. cit.). One other possibility comes to mind; if Sulpicius's work spread the knowledge of St. Martin, it will have done so in all probability while the British church was still intact, that is ca. A.D. 425, the probable period of Sulpicius's death. In any case, Gregory's book, *De virtutibus S. Martini*, will have been well known in Britain before Bede's death, a point overlooked by Wallace-Hadrill. For an eloquent defence of the traditional view of Martin's early importance, as attested by Bede, with a complete review of the evidence and modern scholarship, see Wilson, "The Cult of St. Martin in the British Isles." For an opposing viewpoint, see Thomas, *Christianity in Roman Britain*.

18 For a good recent discussion of the nature of these contacts between Christian Francia and the mission in England, especially in Kent, see John M. Wallace-Hadrill, "Rome and the Early English Church: Some Questions of Tradition," in Wallace-Hadrill, *Early Medieval History*, 115-37 at 119-24.

19 For Augustine's landing in Kent and what he found there, see Bede, *HE* I.25-26, 72-79; for St. Martin's Porch in the Church of Sts. Peter and Paul, see ibid. II.5, 150-51.

20 The evidence is reviewed by Wallace-Hadrill in "Rome and the Early English Church." The marriage of Bertha, daughter of King Charibert, to Aethelberht of Kent was surely not the first contact between Christian Franks and pagan Anglo-Saxons,

To summarize, Anglo-Saxon England continued to be part of the western Roman world even in the dark days between ca. 450 and 600, albeit it may have been a barbarous backwater. The Romano-British church probably continued in existence, as the witness of Gildas attests, even if it did not flourish; soon it was supported by the thriving Celtic church, with which it is too often identified in modern times. Its great enemies were the Anglo-Saxons, admittedly, but the Christians among them probably no less than the pagans (witness Bede on King Cædwalla). And inasmuch as Britain remained part of the Roman world, it was conscious of St. Martin and his cult; indeed Martin's cult seems to have come to Britain around the time of his death, before even the earnest propagandizing of Sulpicius Severus had a chance to reach these shores, to say nothing of the work of Gregory of Tours, a hundred and fifty years later.[21] And the brief entry in Bede's *Martyrologium* for November 11, the feast of St. Martin, amply attests to Martin's reputation at a later period:

> It is not necessary for us to say anything further here (about St. Martin) in as much as his life, his wondrous deeds, and signs have been described quite clearly by Sulpicius in eloquent language; and Gregory the Bishop of that same town (Tours) has written at great length about him in his books of Miracles. (Jacques P. Migne [ed.], *Patrologiae cursus completus*, Series Latina 94 [Paris 1844-64], cols. 1100-01)

One important question remains, but it is probably unanswerable in the present state of our evidence. At what point did the hagiographical works which deal with St. Martin become widely known in Britain? As we have seen, Martin's fame had reached Whithorn even before his death and Canterbury not much later if tradition is to be believed. It was in those same years immediately after Martin's death that Sulpicius Severus, his faithful disciple, was most actively involved in recording and glorifying Martin's deeds (ca. 400-420), and his works may well have come to Britain before the Saxon troubles. If the churches at Whithorn and Canterbury preserved Martin's name, his cult presumably remained known there at least. And Sulpicius's *Life* (if not his further work, the *Dialogues*) would have been part of that cult, as it had been from the beginning elsewhere. Certainly, Martin's fame will have spread widely by the later sixth century, when Gregory of Tours took up the hagiographical task begun by Sulpicius Severus. About the intervening century we must remain in doubt. In any case, it seems unwarranted to assume that knowledge of Sulpicius's work could not have spread in Britain in the period ca. 450-550.

---

even if the extent of communications in the early 500's has been somewhat exaggerated, as Wallace-Hadrill seems to believe.
21 Wilson eloquently defends the value of Bede's clear assertion that the church at Canterbury was dedicated to St. Martin at its foundation; see Wilson, "The Cult of St. Martin in the British Isles" (contra Thomas, *Christianity in Roman Britain*).

But it is time for us to conclude. The rise and function of the Holy Man in late Antiquity are subjects which have attracted some attention in recent years.[22] The increasing importance of Holy Men in that period has been interpreted as a response to the breakdown of the late ancient social order. Their origins are in the chaotic disarray of the social order, but the work of these Holy Men and their followers was to give birth to a new order which we know as medieval Christendom.[23] In the eastern Mediterranean, the Holy Man emerges in a somewhat anarchic fashion, in isolation from—often in opposition to—the established social order. In the western Latin world the situation was somewhat different.[24] However anarchic someone like St. Martin may have been (and his behaviour was a source of great concern to his episcopal colleagues with their Roman respect for law and order), the cult which grew up around the dead saint was "co-opted," if I may use that term, by the newly emerging Christian social hierarchy of Senatorial bishops as the centre for a new social order, for the cult of such saints as Martin (and I would add Oswald and Cuthbert) had the capacity, to an altogether unique degree, to weld the disparate segments of a tragically disordered society into a new consensus, based on *reverentia* for the saintly patron.[25]

Further work on the *patrocinium* of the saints (to use the Roman term) in the world of Gregory of Tours has its starting point here.[26] The Roman institution of *patrocinium* was a highly developed one, with a social ritual and language all its own, governing the form in which an appeal to a patron might be cast and the manner in which that patron might respond. The last generation of Roman historians has made a great advance in our understanding of this most important Roman contribution to Western society,[27] but the wider significance of this social

22 See the works of Brown cited in n. 8 above.
23 Brown, "The Rise and Function of the Holy Man"; this theme is further developed in Brown, *The Cult of the Saints*.
24 Brown, "Eastern and Western Christendom."
25 Brown, "Relics and Social Status," especially pp. 230-32 for *reverentia* in the world of Gregory of Tours. For the social *consensus* on the feast of the saints, see ibid., 246-49. For a detailed exposition and analysis of the data, see Corbett, "The Saint as Patron in the Work of Gregory of Tours."
26 For a clear statement of the central role which *patrocinium* plays in the "phenomenology of the Holy" in late Antiquity, see Brown, "The Rise and Function of the Holy Man," especially pp. 115-20 (for the situation in Syria), and cf. "Eastern and Western Christendom," 178. This theme is further developed in Brown, *The Making of Late Antiquity*.
27 As might be imagined, the recent bibliography on Roman *patrocinium* has grown to a considerable size: it will be convenient to refer to Joseph M. Hellegouarc'h, *Le vocabulaire Latin des relations et des partis politiques sous la République*, 2nd ed. (Paris, 1972), for the data relative to the situation in the later Republic. Louis Harmand, *Le Patronat sur les collectivités publiques, des origines au Bas-empire: un aspect social et politique du monde romain*, Publications de la Faculté des Lettres de l'Université de Clermont, 2ᵉ sér., fasc. 2 (Paris, 1957), considers one important aspect

institution has not yet been fully appreciated. The rich treasure of data and insight in the writings of Gregory of Tours allows us, I believe, to understand how the Christian Holy Men and their representatives, the bishops, took over and developed this Roman social institution, making it the fundamental structure of Western Christianity.[28] Much more remains to be done with this material. But the Roman institution of *patrocinium* is well known. And the detailed anecdotal information which hagiographers such as Gregory (and, I might add, Bede) give us regarding the cult of the Saints in the late Ancient Latin West, can easily be interpreted by any reader (of the Latin text!) in the light of our knowledge of Roman *patrocinium*.

The function of the saint as patron which has been so clearly demonstrated in the case of St. Martin is also evident in Bede's accounts of King Oswald and St. Cuthbert, as we have seen. If we follow the direction of recent work in social history, especially the work of Peter Brown, we can understand that the role of these saints as patrons is much more than a hagiographic convention, and we may be able to appreciate how the Holy Man came to be the centre of a new social order in the Latin West in the time of Gregory and Bede (ca. A.D. 500-750). Much more research is needed into the larger questions of social history in the period and area of concern here, but I am convinced that a careful examination of the evidence will substantiate the view that King Oswald and Saint Cuthbert modelled their conduct as Holy Men, saints and patrons, in large part after the pattern set by their great predecessor, St. Martin.

of *patrocinium*, which clearly prolonged its life into the Middle Ages. Cf. Anton von Premerstein in *Paulys Realencyclopädie der classischen Altertumswissenschaft*, ed. by Georg Wissowa, 4.1 (1900), cols. 23-55, s.v. "clientes." The fundamental work remains Matthias Gelzer, *Die Nobilität der römischen Republik* (Leipzig and Berlin, 1912), and "Die Nobilität der Kaiserzeit," *Hermes* 50 (1915), 395-415; for an English version of both these works see *The Roman Nobility*, trans. by Robin Seager (Oxford, 1969).

28 See further Brown, *The Cult of the Saints*.

6

The Celtic Church in Anglo-Saxon Times

Claude Evans

This paper examines the development of the Celtic church against its historical background during Anglo-Saxon times from the fifth century to the Norman conquest. It attempts to define the originality of that church, to ascertain what differentiated it from the Roman church, and to determine what caused the conflict which culminated in the Synod of Whitby in A.D. 664. It then considers what happened after the Synod and how the Celtic church became integrated into the Anglo-Saxon world.

Historical details about Britain in the fifth and sixth centuries are sparse, and their interpretation is subject to much controversy. What is obvious is that at the beginning of the period, Britain was under the control of the Romano-British; by the end of the sixth century, the Anglo-Saxons and allied peoples were dominant in much of Britain. Apart from a few isolated pockets in the interior, such as the territory south-west of York, known as Elmet, areas that remained free of Anglo-Saxon control were on the periphery: Cornwall, Wales, and southern Scotland. Ireland was not to be invaded by Germanic peoples until the coming of the Vikings in the ninth century. It was in these areas, then, that we should look to find a Celtic Church developing and flourishing.

Archaeological evidence is now making it clear that Christianity was widespread in Britain by the fifth century.[1] This form of Christianity was essentially Roman. Saint Ninian, reported by Bede to have had his episcopal see at Whithorn in Galloway and to have brought Christianity to the Southern Picts, must have been a sub-Roman Briton.[2] According to tradition, Ireland was christianized by Patrick, a Roman Briton, who flourished in the fifth century.[3] From his writings, we know that he equated "Christian" with "Roman."[4] As John Corbett has pointed out above, Roman Christianity did not disappear with the coming of the Germanic settlers.[5] The departure of the Roman troops from Britain in 407 did mean, however, that Britain and Ireland were no longer closely associated with the Roman world;[6] the comparative isolation assisted the development of an original Celtic Church. The fact that Ireland was secure from large-scale invasions until the ninth century provided the ecclesiastical institutions there with a relatively secure environment in which to develop.

The most outstanding element in the Christianity of Ireland, Scotland, Wales, Cornwall, and Brittany was monasticism.[7] Monasteries had not been a prominent feature of the Roman world in the fourth century. They were a product of the Egyptian desert and the Near East.[8] Monasticism quickly took root in Gaul, where it was adopted by Saint Martin of Tours, who died in 397,[9] and it also became established in Italy, where it was adapted by Benedict of Nursia[10] and was to

1 See Charles Thomas, *Christianity in Roman Britain to AD 500* (London, 1981).
2 For the textual evidence on Ninian, see Nora K. Chadwick, "St. Ninian: A Preliminary Study of the Sources," *Transactions of the Dumfriesshire and Galloway Natural History and Antiquarian Society*, 3rd ser., 27 (1948-49), 9-53, and Winifred W. MacQueen, "Miracula Nynie Episcopi," ibid., 3rd ser., 37 [*recte* 38] (1959-60), 21-57; for general treatments, see John MacQueen, *St. Nynia: A Study of Literary and Linguistic Evidence* (Edinburgh, 1961), and Thomas, *Christianity*, chap. 11, 275-94.
3 There is a considerable body of scholarly writing on Saint Patrick. Ludwig Bieler, *St. Patrick and the Coming of Chrisitianity*, History of Irish Catholicism I. 1 (Dublin, 1967), Richard P. C. Hanson, *Saint Patrick: His Origins and Career* (Oxford, 1968), and Thomas, *Christianity*, 307-46, provide a background and discuss some of the controversies.
4 A useful edition is Allan B. E. Hood (ed. and trans.), *St. Patrick, His Writings and Muirchu's Life*, Arthurian Period Sources 9 (London and Chichester, 1978).
5 Above, chap. 5.
6 For evidence on Roman influence on Ireland, see J. D. Bateson, "Roman Material from Ireland: A Reconsideration" and "Further Finds of Roman Material from Ireland," *PRIA* 73 C and 76 C (1973 and 1976), 21-97 and 171-80, respectively.
7 For a qualification of this statement so far as it concerns Wales, see Kathleen Hughes, "The Celtic Church: Is This a Valid Concept?" *Cambridge Medieval Celtic Studies* 1 (1981), 1-19.
8 See Derwas J. Chitty, *The Desert a City: An Introduction to the Study of Egyptian and Palestinian Monasticism under the Christian Empire* (Oxford, 1966).
9 See Rudolf Lorenz, "Die Anfänge des abendländischen Mönchtums im 4. Jahrhundert," *Zeitschrift für Kirchengeschichte* 77 (1966), 1-61.
10 John Chapman, *Saint Benedict and the Sixth Century* (London, 1929) and Lowrie

produce a Roman pope, Gregory the Great, before the end of the sixth century. But it did not come to the British from Rome. On present evidence, it seems most likely that it reached the Celtic world from the eastern Mediterranean via Gaul.[11] The first apparent material evidence for a monastery in Britain seems to be Tintagel in Cornwall, better known today for its associations with the legendary Arthur.[12] This dates from just before A.D. 500. If this site has been interpreted correctly, here are to be found the square buildings characteristic of the Coptic monastery, buildings unlike the round ones to be found in later Irish monasteries.[13] Its appearance in this now isolated area is not surprising in the light of the Mediterranean pottery of fifth-century date which has been found in Cornwall and which bespeaks a healthy sea trade by direct or, more likely, indirect means with North Africa.[14]

The monasteries that sprang up in the Celtic world were different in physical form, ecclesiastical organization, and religious practice from the Benedictine monasticism that was to become the dominant form in early medieval western Europe.[15] In physical appearance, the Celtic monasteries did not represent the ideal of Saint Benedict. They often were a collection of huts surrounded by a wall and situated in an isolated spot; an extreme case is the island rock of Scellig Michael off the west coast of Ireland.

Celtic monasteries also differed from the Roman in their organization. The *abbaye-évêché*, or 'abbey-bishopric,' is characteristic of Celtic lands; in some monasteries such as Tréguier in Brittany, the abbot was also a bishop, and the limits of his diocese were not very well defined.[16] In the Roman world, bishops had been attached to cities, but

J. Daly, *Benedictine Monasticism: Its Formation and Development through the 12th Century* (New York, 1965) place Benedict in his historical background.

11 Jocelyn N. Hillgarth, "The East, Visigothic Spain and the Irish," *Studia Patristica* 4, Frank L. Cross (ed.), Texte und Untersuchungen zur Geschichte der altchristlichen Literatur 79 (1961), 442-56, and "Visigothic Spain and Early Christian Ireland," *PRIA* 62 C (1961-62), 167-94 and 1 plate.

12 Courtenay A. Ralegh Radford, "Tintagel in History and Legend," *Journal of the Royal Institution of Cornwall* 86, Appendix (1942), 25-41.

13 The excavations are described by Courtenay A. Ralegh Radford, "Tintagel: The Castle and the Monastery: Interim Report," *Antiquaries Journal* 15 (1935), 401-19. It should be noted, however, that strong objections to his interpretations have been raised by Ian C. G. Barrow, "Tintagel—Some Problems," *Scottish Archaeological Forum* 5 (1974), 99-103, and by Charles Thomas (supported by Peter Fowler), "East and West: Tintagel, Mediterranean Imports and the Early Insular Church" in Susan M. Pearce (ed.) *The Early Church in Western Britain and Ireland: Studies presented to C. A. Ralegh Radford arising from a Conference organized in his Honour by the Devon Archaeological Society and Exeter City Museum*, BAR 102 (Oxford, 1982), 17-34. Re-excavation is needed to settle the issue.

14 Charles Thomas, "Imported Late-Roman Mediterranean Pottery in Ireland and Western Britain: Chronologies and Implications," *PRIA* 76 C (1976), 245-56.

15 See references cited in n. 10 above.

16 Louis Gougaud, "La Question des Abbayes-Évêchés bretonnes," *Revue Mabillon* 12

the Celts were reduced to (or retreated to) a world that was not marked by major urban settlements. Though bishops seem to have retained some of their power in Wales,[17] it was greatly reduced in Ireland, where the social structure offered no base on which to build a hierarchy following the Roman pattern. The Irish were organized in tribes, each tribe being held together by the ties of kinship.[18] Consequently, each Irish monastery was connected with a single tribe and acknowledged no ecclesiastical superior entitled to control its abbot. In a rural country lacking towns, monasteries offered themselves as natural ecclesiastical centres. Bishops alone still had the power to confirm and consecrate, but from the sixth century, the real leaders of the Celtic church in these places were abbots and learned monks.

Celtic monasticism was also distinguished by its religious way of life. Saint Benedict described his own rule as "this little Rule for beginners."[19] He did insist on self-renunciation, prayer, and physical labour, but did not impose such hardships on his followers as were peculiar to the desert fathers of the East and were adopted especially (though not solely) by the Irish monks. The latters' discipline was severe, to say the least. There were variations in application according to the founder of each monastery and his successors, since at first there were no written rules. The rules attributed to Columba of Iona, Comgall of Bangor, Ailbe of Emly (Imlech), and Carthach of Lismore actually date only from the eighth century and were written in the interests of the eighth-century Culdee revival of discipline.[20] It is thus possible that the rules appear to be stricter than they actually were. Whatever the case, the Celtic monks had a reputation for their asceticism. Fasting was frequent, usually not on just one, but on two days a week; often only one meal a day was eaten, and the sleeping hours were broken by several offices. David, the sixth-century Welsh saint, rationed out bread to his monks and did not permit them to eat meat. He earned the sobriquet of *Aquaticus*, 'the Waterman,' because he demanded complete abstinence from alcohol. (It was normally acceptable for monks in those days to drink wine.)[21]

In Celtic monasteries, penances were a notable feature of the monastic regimen. These included immersion in ice-cold water and

(1922), 90-104; Edmond Durtelle de Saint-Sauveur, *Histoire de Bretagne des Origines à nos Jours*, 4th ed. (Rennes, 1947; rptd. 1975), I, 92-93.
17 See Hughes, "The Celtic Church."
18 Francis J. Byrne, "Tribes and Tribalism in Early Ireland," *Ériu* 22 (1971), 128-66.
19 *Rule*, chap. 73 in *The Rule of St. Benedict*, trans. with introduction and notes by Anthony C. Meisel and M. L. del Mastro (New York, 1975), 106.
20 See Kathleen Hughes, *The Church in Early Irish Society* (London, 1966), 173-93.
21 On David, see Daniel S. Evans, "An Approach to the Historical Dewi—Some Comments," *The Friends of St. David's Cathedral*, 1963 Report (St. David's, 1963), 7-13; and Emrys G. Bowen, *Saint David: Patron Saint of Wales*, St. David's Day Bilingual Series (Cardiff, 1983).

immobility in a standing position with arms raised.[22] Confession was a very important preliminary. Such confessions, including not merely evil acts but also sinful thoughts, were made to a confessor, called in Irish an *anmchara* or 'soul-friend.' This custom is documented in a series of penitential books such as those of Finnian of Clonard and Columban, which list proportionately measured periods of penance for many offences of both clerics and laymen.[23] It should be noted that the penance imposed for a confession was not thought of as a penalty but as medicine for a malady of the soul.[24]

Some of the Celtic missions, like the sixth-century Irish foundations of Iona by Columba and of Luxeuil in Burgundy by Columban, can be explained by the monastic tradition of *peregrinatio pro deo* or 'exile in the name of God.'[25] As a form of penance, a monk would leave everything behind so that he might start anew. He severed his ties with his ecclesiastical place of origin, and it was rare for him ever to return there.[26] Thus, Columba founded his monastery of Iona on an island off the west coast of Scotland in 563, from where other monks set off to preach the Gospel in the northern and western isles.[27]

A number of these *peregrini* reached Wales. Little reliable knowledge of the founding fathers of Welsh monasticism now exists. The saints' lives come mainly from the eleventh and twelfth centuries or later.[28] More can be learned from the dedications of chapels whose names are formed with the prefix *Llan-* 'an enclosure,' followed by the saint's name.[29] Where such dedications are early, they denote the founder of the church or the founder of the monastery from which the founder of the church came. The area of influence of these early saints can be determined by plotting the location of such dedications on a map.[30]

22 See Ludwig Bieler (ed.), *The Irish Penitentials*, Scriptores Latini Hiberniae 5 (Dublin, 1963).
23 Ibid.
24 On the medical analogy, see John T. McNeill, *The Celtic Churches: A History A.D. 200 to 1200* (Chicago and London, 1974), 84.
25 On *peregrinatio*, see Kathleen Hughes, "The Changing Theory and Practice of Irish Pilgrimage," *Journal of Ecclesiastical History* 11 (1960), 143-51.
26 According to the earliest historian of Iceland, Ari Thorgilsson, when the first Scandinavian settlers of the island arrived in the 860's or 870's, they found there "papa," evidently Irish eremites, who promptly left what must have been, up till then, a place of total solitude: Halldór Hermannson (ed. and trans.), *The Book of the Icelanders (Íslendingabók) by Ari Thorgilsson*, Islandica 20 (Ithaca, 1930), 48 (text): 60 (translation).
27 On the saint, see Ian Finlay, *Columba* (London, 1979).
28 The best collected edition of these lives is that by Arthur W. Wade-Evans, *Vitae Sanctorum Britanniae et Genealogiae* (Cardiff, 1944). Canon Gilbert H. Doble's examinations of a number of these lives have now been collectively edited by Daniel S. Evans, *Lives of the Welsh Saints* (Cardiff, 1971).
29 Emrys G. Bowen, *The Settlements of the Celtic Saints in Wales*, 2nd ed. (Cardiff, 1956), 1-3.
30 As Bowen has done (cf. Bowen, *Settlements* and his *Saints, Seaways and Settlements in the Celtic Lands* [Cardiff, 1969]).

In Brittany, it seems that the religious leaders, who, with a few exceptions, were from Wales, often came after the first settlers, most of whom were from Cornwall. Largillière points out that these leaders were priests who came to serve already existing communities.[31] They have often been called "saints," with the meaning not of 'holy men'

---

31 René Largillière, *Les Saints et l'Organisation chrétienne primitive dans l'Armorique bretonne* (Rennes, 1925), 226.

but rather of 'men in orders' or 'literate, educated men.'[32] Settlements were frequently named after them, hence the number of place-names formed with the prefixes *plou-* (Latin *plebs*) 'parish,' or more exactly 'the people belonging to the parish'; *tre-*, 'a subdivision of the *plebs*' or 'a hamlet' (French *trève*); and *lan-*, 'monastery,' followed by the saint's name.[33]

[Map of Brittany showing: Tréguier, St-Pol-de-Léon, Morlaix, Dol, Côtes-du-Nord, Landévennec, St.-Méen, Finistère, Ille-et-Vilaine, Morbihan, Quiberon]

BRITTANY

As the invasions of Britain grew in intensity, the migrations of the Celts increased.[34] There were travels between all Celtic countries, and the same saints' names can sometimes be found on both sides of the

32 Nora K. Chadwick, *The Age of the Saints in the Early Celtic Church* (London, 1961), 3-5.
33 Nora K. Chadwick, *Early Brittany* (Cardiff, 1969), 273-78; Largillière, *Les Saints*, 214; and F. Gourvil, *Noms de Famille bretons d'Origine toponomique* (Quimper, 1970), XXII, XXV, and XXX.
34 It should be noted that the migrations were not solely caused by the invading Anglo-Saxons. Nora Chadwick has argued forcefully in *Early Brittany*, 162-92, and "The Colonization of Brittany from Celtic Britain," *PBA* 51 (1965), 235-99, especially pp. 258-70, that the migration from western Britain to Armorica was caused by the invading Celts from Ireland. See also Léon Fleuriot, *Les Origines de la Bretagne* (Paris, 1980).

English Channel. H. C. Bowen has pointed out the striking recurrence of dedications to Saints Carannog, Pedrog, Briog, and Meugan in Wales, Cornwall, and northern Brittany.[35] For instance, the forms of Llangaranog and Llangrannog appear in Cardiganshire (mid-Wales), as well as the forms Carantoc or Crantock in Cornwall, Carantec near Morlaix, Finistère, and Trécarantec in Léon.[36] Saint Pedrog is patron of Padstow in Cornwall, of St. Petrox in Pembrokeshire, and also of Llanbedrog in Caernarvonshire, and of St-Petreuc, Côtes du Nord.[37] Saint Brioc is patron of Llandyfriog in the extreme south-west of Cardiganshire, as well as of St. Breock in Cornwall, and of St-Brieuc in Brittany.[38] Saint Meugan is remembered at Trevigan near St. David's in Pembrokeshire and at Capel Meugan in western Carmarthenshire, and also in the parish of St. Mewan in Cornwall, and at Trémevan, Côtes du Nord, and St-Méen, Ille-et-Vilaine,[39] to give just a few examples.

The geographic proximity of these dedications is no proof that the saints were contemporaries or even travelled in the same direction.[40] There is a slim possibility that these saints were companions in a missionary enterprise, but it is more likely that these dedications simply represent the widespread influence of various cults. Thus, even if the saints, themselves, did not travel, their followers certainly did.

According to tradition, however, many famous monks laboured in several countries. Saint Cadoc, whose principal monastic foundation was Llancarfan (Nant Carban), near Llantwit Major in south Wales, also had foundations in Cornwall, where a chapel is dedicated to him at Padstow on the north shore, and in Brittany, where his name appears in Pleucadeuc, Morbihan. (*Pleu-* is here the equivalent of *plou-*.) In addition, he had a monastery on the Ile de Cado, north of the Quiberon peninsula in southern Brittany. A Llangadog is recorded from northeastern Anglesey, and Cadoc is the patron of the church at Cambuslang, not far from Glasgow.[41] Paul Aurelian, a Welsh disciple of Saint Illtud, spent some time in Cornwall, but left a greater reputation in Brittany, where he founded St-Pol-de-Léon on the north coast.[42] Saint Budoc is remembered in Saint Budeaux, Devon, but his chief contribu-

---

35 Bowen, *The Settlements*, 89, 91, and Fig. 24.
36 Loc. cit., and Joseph Loth, *Les Noms des Saints bretons* (Paris, 1910), 18.
37 Gilbert H. Doble, "Saint Petroc," in Donald Attwater (ed.), *The Saints of Cornwall* (Truro, 1960-), IV, 132-66, and Loth, *Les Noms*, 103.
38 Bowen, *The Settlements*, 89; Doble, "Saint Brioc," *Saints of Cornwall* IV, 67-104; Loth, *Les Noms*, 16.
39 Bowen, *The Settlements*, 91; Doble, "Saint Mewan and Saint Austol," *Saints of Cornwall* V, 35-58.
40 Siân Victory, *The Celtic Church in Wales* (London, 1977), 34-35.
41 Bowen, *The Settlements*, 39-41 and Fig. 8B; Doble, "Saint Cadoc," *Saints of Cornwall* IV, 55-66; and W. J. Watson, "Saint Cadoc," *Scottish Gaelic Studies* 2 (1927), 1-12.
42 Gilbert H. Doble, "Saint Paul Aurelian," *Saints of Cornwall* I, 10-60; Chadwick, *Early Brittany*, 246-47; Loth, *Les Noms*, 101.

tion was made in Brittany, where we find Beuzec, Lesveuzec, and Tréveuzec in the Finistère.[43] Saint Samson actually provides a link between four Celtic lands. A monk under Saint Illtud in Glamorganshire, he went to Ireland, then Cornwall, where he is patron of Golant and Southill, and ended his career in Brittany, where he founded Dol in 562.[44]

IRELAND

As far as rites are concerned, there were several differences between the Celtic and the Roman Church. Easter was celebrated at a different date in each tradition. There were two problems with the

43 Loth, *Les Noms*, 14.
44 Doble, "Saint Samson," *Saints of Cornwall* V, 80-103; Chadwick, *Early Brittany*, 250-56.

calculation of the date of this festival. The date of the Jewish Passover was the fourteenth day of Nisan, the first lunar month of the Jewish year, and originally, the Christian Easter had been celebrated on that day. But the Council of Nicaea in A.D. 325 forbade the celebration of Easter on the fourteenth of Nisan if it was not a Sunday; Easter had to be on a Sunday. Yet it was not stated at Nicaea whether one should definitely avoid celebrating on the same day as the Jews celebrated Passover or not. The members of the Roman Church believed that one should, and they celebrated between the fifteenth and the twenty-first of Nisan, but the Irish monks and their followers celebrated between the fourteenth and the twentieth of that month, so that whenever the fourteenth of Nisan fell on a Sunday, they celebrated Easter a week earlier than the Roman Church.

To add to the confusion, the Celts did not use the nineteen-year cycle common to the rest of the Christian world. Instead, they used an eighty-four-year cycle, its reputation being attributed (incorrectly) to the late-third-century bishop, Anatolius of Laodicaea.[45]

Other points of divergence were the form of the tonsure, of baptism, of ordination, and of the liturgy. The Roman style of tonsure was a shaven circle on the crown of the head; the tonsure of the Celtic monks differed from that in some way, though the exact form of it is not known.[46] This tonsure was referred to by the eighth-century Anglo-Saxon abbot, Ceolfrith, as that of Simon Magus, Saint Peter's opponent.[47] Strangely enough, the Celts do not seem to have refuted this interpretation of the origin of their tonsure, which seems to have been a gratuitous fiction.[48] There is also some doubt about the exact nature of their baptismal rite. It seems that the Celts performed a single immersion—which was still the custom in Brittany in the early seventeenth century[49]—instead of the three immersions recommended by the apostolic canon and already mentioned in the first-century Didache.[50] Furthermore, there was some objection to their mode of clerical ordination.[51] In the liturgy and the ritual of the mass, the Celtic usage was

---

45 Charles W. Jones (ed.), *Bedae Opera de Temporibus*, Medieval Academy of America Publication No. 41 (Cambridge, Mass., 1934), 15, 20, and 29-33. For further details, see Kenneth Harrison, *The Framework of Anglo-Saxon History to A.D. 900* (Cambridge, 1976), 30-51.
46 Leslie Hardinge discusses the tonsure and provides an illustration of its possible form in *The Celtic Church in Britain*, Church Historical Society Series 91 (London, 1977), 194-96.
47 Bede, *HE* V.21, 548-51.
48 The allegation may have been made because the druids had followed that fashion. See ibid., 548, n. 5.
49 Chadwick, *The Age of the Saints*, 67.
50 For a history of baptism, see John D. C. Fisher, *Christian Initiation: Baptism in the Medieval West. A Study in the Disintegration of the Primitive Rite of Initiation*, Alcuin Club Collections 47 (London, 1965).
51 It is sometimes alleged that the Celts permitted only a single bishop to be present at an

closer to the Gallican rite than to the Roman. For instance, in the seventh-century Columban Church, there were numerous collects (short prayers).[52] Some Eastern influence is also evident. At Bangor in northern Ireland, we know from a seventh-century prayer book that mass was celebrated only on Sunday and that, since Saturday was the vigil, the latter was also kept with solemnity, as was traditional in Egyptian monasteries. During the same period in Roman monasteries, mass was celebrated daily.[53]

In 597, Pope Gregory the Great sent a mission, led by Augustine, to Britain to convert the Anglo-Saxons. Augustine, who had been given authority over the British bishops by the pope, tried to bring the British into conformity with the Roman practice. He first arranged a conference with them near the River Severn close to their territory, but he did not convince them. Bede tells us that a second meeting also failed because Augustine did not rise when the British ecclesiastics approached him.[54] This disagreement about precedence is actually a hint at deeper reasons for the failure of the council. The pupils of ascetics like Saint David could have had only little in common with the Italian monks who had been trained in a less severe fashion, but what was really at stake was Celtic ecclesiastical autonomy.

A synod met at Magh Lene in southern Ireland in 631 to debate the matter of Easter, and the decision was ultimately in favour of Roman usage. By the time of the Whitby Synod, over half of the Irish churches had already made the change.[55] In many places, as at Gilling, northwest of Ripon in Deira, or at Whitby itself, both traditions were intermingled, and this seemed to be well accepted.[56]

Yet in 661, a conflict broke out because of the situation at the Northumbrian court. King Oswy had married Eanfled, daughter of Edwin, who had been brought up in Kent, where she was taught the Roman observance of Easter. She continued to keep it in Northumbria, while the king followed the Irish tradition.[57]

In 664, the question in debate was referred to a synod. The assembly met at *Streonæshalh*, which has been identified as Whitby in northern Yorkshire, and was then the site of an important double monastery.[58] The timing was appropriate for the resolution of the problem, as

episcopal consecration, but this assertion is highly debatable, as Nora Chadwick points out in *The Age of the Saints*, 68.
52 Ibid., 67.
53 Frederick E. Warren (ed.), *The Antiphonary of Bangor: An Early Irish Manuscript in the Ambrosian Library at Milan*, Part 2, Henry Bradshaw Society, Publications 10 (London, 1895), ix-xi, xxiii-xxiv and No. 11, discussed further by Henry Mayr-Harting, *The Coming of Christianity to Anglo-Saxon England* (London, 1972), 163-64.
54 Bede, *HE* II.2, 138-39.
55 McNeill, *The Celtic Churches*, 109.
56 On Gilling, see Mayr-Harting, *The Coming*, 106.
57 See ibid., 105-06, for the political background.
58 On the date of the Synod, see Harrison, *The Framework*, 92-93, *contra* Stenton,

the following year saw Easter falling on the same date, whether calculated according to the Celtic or the Dionysiac mode of reckoning.⁵⁹ At the conference, Bishop Colman from Lindisfarne in Northumbria spoke for the Celtic party. Agilbert, bishop of Wessex, was the senior ecclesiastic on the Roman side, but since he would have needed an interpreter, he left the statement of his case to Wilfrid, who was head of a community at Ripon in Yorkshire and had spent several years studying Roman usages in Italy and Gaul.⁶⁰

As far as we know, the debate was confined to the question of Easter. Colman claimed that his usage was sanctioned by the authority of Saint John, Bishop Anatolius, and Saint Columba. Wilfrid appealed to the authority of Saint Peter. He demonstrated that, in fact, the Celts did not follow John, who celebrated Easter on the fourteenth day of Nisan, regardless of whether it was a Sunday, nor Anatolius, who used a nineteen-year cycle. Saint Columba he referred to with some contempt as "that Columba of yours" (*ille Columba uester*);⁶¹ he was obviously no match for Saint Peter. King Oswy's famous declaration that he would obey Saint Peter, to whom the Lord had given the keys of heaven, was perhaps not the statement of a new conviction, since Eddius, Wilfrid's biographer, notes that when he asked the Synod whether Colman was greater than Saint Peter, he did so "with a smile" (*subridens*).⁶²

It seems that the matter dealt with at the Synod was involved, to a large extent, with Northumbrian politics and may have been, at least in part, a product of rivalry between the house of Bernicia, to which Oswy belonged, and the house of Deira, since Oswy's wife was a daughter of Edwin of Deira. Alfrith, Oswy's son, had been in contact with Wilfrid and took the initiative in organizing the Synod. He held a sub-kingdom in Deira, and we may guess that he hoped that his father would decide in favour of the Celtic party—as might have been expected—and thus weaken his own position. This would explain, as Mayr-Harting points out, Oswy's smile as he moved towards his change of sides, which thwarted his son's plans.⁶³

After their defeat at Whitby, Colman and all the other Irishmen at Lindisfarne left Northumbria, first to go to Iona, and then to found a

---

ASE, 129. The location of *Streonæshalh* is discussed by Christine E. Fell, "Hild, Abbess of Streonæshalch," in Hans Bekker-Nielsen, et al. (eds.), *Hagiography and Medieval Literature: A Symposium* (Odense, 1981), 76-99, at 82-85.
59 Harrison, *The Framework*, 93.
60 The main primary source on Wilfrid is the life written by Eddius Stephanus: Bertram Colgrave (ed. and trans.), *The Life of Bishop Wilfrid by Eddius Stephanus* (Cambridge, 1927). See further David P. Kirby (ed.), *Saint Wilfrid at Hexham* (Newcastle-upon-Tyne, 1974).
61 Bede, *HE* III.25, 306-07.
62 Eddius Stephanus, *The Life*, 20-23.
63 Mayr-Harting, *The Coming*, 108.

new monastery on the island of Innisbofin off the coast of western Ireland. His successors in the bishopric and abbacy of Lindisfarne accepted the Roman order, but the western islands remained the outpost of Irish resistance.[64]

It seems that the reference to Saint Columba at the Synod pointed to the root of the Celts' attachment to their customs. The monks of the Ionan confederacy simply did not want to abandon the tradition of Saint Columba. Even Adamnán, abbot of Iona at the end of the seventh century, who was himself converted to the Roman Easter, could not force his monks to change their customs.[65] It was only in 716 that Egbert, an Anglo-Saxon who had studied in Ireland, got most of the monks of Iona to change their views.[66] Not long thereafter, the Pictish king, Nechtan IV, expelled still recalcitrant monks of the Celtic persuasion from Iona.[67]

In Wales, the change came late, and in Cornwall and Devon, even later.[68] According to the *Annales Cambriae*, the Welsh Latin chronicle, the date of acceptance of the Roman Easter in Wales was 768,[69] and this was due to the influence of Elfodd, bishop of Gwynedd. After Elfodd's death, there was opposition to the reform, but this opposition did not have any lasting effect.[70]

In 705, Aldhelm of Malmesbury wrote to the Cornish king, Geraint, urging him and his clergy to observe Roman practices.[71] Anglo-Saxon political pressure increased in the reign of King Egbert (802-39), and Cornwall was finally brought under the complete control of Wessex by King Athelstan (924-39), who took an active interest in ecclesiastical affairs.[72]

In Brittany, the Celtic customs also continued till very late. In 818, Louis the Pious addressed an order to Matmonoc, abbot of Landévennec, at the western end of the peninsula, enjoining the abandonment of

64 On his successors, see ibid., 110-11.
65 On Adamnán, see Peter H. Blair, *The World of Bede* (London, 1970), 181.
66 Bede, *HE* V.22, 552-55. Bede discusses Egbert in a number of places in the *Historia Ecclesiastica*. See further, Nora K. Chadwick, "Bede, St. Colmán and the Irish Abbey of Mayo," in Nora K. Chadwick (ed.), *Celt and Saxon: Studies in the Early British Border* (Cambridge, 1963), 186-205.
67 Whitley Stokes, "The Annals of Tigernach. Third Fragment. A.D. 489-766," *Revue Celtique* 17 (1896), 225. See also Bede, *HE* V.22, 552-53.
68 See Chadwick, *The Age of the Saints*, 137-38.
69 Nennius, *British History and the Welsh Annals*, ed. and trans. by John Morris, Arthurian Period Sources 8 (London and Chichester, 1980), 47 and 88, s.a. 768.
70 On Elfodd, see McNeill, *The Celtic Churches*, 196-97.
71 Haddan and Stubbs, *Councils*, III, 268-73. On the possible ramifications of this, see Herbert P. R. Finberg, "Sherborne, Glastonbury, and the Expansion of Wessex," in Herbert P. R. Finberg, *Lucerna* (London, 1964), 95-115, esp. p. 100.
72 See Finberg, "Sherborne," esp. pp. 110-13, and William G. Hoskins, *The Westward Expansion of Wessex*, University of Leicester, Department of English Local History, Occasional Papers 13 (Leicester, 1960).

Celtic practices and the adoption of the Roman tonsure and the Rule of Saint Benedict.[73] The change did come, although slowly, but even after its submission in matters of discipline and liturgy, the Celtic church still kept its monastic character.

In the eighth century, there had been a resurgence of the rigorous anchoritic life known as the Culdee revival (from the Irish *Céli Dé*, 'servant of God'). We have already mentioned the written rules it produced. The movement was especially strong in Ireland, where it was led by Máel-ruain.[74] The Scandinavian raids of the ninth century weakened the Celtic monasteries in Britain and Ireland; the monks of Iona were massacred in 806 and again in 986.[75] But it was the Norman kings and their reforming archbishops, Lanfranc and Anselm, who were influential in bringing the Celtic churches into line with Continental practices.[76] Even then, the changes were slow in coming into being; in Ireland, transformations in the religious hierarchy and monastic practice were not far advanced until the mid-twelfth century.[77]

From the point of view of the Anglo-Saxons, the debate over Easter, told so dramatically by Bede, was perhaps not very significant in the long run. What mattered was the order and unity of the Church, and from a practical point of view, it made sense not to be at variance with the rest of Christendom. Yet the Anglo-Saxons were greatly influenced by the medieval Celtic Church. This influence seems to have been predominantly Irish, though it is possible that traditions of the native British Church continued to play some part, as John Corbett suggests. The Christianization of the English kingdoms in the seventh century was mainly the work of Irish monks and their pupils, although it is sometimes hard to separate missions from the Continent from those of the Irish. For instance, the conversion of the West Saxons was begun by Roman missionaries, but an Irish scholar, Maildubh, founded a centre of religion and learning at Malmesbury in Wiltshire.[78] Both the Irishman, Fursa, who established a monastery near Yarmouth in Norfolk, and the Burgundian disciple of Saint Columban, Felix, played a part in the conversion of East Anglia.[79] In Northumbria, on the other hand, it was after the failure of the Roman mission that King Oswald invited the Irish to come, around 635. They were led by Aidan, who

---

73 See Chadwick, *Early Brittany*, 282-83, and references there cited.
74 Hughes, *The Church*, 173-93; Peter O'Dwyer, *Céli Dé: Spiritual Reform in Ireland, 750-900* (Dublin, 1981).
75 Alan O. Anderson (ed. and trans.), *Early Sources of Scottish History A.D. 500 to 1286* (Edinburgh, 1922), I, 258 and 489-90.
76 For their role in Ireland, see Hughes, *The Church*, 257-61.
77 Ibid., 263-74.
78 The history of the monastery is discussed by Dom Aelred Watkin, "Abbey of Malmesbury," in Ralph B. Pugh and Elizabeth Crittall (eds.), *A History of Wiltshire*, Victoria History of the Counties of England (London, 1956), III, 210-31.
79 Stenton, *ASE*, 116-17.

founded on the island of Lindisfarne, off the coast of present-day Northumberland, a monastery which became widely important.[80]

One very significant factor in the influence of Celtic monasteries was their active intellectual life. This was not so much the case in Brittany, where there was so much in the way of violence and threats that the monasteries could do little more than survive, but in Wales and, above all, in Ireland, monastic learning flourished. The pagan Celts had had a great tradition of learning, and the course of study in druidic schools was very exacting.[81] Some of this was kept in monasteries.[82] Illtud, the fifth-century abbot of Llantwit Major in southern Wales, was known for his comprehensive learning and had many students, including Saint Samson, as has been already mentioned.[83] The Irish monks such as Saint Columban show familiarity with various church fathers, as well as with Classical authors. Illuminated manuscripts such as the seventh-century Book of Durrow in Offaly, the Book of Kells (probably started in Iona and completed in Kells in Meath early in the ninth century), and the Lindisfarne Gospels are the products of a consummate art.[84] The Ardagh Chalice, probably a possession of the Clonmacnois monastery in Offaly, could also have been the work of Celtic monks.[85]

The fame of the Irish monasteries as seminaries of learning drew many pupils from the Continent, as well as from England. Bede states that in the plague year, 664, many English people were in Ireland "either for the sake of religious studies or to live a more ascetic life."[86]

So Celtic influence did penetrate Anglo-Saxon culture, sometimes in obvious ways, as we have seen, sometimes less noticeably. For

80 On Aidan, see Mayr-Harting, *The Coming*, 94-99.
81 Joseph Vendryès, "La Religion des Celtes" in *Les Religions de l'Europe ancienne*, "Mana": Introduction à l'Histoire des Religions - 2 (Paris, 1948), III, 290-320.
82 See, for example, McNeill, *The Celtic Churches*, 120-34, and Olivier Loyer, *Les Chrétientés celtiques*, Mythes et Religions 56 (Paris, 1965), 47-62.
83 Above, p. 85.
84 Arthur A. Luce, et al. (eds.), *Evangeliorum Quattuor Codex Durmachensis*, 2 vols. (Olten, Lausanne, and Freiburg i. Br., 1960); Ernest H. Alton, et al. (eds.), *Evangeliorum Quattuor Codex Cenannensis*, 3 vols. (Berne, 1950-51), and *The Book of Kells: Reproductions from the Manuscript in Trinity College Dublin*, With a Study of the Manuscript by Françoise Henry (London, 1974); Thomas D. Kendrick, et al. (eds.), *Evangeliorum Quattuor Codex Lindisfarnensis*, 2 vols. (Olten, Lausanne, and Freiburg i. Br., 1956-60). It should be noted that there is controversy over the provenance of both the Book of Durrow and the Book of Kells; for a discussion and further references, see Isabel Henderson, "Pictish Art and the Book of Kells" in *Ireland in Early Mediaeval Europe: Studies in Memory of Kathleen Hughes*, ed. by Dorothy Whitelock, Rosamond McKitterick and David Dumville (Cambridge, 1982), 79-105.
85 Liam S. Gógan, *The Ardagh Chalice* (Dublin, 1932). Another chalice, together with a paten and a wine-strainer, was found at Derrynaflan, co. Tipperary, in 1980. The hoard will be described in a forthcoming monograph to be published by the National Museum of Ireland.
86 "uel diuinae lectionis uel continentioris uitae gratia," Bede, *HE* III.27, 312-13.

instance, the practice in some English churches of singing the Nicene Creed at mass seems to have come from the Irish, who had borrowed it from Spain. Alcuin, who tried to persuade Charlemagne to have it sung throughout his empire, was using an Irish version of the text, as represented in the Stowe Missal, an Irish mass book of the early ninth century.[87] The Irish influence also appears in books of private prayer, such as the Book of Cerne, which belonged to the monastery of Cerne Abbas in Dorset but which has materials in it from the north of England. Its most striking feature is the importance given to penance. The book includes a prayer which goes through all conceivable types of sin, so that saying it and pondering over it would lead to an examination of one's conscience.[88] This is definitely reminiscent of the Irish private confession to the *anmchara*. The Irish also carried their penitential practices to the Continent in the various missions that led to the establishment of monasteries such as Luxeuil and Bobbio. From Continental sources, these penitentials were to return to England in the tenth century, where their use was fostered, notably by Archbishop Wulfstan of York.[89]

The idea of private confession and of the seal of confession, penance, is indeed a very important part of the Celtic heritage. The examination of one's conscience is necessary if one strives for perfection, and the Celts did yearn for the absolute in religious matters—their taste for asceticism bears witness to this. The Synod of Whitby brought the triumph of Rome, but the question there was one of discipline, not of faith. Because of its faith, of its intense spiritual and intellectual life, the medieval Celtic Church left a lasting mark on the Anglo-Saxon world.

87 See Mayr-Harting, *The Coming*, 181-82, citing Bernard Capelle, "Alcuin et l'Histoire du Symbole de la Messe" in Bernard Capelle (ed.), *Travaux liturgiques de Doctrine et d'Histoire* (Louvain, 1955-67), II, 211-21.
88 *The Prayer Book of Aedeluald the Bishop, commonly called the Book of Cerne*, ed. with intro. and notes by Dom Arthur B. Kuypers (Cambridge, 1902), discussed by Mayr-Harting, *The Coming*, 182-87, with further references to secondary studies.
89 Allen J. Frantzen provides a full discussion of this subject in "The Tradition of Penitentials in Anglo-Saxon England," *ASE* 11 (1983), 23-56; the Continental background is discussed in his book, *The Literature of Penance in Anglo-Saxon England* (New Brunswick, N.J., 1983).

7

Anglo-Saxon Use of the Apocryphal Gospel

Antonette di Paolo Healey

The Anglo-Saxon church had an ambivalent attitude towards New Testament apocrypha. On the one hand, there is popular and frequent use of apocryphal literature; on the other, there is ecclesiastical censure of it. As I have remarked elsewhere,[1] both Aldhelm and Ælfric, writing three centuries apart, condemn the *Vision of St. Paul*, a well-known medieval guidebook to the next world. Aldhelm describes its scenes as "fevered fancies" and urges the faithful to deny its authority.[2] Ælfric is equally orthodox in his homily for Tuesday, "On the Greater Litany." Here he refers to St. Paul being caught up to the third heaven and wonders at the naïveté of men who read this "false composition." He writes: "How do some men read the false composition which they call the vision of Paul, when he himself said that he heard the secret words, which no earthly man may speak?"[3]

---

1 Antonette di Paolo Healey, *The Old English Vision of St. Paul*, Speculum Anniversary Monographs 2 (Cambridge, Mass., 1978), 41.
2 Rudolf Ehwald, *De Virginitate*, MGH, Auctores Antiquissimi 15 (1919; rptd. 1961), 256, lines 7-14. Cited by Theodore Silverstein (ed.), *Visio Sancti Pauli: The History of the Apocalypse in Latin together with Nine Texts*, Studies and Documents 4 (London, 1935), 6.
3 Malcolm Godden, *Ælfric's Catholic Homilies: The Second Series*, EETS, SS 5 (Lon-

Ælfric's attack on this apocryphon is what we would expect of him, for he was always concerned with soundness of doctrine. As Gatch reminds us,[4] Ælfric differed from many of the anonymous homilists in that he possessed a mind which discriminated about the reliability and authority of his sources. As Clemoes has argued,[5] the informing principle in Ælfric's work was to provide England with orthodox teaching in vernacular prose.

Not all Anglo-Saxon writers shared his concern. For them, apocryphal literature was at least accessible and instructive, and frequently memorable and dramatic. In short, it provided material for both translation and editing into homilies. The editing could take various forms: at its most basic level, a writer summarized or amplified the existing story; occasionally, he adjoined other apocryphal material; and occasionally, he excised heretical elements, thus providing a semblance of orthodoxy. However, he would always add a phrase of direct address, such as *men þa leofestan*, to indicate his awareness of an audience, either reading or listening. This apocryphal material, disseminated through translations and the homilies based on them, exerted a perceptible influence on other areas of Anglo-Saxon culture: poets allude to it; workers in stone carve scenes from it; and even Anglo-Saxon medical men appropriate details from it for their charms and recipes.

Angus Cameron in his *List of Old English Texts*[6] has identified five New Testament apocrypha: *The Gospel of Pseudo-Matthew*, *The Gospel of Nicodemus*, *The Vindicta Salvatoris*, *The Vision of St. Paul*, and *The Apocalypse of Thomas*. The last two, *The Vision of St. Paul* and *The Apocalypse of Thomas*, both treat the fate of souls. *The Vision of St. Paul* is concerned with documenting the individual judgment each soul undergoes at the moment of death, and *The Apocalypse of Thomas* is concerned with heralding the general judgment by means of cosmological signs on seven days. *The Vision of St. Paul* draws upon the contents of several visions for its material. Its very lack of originality is an assurance of its truth. The more familiar it sounded, the more authentic it seemed. *The Apocalypse of Thomas*, in turn, draws upon the familiar language and images of St. John's *Apocalypse*. Eschatological in content, these two apocrypha cannot be strictly considered gospels, and they will be mentioned only in passing here.[7]

don, 1979), 190, lines 14-16: *Humeta rædað sume men. ða leasan gesetnysse. ðe hi hatað paulus gesihðe. nu he sylf sæde. þæt he ða digelan word gehyrde. þe nan eorðlic mann sprecan ne mot.*

4 Milton McC. Gatch, *Preaching and Theology in Anglo-Saxon England: Ælfric and Wulfstan* (Toronto, 1976), 14-15.

5 Peter Clemoes, "Ælfric," in Eric G. Stanley (ed.), *Continuations and Beginnings: Studies in Old English Literature* (London, 1966), 183.

6 Angus Cameron, "A List of Old English Texts," in Roberta Frank and Angus Cameron (eds.), *A Plan for the Dictionary of Old English*, TOES 2 (Toronto, 1973), 118-19.

7 For a recent survey of the content and influence of *The Vision of St. Paul*, see

By far the most popular of the New Testament apocrypha, and the one on which this discussion focusses, is the *Gospel of Nicodemus*, whose development has been recently sketched by H. C. Kim and Jackson J. Campbell.[8] Originally composed in Greek about 600, the *Gospel of Nicodemus* first contained only the details of Christ's trial and crucifixion. However, by the time of the late Latin recension of the text, the famous Descent to Hell material had been added and the Letter of Pilate to Claudius, testifying to Christ's death and resurrection, had been appended to it, and thus the whole gospel comes to be called the *Acts of Pilate*.[9]

The Harrowing of Hell, the belief that in the three days between Christ's death and resurrection, he harrowed Hell, conquered the Devil, and led out the souls of the righteous, is the most striking episode of the entire gospel. Those of us raised on the Apostles' Creed find it difficult to believe that the notion of the Harrowing of Hell has no real basis in scripture and was originally unorthodox—as David Dumville has reminded us.[10] However, passages such as Psalm 24:7, "Gates, raise your arches, rise you ancient doors, let the king of glory in!" allow for the natural development of Christ's storming Hell's gates, his rescue of the just, and his return in glory with them to the gates of Heaven. By about the year 1000 in England, the Latin formula *descendit ad inferos*, noticed by David Dumville in Irish manuscripts,[11] is given legitimacy in an Old English translation of the Apostles' Creed: *he nider-astah to helle*.[12] Moreover, in the *Durham Hymnal*, dated by Ker as of the first quarter of the eleventh century,[13] we find a hymn on

---

Healey, *The Old English Vision of St. Paul*. For the *Thomas* material, see Max Förster, "Der Vercelli-Codex CXVII nebst Abdruck einiger altenglischen Homilien der Handschrift," *Festschrift für Lorenz Morsbach*, dargebracht von Freunden und Schülern, ed. by Ferdinand Holthausen and Heinrich Spies, Studien zur englischen Philologie 50 (Halle a S., 1913), 116-28; Max Förster, "A New Version of the Apocalypse of Thomas in Old English," *Anglia* 73 (1955), 6-36; and Milton McC. Gatch, "Two Uses of Apocrypha in Old English Homilies," *Church History* 33 (1964), 379-84, 388.

8 Hackchin Kim (ed.), *The Gospel of Nicodemus*, Toronto Medieval Latin Texts 2 (Toronto, 1973), 1-7; Jackson J. Campbell, "To Hell and Back: Latin Tradition and Literary Use of the 'Descensus ad inferos' in Old English," *Viator* 13 (1982), 107-58, gives an excellent and full treatment of this tradition from a perspective different from my own.

9 G. C. O'Ceallaigh, "Dating the Commentaries of Nicodemus," *Harvard Theological Review* 56 (1963), 23-25; cited by Kim, *Nicodemus*, 1-2.

10 David N. Dumville, "Biblical Apocrypha and the Early Irish: A Preliminary Investigation," *PRIA* 73 C (1973), 301.

11 Ibid.

12 Cambridge University Library MS Gg. 3. 28 is dated by Neil R. Ker, *Catalogue of Manuscripts Containing Anglo-Saxon* (Oxford, 1957), 13, No. 15, as "s. x/xi" (hereafter all dates of manuscripts are taken from Ker without notice); for the text of the Apostles' Creed, see Benjamin Thorpe (ed.), *The Homilies of the Anglo-Saxon Church*, 2 vols., Ælfric Society (London, 1844-46), II, 596.

13 Ker, *Catalogue* 146, No. 107.

the Resurrection, alluding to Christ's return from the Harrowing. The Latin phrase *victor redit de barathro* is glossed by Old English *sigefæst he gehwerfde of helle*.[14] The explicit mention of the descent to Hell in both the Apostles' Creed and the *Durham Hymnal* demonstrates the English Church's tolerance and, in fact, active encouragement of this notion of the Harrowing of Hell.

As we turn to the *Gospel of Nicodemus* material in Old English, we notice that Anglo-Saxon writers not only were interested in providing plain translations of the gospel, but were also concerned with recasting it into homilies. What primarily distinguishes the two is the absence or presence of a hortatory voice. In the homilies, we hear intruding into the narrative a voice urgent and compelling in articulating the need to repay Christ for his act of redemption. The translations, on the other hand, are characterized by the absence of an authorial/scribal voice commenting on the action of the narrative. The characters simply speak for themselves; and it has been suggested that the Latin translation of the Harrowing of Hell found in the Book of Cerne (manuscript dated between 800 and 825) may perhaps be our earliest example of the development of liturgical drama.[15]

The Old English translation of the *Gospel of Nicodemus* is preserved in two manuscripts: Cambridge University Library MS Ii. 2. 11, dated by Ker as written between the third quarter of the eleventh century and the first quarter of the twelfth century,[16] and BL MS Cotton Vitellius A. xv, Part I, dated by Ker as the middle of the twelfth century.[17] As the Cambridge University Library translation is both older and fuller, I will concern myself only with that. If we disregard Thwaites's edition of 1698,[18] which was a mere reprint of Junius's transcript, the first modern edition of the text was by W. H. Hulme in 1898.[19] It is a rather loose translation of the late Latin recension, and like the late Latin recension, it follows, on the whole, the canonical gospels in its treatment of Christ's trial by Pilate and his resurrection and ascension. Also like the late Latin recension, the Old English translation incorporates some interesting apocryphal elements.[20] It

---

14 Joseph Stevenson (ed.), *The Latin Hymns of the Anglo-Saxon Church with an Interlinear Anglo-Saxon Gloss*, Publications of the Surtees Society 23 (Durham, 1851), 83, cited by Michael Swanton (ed.), *The Dream of the Rood*, Old and Middle English Texts (Manchester, 1970), 135, s.v. *sigorfæst on þam sið fate*.
15 David N. Dumville, "Liturgical Drama and Panegyric Responsory from the Eighth Century? A Re-examination of the Origin and Contents of the Ninth-Century Section of the Book of Cerne," *Journal of Theological Studies* 23 (1972), 381.
16 Ker, *Catalogue* 28, No. 20.
17 Ibid. 279, No. 215.
18 Edward Thwaites (ed.), *Heptateuchus, Liber Job et Evangelium Nicodemi; Anglo-Saxonice. Historiae Judith Fragmentum; Dano-Saxonice* (Oxford, 1698).
19 William H. Hulme, "The Old English Version of the Gospel of Nicodemus," *Publications of the Modern Language Association of America* 13 (1898), 457-542.
20 Kim, *Nicodemus*, 3-5, notes the apocryphal elements in the Latin text.

narrates the story of Pilate's messenger who bows down before Christ and extends a piece of cloth in front of him[21] (although it does not preserve the strange story found in the late Latin of the standards bowing before Christ as he enters the presence of Pilate; in the Old English, only the *heads* of men, not their standards, bend to Christ).[22] Like the Latin, the Old English identifies Pilate's wife as Procula,[23] a detail not found in the New Testament, although the account of her fear is given in Matthew 27:19; and like the Latin, the Old English presents the flight of Mary and Joseph into Egypt as caused, not by fear of Herod, as Scripture tells us (Matthew 2:13-15), but by a basic mistrust of everyone.[24] The Old English translation also preserves the mistaken notion found in the Latin that Christ is brought before Pilate, and not the high priest Caiaphas, to be charged for his statement about the destruction and reconstruction of the temple.[25] As chapters six through eleven of the late Latin gospel are omitted in the Old English translation, the Old English does not retain the interesting identification of the woman suffering from a bloody issue for twelve years, who is cured by touching the edge of Christ's cloak, with Veronica, the woman who wipes Christ's face with her veil and receives the imprint of it on the garment;[26] and due to the same gap in the Old English translation, the names of the good and bad thieves, Dismas and Gestas, and the name of Longinus, the man who pierced Christ's side, are omitted—all memorable contributions of the *Gospel of Nicodemus* to the crucifixion story.[27] Finally, like the Latin, the Old English translator expands the Joseph of Arimathea legend, narrating how the Jews angrily imprison Joseph and how the risen Christ miraculously releases him.[28]

Almost all the remaining material treats of the Harrowing of Hell. The story is told by Karinus and Leuticus (Lat. Leucius), the sons of "Blessed Simeon," who were among those resurrected from the dead by Christ. The choice of narrators is no doubt an attempt to give authenticity to the Harrowing episode. The Harrowing is marked first by the presence of light in darkness, a light so bright it seems "as if the golden sun were on fire there,"[29] then by the consternation of Satan and all his "cruel company"[30] and the joy of all mankind; and as in life, so too in death, John the Baptist heralds the coming of Christ. The ensuing dialogues between Hell and Satan and the supplications of

21 Hulme, "Nicodemus," 472, lines 6-8; Kim, *Nicodemus*, I.2.
22 Hulme, "Nicodemus," 474, lines 7-9; Kim, *Nicodemus*, I.5.
23 Hulme, "Nicodemus," 474, line 11; Kim, *Nicodemus*, II.1.
24 Hulme, "Nicodemus," 474, lines 25-27; Kim, *Nicodemus*, II.3.
25 Hulme, "Nicodemus," 478, lines 21-31; Kim, *Nicodemus*, IV.1.
26 Kim, *Nicodemus*, VII.
27 Ibid., IX.5 and X.1.
28 Hulme, "Nicodemus," 482, line 18 to 486, line 22; Kim, *Nicodemus*, XII-XIII.
29 *swylce þær gylden sunna onæled wære*, Hulme, "Nicodemus," 496, lines 10-11.
30 *reðe werod*, ibid., 496, line 12.

Adam (Eve is *not* mentioned in the Old English translation) and the good thief create exciting drama. The gospel ends with Pilate's letter to Claudius, which attests to the truth of Christ's resurrection and the deceit of those who killed him.

The manuscript in which the Old English *Gospel of Nicodemus* is found gives us some indication of how this translation was received by its Anglo-Saxon audience. Cambridge University Library MS Ii. 2. 11, dated from the third quarter of the eleventh century to the first half of the twelfth century, is most famous for the material which precedes the *Gospel of Nicodemus*, namely, the West-Saxon translation of the four gospels. The placement of the *Gospel of Nicodemus* immediately after them suggests that this apocryphal gospel, if not equal, was almost equal in authority to the canonical gospels. By mere juxtaposition with Matthew, Mark, Luke, and John, Nicodemus nearly attains the status of a fifth gospel;[31] and to answer the question "In what relation did these apocrypha stand to the Canon itself?"[32] we would have to reply from the evidence of this manuscript, late though it is, that they were almost indistinguishable from it. Not only in content, but also in placement, the *Gospel of Nicodemus* supplements and completes the canonical gospels.

As I mentioned earlier, the Anglo-Saxon impulse was not only to translate the gospel but also to rework it into homiletic form. Folios 87b-100 of BL MS Cotton Vespasian D. xiv, dated as mid-twelfth century, provide a translation of the *Gospel of Nicodemus* which is on its way to becoming a homily. It gives, in abbreviated fashion, Part I of the *Gospel of Nicodemus*: the crucifixion scene, Joseph of Arimathea's role in burying Christ, Joseph's imprisonment and release by Christ, and an account of the Lord's resurrection. The remainder of the text treats of the Harrowing of Hell. W. H. Hulme, the first editor of the piece,[33] calls attention to the "decidedly homiletic character" (p. 580) of the manuscript in which the text has been preserved, and notices two passages which have no source in the usual narrative of the *Gospel of Nicodemus*. The two passages are these: "Oh, dearest men, how loathly and how horrible was the meeting of the devils when Hell and the Devil quarreled between themselves"[34] and "Oh men, how horrible it was when diabolical Hell seized the fiend Beelzebub and held him

---

31 Most recently noticed by Angus Cameron in "Anglo-Saxon Literature," *Dictionary of the Middle Ages*, ed. by Joseph R. Strayer (New York, 1982-), I, 285.
32 Dumville, "Biblical Apocrypha," 332, has recently asked the question.
33 William H. Hulme, "The Old English Gospel of Nicodemus," *Modern Philology* 1 (1903-04), 579-610; later edited by Rubie D.-N. Warner, *Early English Homilies from the Twelfth Century MS. Vesp. D. xiv*, EETS, OS 152 (1917; rptd. New York, 1971), 77-88.
34 *Eala, mæn þa leofeste, hwu laðlic and hwu grislic wæs þære deoflene gemot, þa seo helle and se deofel heom betweonen cidden!* (Hulme, 1903-04, 603).

fast because the Devil had been lord of Hell and of all the diabolical things which were in it."[35] We notice that the text is given a homiletic title "De Resurrectione Domini" (fol. 87b) which places it firmly in the *temporale*, whereas our plain translations have no medieval titles, and that the homilist uses the first person plural in the opening sentence— an acknowledgement that he is writing for an audience: "On that day in which *our* Saviour suffered pain on the holy cross for *our* redemption, there was a certain man standing near there who was called Joseph" (emphasis mine).[36] It is always difficult to make comments about the originality of a homilist when his precise source is unknown. We do not know what was in his source and what were his deviations from it. Yet, in these particular passages I have cited, we clearly suspect that the homilist is making his own contribution to sermon literature. The sermon on the "Resurrection of the Lord" in MS Cotton Vespasian D. xiv, although it is a twelfth-century text, shows us the earliest stages by which a gospel translation can become a homily. It is also interesting to observe that the *Gospel of Nicodemus* text immediately follows a translation of John 14:1-13, verses in which Christ tries to strengthen his apostles at the Last Supper after his prediction of Peter's denial. Once again, as in Cambridge University Library MS Ii. 2. 11, we find the apocryphal gospel not inappropriately placed side by side with the canonical, and once again, it supplements and completes the Passion narrative.

The margins of pages 295-301 of Corpus Christi College, Cambridge MS 41, the famous Bede manuscript of the *Ecclesiastical History*, show what usually happened to the *Gospel of Nicodemus* in the Old English period.[37] In this text, dated as first half of the eleventh century or mid-eleventh century, only the Harrowing of Hell episode, the most important part of the *Gospel of Nicodemus* in literary interest and influence, is given a homiletic reworking; moreover, other apocryphal matter is attached to it. The sermon begins with the Latin heading "*Hec est dies quam fecit dominus...*" and with the Old English direct address "*Men þa leofestan....*" The scribe is obviously copying out his text, and his exemplar seems to be in front of him as he is writing, for in the early part of the sermon, the phrases *her sægeð* and *hit sagað* continually remind us that he is *scribe* not *composer*,[38] and he reinforces this distinction by stating that *se writtere* 'the author,' not

---

35 *Eala mæn, hwu grislic hit wæs þa-þa seo deofellice helle þone feond, Beelzebub, underfeng and hine fæste geheold! For-þan se deofol wæs ær þære helle hlaford and eallra þære deofellicre þingen þe hire on wæron* (Hulme, 1903-04, 606).
36 *Ðæs dæiges þe ure Hælend for ure alesednysse geðolede pine on þær halgen rode, þa wæs þære neh sum were standende, se wæs Ioseph genæmned* (Hulme, 1903-04, 591).
37 Ibid., 610-14.
38 Ibid., 610, lines 1, 9, 11, 13.

he, draws a comparison between the first Easter and the general resurrection at the end of the world.[39] It is at this point that the homilist turns away from the Harrowing of Hell material and takes up material from the *Apocalypse of Thomas*, which describes the signs of the end of the world and relates the intercessions of Mary, Michael, and Peter for the souls of the just. The transition between the two texts is not a smooth one, and we are left with the impression of a disjointed narrative. Not all homiletic recastings of the *Gospel of Nicodemus* are skillful ones. This particular homily appears directly after the *Apocalypse of Thomas* in the margins of Corpus Christi College, Cambridge MS 41, and the use of material from *Thomas* in the homily itself may be the cause for their juxtaposition; but before we too hastily make a statement about apocryphal legends attracting other apocryphal legends in manuscript compilations, we should note that a copy of this same homily is found in Corpus Christi College, Cambridge MS 303, where it follows Ælfric's Easter homily for the First Series titled "Ewangelium In Resurrectione Domini. Secundum Marcum" (Ker, *Catalogue*, no. 57, item 16). Once again, the *Gospel of Nicodemus* is associated with the orthodox tradition.

Where the Easter homily written in the margins of Corpus Christi College, Cambridge MS 41 fails, Blickling Homily 7 succeeds.[40] It draws upon the same apocryphal material, combining the Harrowing of Hell with the *Apocalypse of Thomas*, but it does so gracefully and coherently. Marcia Dalbey, in her authoritative and sensitive analysis of the patterns of preaching in this homily,[41] suggests how the homilist structures his sermon to reflect the typological implications of Easter; the final event of the process of redemption is the Last Judgment, and therefore there is a natural association of the Harrowing of Hell material with that of the *Apocalypse of Thomas*. The promise to each of us in the Harrowing episode receives its fulfillment on Doomsday; Christ's past mercy may be predictive of his future mercy, and just as Christ responds to Adam in Hell, so too he may respond to all mankind on Judgment Day. Past and future become identical in time. The achievement of the Blickling homilist in this sermon should not be underestimated. As Dalbey has shown, the text is a *sermon* and moves from "what Christ has done and will do" to "what man must do," from divine dispensation to human responsibility.[42] Resonating through the text is the pleading voice of the homilist, urging us and himself to right action and right thinking: "*Uton beon eaþmode & mildheorte & ælmes-*

---

39 Ibid., 611, line 31.
40 Richard Morris (ed.), *The Blickling Homilies*, EETS, OS 58, 63, 73 (London, 1874-80; rptd. as one volume 1967), 83-97.
41 Marcia A. Dalbey, "Patterns of Preaching in The Blickling Easter Homily," *American Benedictine Review* 24 (1973), 478-92.
42 Dalbey, "Patterns," 491.

georne"; "*Uton nu, men þa leofestan, þas þing geþencean* . . . ."[43] The sermon ends appropriately with a prayer, the communal voice of the Church. Although there is one other homily which can be termed a *Gospel of Nicodemus* homily, folios 148v-54v of MS Junius 121, recently edited by Anna Maria Luiselli Fadda,[44] Blickling Homily 7 is by far the most successful of all the prose sermons.

Old English poetry, too, reflects the influence of the *Gospel of Nicodemus*. Cynewulf, in *Christ II*, his Ascension poem found in the Exeter Book,[45] improves upon Gregory the Great's striking image of the *leap*, five in all in Gregory,[46] to depict the significant phases of Christ's ministry. He adds in lines 558-76 another leap, not found in Gregory, of the Harrowing of Hell. These lines show familiarity with the *guþplega* 'battleplay' (line 572) between the King of Glory and Satan, and with the release of a countless number of people from bondage. Another Exeter Book poem, *The Descent into Hell*,[47] is wholly based on Part II of the *Gospel of Nicodemus*, with due allowance for recastings and omissions. This poem represents a later stage than the homilies in the process of translation of the *Gospel of Nicodemus*, for here not only is there an authorial voice, but the voice tends to take over and dominate the voice of the imagined prophet, John the Baptist. The speeches blend, and it is difficult to distinguish between prophet and poet.[48] This results in an interesting widening of the reader's perception of time in the poem and makes relevant the truth that redemption is not limited to a particular place or a particular time. The last poem in MS Junius 11, *Christ and Satan*,[49] also shows knowledge of the *Gospel of Nicodemus*.[50] In its middle section, it treats some of the events of Christ's life, including the Harrowing of Hell (lines 363-455), and ends the section with the Last Judgment. This poem repeats the pattern that we have seen in two of the homilies: the association of the Harrowing of Hell material with that of Doomsday.

43 Morris, *Blickling Homilies*, 95, line 26, "Let us be humble and merciful and charitable"; p. 97, line 1, "Let us now, dearest men, consider these things."
44 Anna Maria Luiselli Fadda, "'De descensu Christi ad inferos': una inedita omelia anglosassone," *Studi Medievali*, Ser. 3, 13.2 (1972), 989-1011.
45 George P. Krapp and Elliott van K. Dobbie (eds.), *The Exeter Book*, ASPR 3 (New York, 1936), 15-27.
46 *Homiliarum in Evangelia* II.29, paragraphs 9-11, in Jacques P. Migne (ed.), *Patrologiae Cursus Completus*, Series Latina 76, cols. 1218-19.
47 Krapp and Dobbie, *Exeter Book*, 219-23.
48 The most recent editor of the poem, Thomas A. Shippey, *Poems of Wisdom and Learning in Old English* (Cambridge and Totowa, N. J., 1976), 41, suggests that the two "personae," John the Baptist and the poet, substantially agree with one another, and therefore there is no need to distinguish between their voices.
49 George P. Krapp (ed.), *The Junius Manuscript*, ASPR 1 (New York, 1931), 135-58.
50 For a modern survey of the relationship between *Nicodemus* and *Christ and Satan*, see Robert E. Finnegan (ed.), *"Christ and Satan": A Critical Edition* (Waterloo, Ontario, 1977), 49-55.

Finally, *The Dream of the Rood*,[51] in which the Cross is personified, has an allusion in lines 148-49 to the renewing of hope for those creatures who endured the burning. These lines suggest that the *Gospel of Nicodemus*, late though our extant manuscripts may be, had such a secure place in English literary tradition that a mere reference to it suffices to evoke in the mind the whole apocryphal legend.

We should note one other detail which clearly reveals the wide-reaching effect of the *Gospel of Nicodemus* on its Anglo-Saxon audience. There is a stone slab at Bristol Cathedral, dated around mid-eleventh century by Lawrence Stone,[52] which shows the figure of Christ standing erect, his right hand holding a cross, his feet treading on the demonic figures below him, his left hand raising up two, or possibly three, other figures. This carving in stone portrays vividly and accurately the essential promise contained in the Harrowing of Hell story, and may indicate the reason for its continual popularity in the Middle Ages.[53]

The other two apocryphal gospels in Old English are much slighter in influence, although they are not without interest. The *Gospel of Pseudo-Matthew* is a narrative on the infancies of both Mary and Christ. A homily on the birth of Mary, a translation of chapters 1-12 of the *Gospel of Pseudo-Matthew*, treating from Anna's infertile marriage to Joachim to the Doubting of Mary, is found in three manuscripts: MS Hatton 114, MS Bodley 343,[54] and imperfectly in Corpus Christi College, Cambridge MS 367, all of which contain principally Ælfrician material. Since Ælfric was always concerned with orthodoxy and himself wrote, in Clemoes's words, "a cautiously correct homily"[55] on the Nativity of Mary, we are surprised that the cautious homily is absent from these Ælfrician manuscripts, whereas the homily based on *Pseudo-Matthew* appears there. Homily 6 in the Vercelli Book,[56] a sermon on Christ's nativity, is a loose and sporadic translation of chapters 13-25 of the *Gospel of Pseudo-Matthew*, treating of the birth of

---

51 George P. Krapp (ed.), *The Vercelli Book*, ASPR 2 (New York, 1932), 61-65.
52 Lawrence Stone, *Sculpture in Britain: The Middle Ages*, Pelican History of Art (Harmondsworth, 1955), 39 and Plate 24; see also M. Q. Smith, "The Harrowing of Hell Relief in Bristol Cathedral," *Transactions of the Bristol and Gloucestershire Archaeological Society* 94 (1976), 101-06. I am grateful to my colleague Professor Robert Deshman, who provided me with these references.
53 The correspondence between the *Gospel of Nicodemus* and the stone slab at Bristol Cathedral has been noticed recently by Jack D. A. Ogilvy, *Books Known to the English, 597-1066*, Medieval Academy of America Publication No. 76 (Cambridge, Mass., 1967), 71.
54 Bruno Assmann (ed.), *Angelsächsische Homilien und Heiligenleben*, Bibliothek der angelsächsischen Prosa 3 (1889; rptd. with a supplementary introduction by Peter Clemoes, Darmstadt, 1964), 117-37 (an edition of the text in MS Hatton 114 and Bodley 343).
55 Ibid., xxix.
56 Max Förster (ed.), *Die Vercelli-Homilien*, Bibliothek der angelsächsischen Prosa 12 (1932; rptd. Darmstadt, 1964), 131-37.

Christ, the Flight into Egypt, and the Holy Family's return to Judea. Perhaps of even more interest is that the Pseudo-Matthew material, represented by Vercelli Homily 6, probably influenced the choice of the Flight into Egypt as one of the scenes on the Ruthwell Cross.[57] In this scene, Mary with the Christ Child in her arms is sitting on a beast. The remains of a figure which must be Joseph is discernible in the upper left corner. Above the scene is a fragment of an inscription: Maria et IO(SEPHUS). As Swanton[58] has noted in his study of the figures of the Ruthwell Cross, it is the *Gospel of Pseudo-Matthew* which elevates the Flight into Egypt into a miraculous festival in which the wild beasts of the desert, dragons, lions, and panthers, worship and follow the Holy Family. In the canonical gospels, the Flight into Egypt is a relatively insignificant episode, and the Church has never thought it important enough to give it a particular feast day. If Swanton's thesis be accepted, we have new evidence of an apocryphal text influencing a form of art other than literature.

The final apocryphal gospel we find in Old English is the *Vindicta Salvatoris*, more familiarly called the *Legend of St. Veronica*.[59] It functions as a kind of supplement to the *Gospel of Nicodemus*, and in fact, in Cambridge University Library MS Ii. 2. 11, it follows immediately after the *Gospel of Nicodemus*. This gospel recounts, through the testimony of Nathan the Jew, the miracles which Christ wrought in his own country, the most important of which, for our purposes, is the healing of the woman with the issue of blood, who is given the name Veronica. Nathan's testimony is effective, for it encourages Titus, King of Libya, and his friend Vespasianus, to avenge Christ's death. They go to Jerusalem where they meet Veronica, who possesses a cloth with Christ's image on it, and the rest of the gospel treats of the various attempts to separate Veronica from this unique piece of cloth. Although there is an abbreviated version of this gospel, known as the *Legation of Nathan the Jew* in MS Cotton Vespasian D. xiv,[60] which omits all the Veronica material, it is the full version of the legend which influences another area of Old English literature, that of medical charms.[61] An Anglo-Saxon leech uses her name to bring about a cure for a form of malaria: "For tertian fever: A man shall in silence write 'Thine Hand Vexeth' and silently put the words on the left breast. And also in silence [the names] Emmanuel, Veronica."[62] As Grattan and Singer suggest (p. 34), St. Veronica's name is invoked for

---

57 Cited by Ogilvy, *Books*, 70.
58 Swanton, *Dream*, 15-16.
59 Assmann, *Homilien*, 181-92.
60 Ibid., 193-94; Warner, *Homilies*, 88-89.
61 Cited by Ogilvy, *Books*, 71.
62 John H. G. Grattan and Charles Singer (eds.), *Anglo-Saxon Magic and Medicine*, Publications of the Wellcome Historical Medical Museum, N.S. 3 (London, 1952), 34.

this cure made in silence, because her own cure was brought about in silence when she touched the hem of Christ's cloak.

As we can see, diversity characterizes the Anglo-Saxon uses of the apocryphal gospel. It was translated, reworked into homilies, associated with orthodox texts such as the canonical gospels and the homilies of Ælfric, and juxtaposed with unorthodox ones such as the *Apocalypse of Thomas* and the *Legend of St. Veronica*. It furnished significant parts of at least three Old English poems, *Christ II*, *The Descent into Hell*, and *Christ and Satan*, and provided an allusion for *The Dream of the Rood*, which suggests the assured place of one apocryphal gospel in Old English. It even had its effect on Anglo-Saxon magic and medicine. Finally, it seems to have been the inspiration to at least two stonemasons in England: that eighth-century Northumbrian who carved the scene depicting the Flight into Egypt on the Ruthwell Cross and that eleventh-century Englishman who portrayed the promise in the Harrowing of Hell on the stone slab of Bristol Cathedral.

8

The Image of the Worm: Some Literary Implications of Serpentine Decoration

Andrew J. G. Patenall

The progenitor of this topic is Professor Roy Leslie, who, in a paper first published in 1959, assessed current approaches to the analysis of Old English Syntax.[1] He perceived that an emerging recognition of a dominant hypotaxis in the literature had significant implications for stylistic and structural analysis. If analysts of syntax could define a larger sense and purpose in what were hitherto regarded as discrete, often awkwardly parallel, syntactical units, then it followed that in the larger structure, that which was formerly seen as digressive, accidentally echoic, and inorganically ornamental might in fact be related in accord with a series of complex aesthetic principles. Professor Leslie implied that just as the paratactical devices of repeated phrases, antitheses, *et cetera* constituted a plurilinear series, so too in the larger structure of a poem there might be a counterpoint of series of themes and perceptions. While each of these perceptions has a vigour of its own, it is related to others by rhythmic character, sometimes by a shared vocabulary, and by a common perceptual mode. Professor Les-

---

1 Roy F. Leslie, "Analysis of Stylistic Devices and Effects in Anglo-Saxon Literature," in Paul Böckmann (ed.), *Stil- und Formprobleme in der Literatur* (Heidelberg, 1959), 129-36.

lie called this practice interlacing. He was not the first to use the term in reference to Old English (OE) syntax, but, I believe, he was the first to develop the association between syntax, style, and structure.

The term was used again in 1967 by Professor Leyerle, who, in a paper entitled "The Interlace Structure of Beowulf" (subsequently published in *The University of Toronto Quarterly*), extended the principle of plurilinear interlace through the structure of a substantial poem.[2] Professor Leyerle definitively associated the aesthetic principle of interlace in manuscript illumination, decorative and functional furniture, memorial sculpture, and poetry. Subsequent critical literature has shown that paper to be one of those rare critical watersheds that inexorably alter the perspectives of readers who follow. The observation that plurilinear, allusive, associative art is closer to the natural processes of the human imagination is especially useful. For myself, whose involvement with the poetry of the Anglo-Saxons is primarily as an instructor of beginning students, the principle and implications of a literature and art that are both—in the manner of Beowulf's giant-sword—*wreoþenhilt ond wyrmfah* 'with braided hilt and worm-like decoration' (line 1698) is an irresistible notion with which to dispel the novice's characteristic vision of Anglo-Saxon society as rude, senselessly militant, and imaginatively coarse.

It is a commonplace that serpentine decoration is the predominant motif in Anglo-Saxon art. As well as the braided hilt and serpentine decoration of the sword attained by Beowulf, there are other poetic evocations of worm-like art. The narrator of *The Wanderer*, of the Exeter Book, must forego *wunden gold* 'braided gold' (line 32b), and he sees the deserted, ruined halls of a lost, high civilization as being *wyrmlicum fah* 'embellished in a serpentine pattern' (line 98b). The OE Riddles, too, are both rich in serpentine reference and themselves indicative of a cultural taste for an elliptic, tightly knotted, and enigmatic art. Riddle XXXV, for which the solution is "coat of mail," exhibits a marvellous consonance of subject-matter—the interlocking rings of the coat—lexicon, and structure; the whole presents a convoluted, endless knot that teases and delights the imagination.

Pictorial images particularize this taste and provide analogues for the poetry. The most dramatic instances are probably to be found in the so-called carpet pages of the books of gospels. These invariably occur on the verso of the leaf and form an imaginative preface to the text or title that begins on the facing folio. Thus they constitute a breach of the linear continuity of the text and serve as meditative interludes or embellishments on that which is to follow. In the carpet page facing the beginning of the gospel of John in The Book of Durrow, the two smaller

---

2 John Leyerle, "The Interlace Structure of *Beowulf*," *University of Toronto Quarterly* 37 (1967), 1-17.

side panels correspond exactly; the zoomorphs are elaborated by an interlace of tails. In the panels immediately above and below the medallion, serpentine figures intertwine in a figuration amplified by curious limbs springing from a lozenge-like joint on each body. The upper and lower panels again correspond, although the colours of gold and carmine are now reversed. The eye of the viewer is led, not back and forth across the page, but into the medallion in which, among the elaborate serpentine braids of gold, green, and carmine, are three peripheral and cruciform rivets in black and white; and at the centre, in a fourth, is the small essential cross. In colour and in form, the page has the succinctness of a charm and the ritual repetitiveness of a prayer. The carpet page that prefaces Mark's gospel in the Lindisfarne Gospels is also built around a cruciform heart. Serpentine zoomorphs in inner panels are echoed by knotted excrescences on the border, and four medallions rivet the design to the page; but what is so extraordinary about this folio is the tissue of fine interlaced ribbons that bubbles past and around all the panels. Our eyes swim as the pattern vibrates and leads us inexorably to the stationary cubes that constitute the cross in the centre.

The *nomen sacrum*, Chi-Rho, at Matthew 1:18—the incarnation of Christ—traditionally received glorious treatment. In the Lindisfarne Gospels, the whole monogram is bordered with interlaced zoomorphs. The lower left tail of the Chi rises from a swirl of medallions and sweeps through a climbing braid of serpentine figures to the upper right. The upper left arm of the Chi swings down in an elegant chiasmus to the centre of the folio by the same means, and ends in a nesting, curving galaxy of tailed medallions, which takes us to the curve of the Rho and so through knots and whorls to the stems of the initial. This ecstatic art which forces the viewer to dwell on the name of Christ, just as he was forced into the cruciform heart of the carpet panels has, I believe, precise parallels in OE poetry.

One further device of manuscript illumination for which I find literary analogues is well illustrated in the Book of Kells. This is the regular practice of small ornamental initials within the text itself. The device has rhetorical significance since it characteristically emphasizes and identifies a logically associated group of verses. The grotesques consist usually of serpent-cum-bird-cum-fish figures, but quite often anthropomorphic figures, in detail or in whole, are portrayed. Nearly all the images are bound in braids and lacertine knots; and within each folio, and to some extent within each gospel, there is a unity of style, colour, and execution. Their effect seems to correspond quite closely to the recurring phrase, the formulaic expression, and the lexical reiteration that appears in the poetry.

The literary implications that I draw from the taste for serpentine decoration in Anglo-Saxon art can be discovered in *The Phoenix*, a poem of some 680 lines preserved in the Exeter Book. It dates from the late eighth century (according to Professor Dobbie[3]) or from the late ninth century (according to Professor Blake[4]). The first 380 lines of *The Phoenix* are derived fairly obviously from the enduring and presumably popular *Carmen de ave Phoenice* attributed to Lactantius; and thus the poem's pedigree extends to the first part of the fourth century. The *Carmen*, extant in an eighth-century manuscript, runs to 170 lines. The first line of the *Carmen* occupies six lines in *The Phoenix*; the first thirty in the original become the introductory eighty-four in Old English; and on average, each line of Lactantius is expanded to two and a quarter lines in *The Phoenix*. Professor Blake, in his edition of the poem, says: "*The Phoenix* is verbose, and one might almost say diffuse."[5] This verbosity will bear some examination.

The first passage that will serve to demonstrate *The Phoenix* poet's method is comprised of lines 7-27. In the first six lines of the poem, the poet has told us that he has learned of a distant eastern paradise. The extract with which we are concerned begins, in lines 7-10, with a section—or panel—describing the paradise.

> Wlitig is se wong eall,   wynnum geblissad
> mid þam fægrestum   foldan stencum
> ænlic is þæt iglond,   æþele se Wyrhta
> modig meahtum spedig,   se þa moldan gesette.

> Fair is that meadow throughout,   blessed with joys,
> with the fairest   perfumes of the field;
> exquisite is that region,   noble its creator,
> mighty, abounding in powers   he who made that land.

In the first two lines (7-8), *se wong* 'the meadow' is depicted in earthly terms; and in the next two lines (9-10), it is described again, now as a creature of the Maker. The parataxis exhibited here surely corresponds to the zoomorphs in the carpet page from the Book of Durrow, where identical serpentine figures are played first in scarlet, then in gold. The Heavenly Creator becomes the bridge to the next two lines (11-12), where a perspective of heaven from the glorious meadow is presented.

> Ðær bið oft open,   eadgum togeanes
> onhliden hleoþra wyn,   heofonrices duru.

> There is often revealed   before the faces of the blest,
> manifested the delights of melody,   the door of the heavenly mansion.

In the next line and a half (13-14a), the poet returns to the *wynsum wong* and restates the theme with which the passage began.

---

3 George P. Krapp and Elliott Van K. Dobbie (eds.), *The Exeter Book*, ASPR 3 (New York, 1936), xxxvi.
4 Norman F. Blake (ed.), *The Phoenix*, Old and Middle English Texts (Manchester, 1964), 24.
5 Blake, *Phoenix*, 25.

Ðæt is wynsum wong,   wealdas grene
rume under roderum.

That is a pleasing meadow,   green the woodlands,
spacious beneath the skies.

The leitmotif has now been introduced, varied, and restated. Between 14b and 19a, a vivid antithesis to the motif occurs:

Ne mæg þær   ren ne snaw
ne forstes fnæst   ne fyres blæst
ne hægles hryre   ne hrimes dryre
ne sunnan hætu   ne sincaldu
ne wearm weder   ne winterscur
wihte gewyrdan,

Nor may there   rain nor snow,
nor crack of frost   nor blast of heat
nor tumult of hail   nor crust of rime
nor scorch of sun   nor bitter cold
nor close weather   nor winter storm
harm aught.

In five lines, nine subject phrases, embedded in their verbal cluster—*mæg* in 14b and *gewyrdan* in 19a—form a web of contrast to the original theme. There is no forward movement of narrative; instead there is an atemporal expansion and embellishment against which the motif stands out vividly. The motif returns in the next two lines (19b-21a).

                ac se wong seomað
eadig ond onsund.   Is þæt æþele lond
blostmum geblowen.

                but the meadow stands
blessed and wholesome.   That noble land is
abloom with blossoms.

At first, the meadow is referred to abstractly as *eadig ond onsund* 'blessed and wholesome'; and then, at the heart of this medallion, we have the vividly realized phrase *blostmum geblowen*; 'abloom with blossoms' is a lame rendering of the picture that is conjured. Following this, the poet returns for another five lines (21b-26a) to a monochromatic interlace of images of the world of common experience *her mid us*, 'here among us':

              Beorgas þær ne muntas
steape ne stondað,   ne stanclifu
heah hlifiað,   swa her mid us,
ne dene ne dalu   ne dunscrafu,
hlæwas ne hlincas,   ne þær hleonað oo
unsmeþes wiht,

rear up steeply,	There neither crags nor mountains
tower high	nor stony cliffs
neither glade nor dale	(as here among us);
outcrop nor hill;	nor upland cave,
anything rugged.	nor towers there ever

The whole passage is brought to an end by a brief one-and-a-half-line coda in which the essential notions of the field of paradise and the heaven above it are restated:

	ac se æþela feld
wridað under wolcnum,	wynnum geblowen.
	but the noble field
spreads out beneath the skies,	abloom with delights.

As well as thematic restatement, there is lexical repetition; *blostmum geblowen* of the middle medallion becomes *wynnum geblowen* 'abloom with delights' in the last, and the epithet *æþele* 'noble,' associated with the Creator in the initial panel, is transferred to *lond* in the middle section (20b), and to *feld* in the coda (26b).

The symmetry of this passage is remarkable. The opening statement consists of fifteen verses; the first antithetical section of ten verses; the medallion of four verses; another ten-verse antithesis; and a three-verse coda. Throughout the passage there is no forward action. Only from line 28 does the poet advance his narrative and introduce further themes. The Phoenix, itself, is not introduced until line 85. The first eighty-four lines of the poem are an introductory carpet concerned only with the paradise in which the bird is found. The twenty-one lines we have considered are thus a panel within this introduction. The motifs observed in this panel variously recur in the larger introduction.

Grey, bleak references to the hardships of our world, for instance, recall the elaborately stated antitheses (14b-19a and 21b-26a) on seven occasions in the introductory carpet. They range from a two half-line interpolation (81b-82a) to a twenty-five half-line interlude (50a-62a).[6] These recurrences are either directly echoic of the lacertine fabric of the antitheses we have considered, or they may be inversions of the positively stated motifs: *Is þæt æþele lond / blostmum geblowen* 'That noble land is abloom with blossoms' (20b-21a) becomes in line 74 *ne feallað þær on foldan fealwe blostman* 'nor fall there to the field withered blossoms.' As a panel, the twenty-five verse interpolation between lines 50 and 62 matches closely the twenty-four verse antithesis—with the four-verse medallion—dealt with earlier. These two extended antitheses balance each other in the eighty-four line introductory carpet.

6 See also 31-32, 38b-41a, 72b-74.

As well as thematic echoes, there is an even more finely wrought development of lexical resonance. *Æþele* 'noble,' attached first to the Creator (9b), then to *lond* (20b), and to *feld* (26b) becomes *se æþele wong* 'the noble meadow' in line 43b. In the section introducing the bird, which follows line 84, first the sun is described as *se æþelast tungla* 'most noble of stars' (93b) and then, in line 104a, the epithet is finally attached to the Phoenix itself—'the noble bird.' Similarly, the words *eadig* 'blessed,' *tir* and *tirfæst* 'glorious,' and *wlitig* 'lovely' or 'fair' are carried through the introduction with harmonious variations, and then used splendidly and intensely to describe the Phoenix; *wlitig* becomes *wlitigfæst* 'of lasting beauty' (105a) and *eadig* becomes *se tireadga* 'the gloriously blessed one' (106a). The colours of the introduction thus become the palette for the depiction of the bird. Rather than proceeding linearly through sequential episodes of the poem, the reader is drawn into its heart, just as the viewer is drawn irresistibly into the cruciform at the heart of a carpet page.

There is evidence in the vocabulary that a sense of serpentine ornament was dominant in the author's aesthetic creed. *Wrætlic* (*wrætlice* adverbially), meaning 'beautiful' generally, because of its association with *wrætt* 'jewel' or 'ornament,' connotes 'curious' and 'intricate,' as well. The springs that water the Phoenix's paradise are described by Lactantius as *perspicuus, lenis, dulcibus uber aquis* (26): 'pellucid, gentle, rich in sweet waters.' The Old English poet ignores these attributes and describes his well-springs as *wundrum wrætlice* 'strangely beauteous' (63a)—with a sense of their windings and curiosity. The image is developed subsequently in the description of the Phoenix itself: *Wrætlic is seo womb neoþan* 'Intricate is its breast beneath' (307a) and *Is him þæt heafod hindan grene, / wrætlice wrixleð, wurman geblonden* 'behind its head it is green, curiously dappled, mingled with purple' (293-94). Both *wrixleð* and *geblonden*, 'variegated' and 'mingled,' heighten the artificiality of the bird, and the phrases recall the peacocks attendant on Christ in Judgment in the Book of Kells (folio 32v) or the elaborate symmetry of St. John's eagle in the Echternach Gospels (folio 176v).

Not only are the well-springs *curious* but a little further in the introduction the poet describes the trees, which, like Milton's, blossom and fruit simultaneously, as *wrætlic* (75) and *gehroden hyhtlice* 'adorned joyously' (79); and *gehroden* means more than is conveyed by 'adorned.' Etymologically, it is closely associated with *hreod* meaning 'rush' or 'reed.' Thus, there is implicit in the adorning that the poet describes a woven texture or web-like characteristic that corresponds to the fields of braided ribbons so common in illumination.

Although *gehroden* only occurs once in the poem, the mode it implies is developed. Of the bird, we are told:

> Is ymb þone sweoran, swylce sunnan hring,
> beaga beorhtast   brogden feðrum. (305-06)

> There is around its neck, like a ring of sunlight,
> a most bright chain of embroidered feathers.

A little later, this is metamorphosed into the divine halo of the company of saints.

> Þær se beorhta beag, brogden wundrum
> eorcnanstanum   eadigra gehwam
> hlifað ofer heafde. (602-04a)

> There the bright ring, marvellously embroidered
> with costly stones, stands over the heads of the
> blessed ones.

This graphic metaphor recalls the frontispiece to the gospel of St. John in the Lindisfarne Gospels, where the line of the eagle's collar is carried into a halo, which, of course, corresponds to that of John himself. The poet's view of the collar is more complex than that of the artist; the poet's collar and halo are distinguished by the omnipresent serpentine braids, visually present in the central medallion of the Durrow carpet page already described, or perhaps more modestly, in the rim of the halo of John's eagle in the Book of Kells (folio 27v). It should be stressed again that this lexicon of particularly serpentine and generally pictorial images is not a characteristic of Lactantius, but is a deliberate aesthetic innovation of the Old English poet.

Following the eighty-four introductory lines with which we have been primarily concerned, the Phoenix is described. Then we are told of its immolation and curious regeneration—from the ashes grow *wyrm wundrum fæger* 'a worm marvellously fair' (232); its departure is recorded, and then, from the point where Lactantius apparently ceased, the poem becomes an increasingly abstract disquisition on resurrection and redemption. Perceived from a later tradition of printed literature, it is understandable that Professor Blake charged the poem with verbosity and diffuseness. I will be further concerned with the verbosity, but the diffuseness can be refuted, I believe, by visual analogues. In the larger view of the poem, we begin with the Phoenix, and from it the poem widens to explore the implications of what has been initially stated, according to much the same principle as that of a rose-window; from a golden-yellow heart, the lozenges of glass spread outward through orange to scarlet to crimson and blue and purple. It is diffuse in a non-pejorative sense only. It demands a specific imaginative attitude to digest the form of the work. Separate panels, be they coloured glass, illuminated device, or verse, may be static or possessed of an intrinsically completed action—like the familiar device of the knotted snake turned back and feeding on itself; but these panels also are united and given a dynamism both by a fabric of interlaced ribbons around them and by repetition of words, motifs, and colours within them.

Panels similar in scale to that between lines 7 and 27 occur frequently in *The Phoenix*, and with no less remarkable symmetry. The great *aubade* of the Phoenix (120-45) is one such panel. The poet has previously moved the action of the poem forward by telling us of the bird's symbolic washing in the waters of paradise and of its subsequent waiting in the high branches of a tree, where it may soonest see the first rays of *swegles tapur* 'the taper of heaven' (114b).

> Sona swa seo sunne   sealte streamas
> hea oferhlifað,   swa se haswa fugel
> beorht of þæs bearwes   beame gewite,
> fareð feþrum snell   flyhte on lyfte,
> swinsað ond singeð   swegle toheanes.
> Ðonne bið swa fæger   fugles gebæru,
> onbryrded breostsefa   blissum remig;
> wrixleð woðcræfte,   wundorlicor
> beorhtan reorde   þonne æfre byre monnes
> hyrde under heofonum,   siþþan Heahcyning,
> wuldres Wyrhta   woruld staþelode,
> heofon ond eorþan.   Biþ þæs hleoðres sweg
> eallum songcræftum   swetra ond wlitigra
> ond wynsumra   wrenca gehwylcum;
> ne magon þam breahtme   byman ne hornas
> ne hearpan hlyn   ne hæleþa stefn
> ænges on eorþan   ne organan,
> swegleoþres geswin   ne swanes feðre
> ne ænig þara dreama   þe Dryhten gescop
> gumum to gliwe   in þas geomran woruld.
> Singeð swa ond swinsað   sælum geblissad
> oþþæt seo sunne   on suðrodor
> sæged weorþeð.   Ðonne swiað he
> ond hlyst gefeð,   heafde onbrygdeð
> þrist þonces gleaw,   ond þriwa ascæceð
> feþre flyhthwate: fugol bið geswiged.[7]

The position of the Phoenix in this panel is established in the first five lines (120-24). The bird and the sun, perhaps envisaged as a halo, to-

---

[7] 'As the sun rises high over the salt streams, the dove-grey bird—bright in that grove—departs the tree, swift on the wing travels aloft in flight, into the heavens, he carols and he sings. Then is so lovely, the tongue of that bird, its soul exultant in joys is inspired. He sings song-skillfully, with a more wondrously bright voice than ever child of man heard this side of heaven, since the High King, the Maker of Glory, founded the world, the heaven and the earth. Is the sound of that music sweet and more gorgeous and more winsome than all songcraft, any musical skill; nor may be compared to that sound trumpets or horns or cadence of harp or the singing voice of any on earth or organs or the strains of melody or the whistle of the swan or any of those joys which the Lord made to comfort man in this sad world. He carols thus and sings, blessed with delights, until the sun in the southern sky begins to sink. Then he falls silent, and seems to listen, with head upraised, brave sage in thought; and three times he spreads his flight-eager wings; the bird grows still.'

gether rise into the sky. The fifth line introduces the song: *swinsað ond singeð* 'he carols and he sings.' There then follow fifteen lines (125-39) in which the ornate glory of the song is extolled; to this passage, we shall return. The panel concludes (140-45) with a six-line description of the ending of the song, the settling of the bird, and the sinking of the sun. As the first passage ended with *swinsað ond singeð*, so the last section begins *singeð swa ond swinsað*. In the middle section, the praise of the song, there is symmetry and a ribbon of reference to mortal concepts of sweet music which is interlaced about two medallions (129b-31a and 138-39), extolling God the creator. This aspect of God permits allusion to *þas geomran woruld* 'this sad world,' which phrase, in turn, echoes the incapacity of mortal ear to hear or to imagine the loveliness of the Phoenix's song. In approaching even closer to the "verbose" detail of the panel, we find that the singing itself depends on a suggestively serpentine vocabulary. *Wrixleð woðcræfte* 'the skilled in song one sings' (127a) recalls the curious and intricate art of the bird's performance. Even more dramatically, the term *wrenc* 'device' (133b) declares that high art, not nature, is the business of the Phoenix. *Wrenc* often signifies 'guile' or 'deceit'; and when applied to music, it refers especially to technical detail. The reader is thereby obliged to consider the craft or skill of the piece, rather than the effect. The accumulating sequence of negative phrases (134-39) is an unselfconscious and efficient depiction of other-worldly beauty in terms of common experience.

Not only in its song is the Phoenix a creature of Art; its colouration and form manifestly allude to the stylized birds of manuscript illumination. Its breast is *bleobrygdum fag* 'of variegated hue' (292a); its head is green and purple; the tail is *fægre gedæled / sum brun sum basu sum blacum splottum / searolice beseted* 'beautifully mottled with brown and crimson and with some white spots ornately decorated' (295b-97a). The beak is *swa glæs oþþe gim* 'like glass or gemstone' (300a); and the form of eye *stearc ond hiwe stane gelicust, / gladum gimme, þonne in goldfate / smiþa orþoncum biseted weorþeð* 'piercing and coloured most like precious stone, a gorgeous gem, when, by the skill of smiths it has been set in gold' (302-04). The reference to the *cloisonné* and filigree of Anglo-Saxon jewelry is unmistakable.

Thus the premises of visual art govern the conception of the bird itself, as well as the form and structure of the poem. The syntax, too, is governed by these non-literary, non-verbal assumptions. A serpentine style in syntax presents problems in analysis that are not encountered in consideration of larger structural units. The greatest difficulty is in perceiving the distinctions between a conscious artistic manipulation of syntax for the purposes of *The Phoenix* and aspects of syntax which were implicit in the literature, and which, moreover, remained idiosyncrasies of literature subsequently. Fortunately, syntactic interlace has been quite extensively investigated, and seems to have been an aesthetic preoccupation from which literature never fully escaped. However, although perhaps native to the tradition, certain syntactic and stylistic devices are splendidly suited to the aesthetic of *The Phoenix*. The most obvious feature is pleonastic embellishment of the most significant element of the sentence; a subject or verb may be treated, varied, and reiterated five or more times within the sentence; or a single verb may sustain a florid display of verb modifiers. In the antithetical passage lauding the song of the bird (134-39), eight of the twelve verses are committed to subjects and subject phrases, ranging from the particularized *byman* and *hornas* 'trumpets' and 'horns' to the generalized *ænig þara dreama* 'any of those joys.' The passage then dissolves into reference to God and this sorrowful world. This progression from concrete to abstract corresponds precisely to the serpentine ornament of illumination which so often travels from a zoomorphic precision at the head to an ambiguous series of flourishes at the other end.

Another quirk of syntax, and one which has become inseparable from the English literary tradition, is the practice of concluding an ornate and circuitous paragraph with a syntactically separate and epigrammatic half-line, which distills and condenses what has gone before. Thus, the panel of the Phoenix's song (125-45), which consists of five parallel sentences—the action is not advanced in their course—concludes with *fugol bið geswiged* 'the bird falls silent.' Similarly, the preparations for immolation (182-208a) are described in four sentences of fifteen, six, fourteen, and seventeen verses. The passage concludes with the single verse *Siteþ siþes fus*, 'He sits ready to depart.' Such epigrams constitute the rivets or devices with which the swirling ribbons are tied off.

The Phoenix shares several of its characteristics with other Old English poems. The various and varying perspectives of manuscript illumination are imitated by inconstancy of perspective in *The Dream of the Rood*, where the narrative data of the poem alter to suit the artistic spirit of the moment. Thus, not only is the Cross used for the crucifixion of Christ, but it also becomes the instrument of many a criminal's death. Questions of unity which have plagued such poems as *The Seafarer* and *The Wanderer* are seen in a different light when the poems are considered as groups of associative panels, and not necessarily as continuous narratives. Perhaps the proximity and relationship of the early and late *Guthlac* poems in the Exeter Book may be explained by an aesthetic attitude which perceived a poem to be a series of tableaux.

A feature of *The Phoenix* which is both extraordinary and inseparable from the precepts of visual art is the sudden peroration at the end of the poem. In a twenty-two verse macaronic gloria, Latin and English are triumphantly fused, and the passage ends in a word neither Latin nor English; the interlaced tongues lead to the ecstatic apostrophe, *Alleluia*.

  Hafað us alyfed lucis auctor
  þæt we motun her   merueri,
  goddædum begietan   gaudia in celo,
  þær we motum maxima regna
  secan ond gesittan   sedibus altis
  lifgan in lisse lucis et pacis,
  agan eardinga alma letitie,
  brucan blæddaga,   blandem et mittem
  geseon sigora Frean   sine fine
  ond Him lof singan   laude perenne
  eadge mid englum. Alleluia.[8]

8 'Has granted to us the author of Light
  that we may here obtain,
 earn by merit joy in the heavens;
 where we may in the mightiest kingdom
 repair and repose; by the high throne
 live in bliss in light and in peace;
 possess the abode of merciful joy,
 enjoy a time of glory, gracious and mild
 behold the Lord of Victories without end,
 and sing to him praise, everlasting glory,
 blessed among angels. Alleluia.'

9

Slavery in Anglo-Saxon England

David A. E. Pelteret

Slavery was an important institution in most of the Ancient Civilizations of the Near East and Mediterranean area.¹ Rome, in particular, seems to have been heavily dependent on slaves, especially during the late Republican and Imperial periods. In the Ger-

---

1 As an introduction to slavery in Asia, see Isaac Mendelsohn, *Slavery in the Ancient Near East* (New York, 1949); for slavery in the world of Greece and Rome, see the collection of papers edited by Moses I. Finley, *Slavery in Classical Antiquity* (Cambridge, 1960; rptd. 1968). The *status quaestionis* on slavery in Ancient Greece, Rome, and Egypt is analyzed by Jean Gaudemet, who also provides a select bibliography, in "Esclavage et dépendance dans l'antiquité: bilan et perspectives," *Tijdschrift voor Rechtsgeschiedenis* 50 (1982), 119-56. An approach that is stimulating and could have wider application is that of Ignace J. Gelb, "From Freedom to Slavery," in Dietz O. Edzard (ed.), *Gesellschaftsklassen im Alten Zweistromland und in den angrenzenden Gebieten*, XVIIIe Rencontre Assyriologique Internationale, Bayerische Akademie der Wissenschaften, Phil.-historische Klasse, Abhandlungen, Neue Folge, Heft 75 (Munich, 1972), 81-92. His promised monograph on Mesopotamian slavery has yet to appear. Slavery as an institution in world history has been recently examined by Orlando Patterson, *Slavery and Social Death: A Comparative Study* (Cambridge, Mass., 1982). Moses I. Finley has written a critical assessment of the historiography of slavery in the Ancient world in his *Ancient Slavery and Modern Ideology* (New York, 1980). Some qualifications to his arguments are made by Ernest Badian in a review, "The Bitter History of Slave History," *New York Review of Books* 18, No. 16 (October 22, 1981), 49-53.

manic world, on the other hand, slavery does not seem originally to have been a significant social feature. Once the Germanic peoples had come in contact with the Roman Empire, however, the attractions of the finished goods of the technologically more advanced civilization soon made their mark on the underdeveloped Germanic realms, and the tribes beyond the Roman frontier were more than ready to barter primary products, including slave manpower, in return for the wine, cloth, and luxury goods of the Romans. By the time that the administration of the Empire was crumbling in the fifth century, slavery had become a familiar institution among the Germanic peoples.[2]

It was in this century that Germanic colonists from Denmark and the coasts of Germany and Holland were appearing in sizeable numbers in England.[3] Our sources show that slavery existed in Anglo-Saxon England from this early period, as it had done in Roman Britain.[4] Slaves were to remain part of English society right into the twelfth century, at least two centuries longer than in neighbouring France.[5] England was, however, in advance of Spain, where slavery survived the Middle Ages, to be transported to the Americas as an unfortunate relic of Ancient Times in the midst of the New World.[6]

To discuss within the compass of a brief paper the history of slavery in England during the seven centuries of the Anglo-Saxon era would not be a useful exercise. Instead, I shall seek to answer three of the most obvious questions one would raise when examining this topic. The first of these questions is a composite one: Who were the slaves in Anglo-Saxon society, and how did they acquire this status? The second is: What was it like to be a slave in England? And finally: How did slavery come to disappear?

To begin with, the identity of the slaves in Anglo-Saxon society is difficult to determine with great precision, at least for the earliest part of the Anglo-Saxon period. The paucity of sources covering the cen-

---

2 On Germanic slavery, see Edward A. Thompson, "Slavery in Early Germany," in *Slavery in Classical Antiquity*, 191-203.
3 On the history of Britain in this period, see Leslie Alcock, *Arthur's Britain: History and Archaeology AD 367-634* (Harmondsworth, 1973), and John N. L. Myres, *Anglo-Saxon Pottery and the Settlement of England* (Oxford, 1969). In reading these, one should bear in mind the cautionary comments on the hazards of writing a history of this period made by David Dumville in "Sub-Roman Britain: History and Legend," *History* 62 (1977), 173-92.
4 For evidence of slavery in Roman Britain, see Robin G. Collingwood and Richard P. Wright, *The Roman Inscriptions of Britain* I (Oxford, 1965), Nos. 21, 445, 712, (?)760, 902, and 1436.
5 See Marc Bloch, "How and Why Ancient Slavery Came to an End," in Marc Bloch, *Slavery and Serfdom in the Middle Ages*, trans. by William R. Beer (Berkeley, 1975), 1-31.
6 See Charles Verlinden, *L'Esclavage dans l'Europe médiévale I: Péninsule Ibérique-France*, Universiteit te Gent, Werken uitgaven door de Faculteit van de Letteren en Wijsbegeerte 119 (Bruges, 1955), 41-46.

turies between A.D. 400 and 600, when Roman rule in Britain disintegrated, and the early Anglo-Saxon kingdoms were established, has led many historians to call it the "Dark Age" period of English history.[7] There is some evidence of cultural, and probably also agricultural, continuity between the Roman and Anglo-Saxon eras in England.[8] There is thus the possibility that some who were slaves under Roman or Romano-British masters found that their owners had become Anglo-Saxons. Nothing more definite than this can be asserted. We can be sure, however, that the invasions did lead to the enslavement through conquest of some of the indigenous inhabitants. Our best evidence for this is the tract *De excidio Britanniae* ('The Ruin of Britain') composed perhaps about 547 by a British monk called Gildas. He paints a gloomy picture of the fate of those British attacked by the invaders. "So a number of the wretched survivors," he writes, "were caught in the mountains and butchered wholesale. Others, their spirit broken by hunger, went to surrender to the enemy; they were fated to be slaves for ever."[9] We must be careful how we interpret this. Gildas was, after all, primarily a preacher, not an historian.[10] It would be out of place, therefore, to expect him to be too precise about the specifics of time and place referred to in his account. In some cases, the full horror of what Gildas portrays indeed may have struck a community. His description of events in Britain is, however, too simplistic. Archaeological evidence suggests that the settlement must have at times involved infiltration rather than conquest;[11] and some of the earliest

7 See, for example, John Morris, "Dark Age Dates," in Michael G. Jarrett and Brian Dobson (eds.), *Britain and Rome: Essays presented to Eric Birley on his Sixtieth Birthday* (Kendal, 1966), 145-85.
8 The problem is a complex one since it is now realized that the term "continuity" itself needs to be more closely defined, as is stressed by Walter Janssen, "Some Major Aspects of Frankish and Medieval Settlement in the Rhineland," in Peter H. Sawyer (ed.), *Medieval Settlement: Continuity and Change* (London, 1976), 41. For a discussion of a possible example of agrarian continuity, see Herbert P. R. Finberg, "Roman and Saxon Withington," in Herbert P. R. Finberg, *Lucerna* (London, 1964), 21-65, and for cultural continuity, see P. A. Wilson, "The Cult of St. Martin in the British Isles, with Particular Reference to Canterbury and Candida Casa," *Innes Review* 19 (1968), 129-43. For recent findings, see Trevor Rowley (ed.), *Anglo-Saxon Settlement and the Landscape: Papers presented to a Symposium, Oxford 1973*, BAR 6 (Oxford, 1974).
9 Gildas, *The Ruin of Britain and Other Works*, ed. and trans. by Michael Winterbottom, Arthurian Period Sources 7 (London, 1978), Ch. 25, p. 27 (translation); p. 98 (text).
10 He is, nevertheless, our major source for the history of Britain in the fifth and first part of the sixth century; see Dumville, "Sub-Roman Britain" and Molly Miller, "Bede's Use of Gildas," *EHR* 90 (1975), 241-61. The authenticity and unity of the work is defended and a somewhat earlier date of composition (A.D. 515x520) argued by Thomas D. O'Sullivan, *The De Excidio of Gildas: Its Authenticity and Date*, Columbia Studies in the Classical Tradition 7 (Leiden, 1978).
11 For the likely contemporaneity of late Roman and early Anglo-Saxon occupation of Abingdon, see Martin Biddle, H. T. Lambrick, and John N. L. Myres, "The Early

Anglo-Saxon documents, the West Saxon laws from the late seventh century, show that not all the indigenous inhabitants were reduced to slavery: on the contrary, the Celtic aristocracy retained their noble status in the laws, though their wergeld was lower than that of the Anglo-Saxon nobility.[12]

Where conquest occurred, it was not always the native British that suffered. As the various Anglo-Saxon tribes expanded their control over the country, it was inevitable that they would clash with one another, and I suspect that a substantial number of slaves from the early centuries of the settlement were those captured in inter-tribal warfare. Some of these captives were traded out of the country and ended up in such slave markets as the one in Marseilles in the south of France.[13] It was this trade in slaves of Anglo-Saxon origin that led to the charming, if apocryphal, story of what prompted Pope Gregory the Great to send Augustine to Kent in 597 to convert the English. The story goes that on being told that some slave boys whom he had seen in a Roman market were *Angli*, or Anglians, the pontiff allegedly punned, "They have the face of angels, and such men should be fellow-heirs of the angels of heaven." He then made a further play on the name of their tribe and of their king. (In defence of Pope Gregory, it is not inapposite to note that this story appears in Anglo-Saxon sources and not in Gregory's own correspondence.[14] It is evident that the Englishman's penchant for puns has a long ancestry.)

An illustration of how the Anglian boys could have been enslaved appears in the *Ecclesiastical History* written by the Venerable Bede in the 730's. He recounts how, after a skirmish between Northumbrians and Mercians in 697, a Mercian thegn, Imma, was found on the battlefield by a Northumbrian who had had relatives killed in the battle. Imma initially claimed that he was only a peasant who had brought supplies for the warriors. He did, however, subsequently admit his true status and though his captor wanted to kill him, he was for some reason spared. A Frisian in London bought him and later permitted him to buy back his own freedom. The story implies that there was a warrior class, who, if captured, might be killed, but there was also a peasant class who would simply be enslaved if their tribe was defeated.[15]

Warfare and conquests, then, were major sources of slaves in the first three centuries of the Anglo-Saxon period, and those who were

History of Abingdon, Berkshire, and its Abbey," *Medieval Archaeology* 12 (1968), 26-69.
12 See the Laws of Ine in EHD I, 398-407, No. 32.
13 On Marseilles, see Verlinden, *L'Esclavage* I, 670.
14 Bede, *HE* II.1, 132-35. The story is also told by the anonymous biographer of Gregory, who does not, however, describe them as slaves. See Bertram Colgrave (ed. and trans.), *The Earliest Life of Gregory the Great* (Lawrence, Kansas, 1968), 90-91.
15 Bede, *HE* IV.22 (= 20), 400-05.

enslaved included both the indigenous Celts and the invading Anglo-Saxons. Slavery through capture did not cease in the eighth century, however. At the end of that century, the first Vikings made their appearance in England. Slaves were a major item of interest to these marauders, who were not simply plunderers but traders as well.[16] They retained their interest in this marketable commodity, and when in the late tenth century the intensity of their attacks again increased, they once more took slaves. Our most graphic evidence for this comes from another jeremiad not uninfluenced by Gildas's diatribe, the Sermon of Archbishop Wulfstan of York to the English, written in ca. 1014:

> Often two seamen, or maybe three, drive the droves of Christian men from sea to sea, out through this people, huddled together, as a public shame to us all, if we could seriously and rightly feel any shame. But all the insult which we often suffer we repay with honouring those who insult us; we pay them continually and they humiliate us daily; they ravage and they burn, plunder and rob and carry on board; and lo, what else is there in all these events except God's anger clear and visible over this people?[17]

We might feel that most of these captives were destined for sale abroad, as was the case with many of those taken in the sixth and seventh centuries. This was certainly true, but the tenth-century *Life of Saint Swithun* shows that there was also a market for slaves within the country. The *Life* mentions that a slave-woman stolen from her owner in the north of England was later sold in Winchester, the West Saxon capital.[18]

This last account does not suggest that the parties to the transaction were other than Anglo-Saxons, and there is interesting linguistic evidence to show that the Anglo-Saxons continued to capture and enslave people right into the tenth century. From that century on, in southern dialects of Old English, the word *wealh* appears as a designation for a slave. The word is related to the Modern English "Welsh." Originally *wealh* seems to have meant 'foreigner' and then 'Celt.'[19] That 'Celt' became synonymous with 'slave' points to an ominous fate for many of those Celts from the south-west of England, especially present-day Cornwall, an area that was only fully integrated into the West Saxon Kingdom in the second quarter of the tenth century during

16 See especially Peter Sawyer, *The Age of the Vikings*, 2nd ed. (London, 1971).
17 EHD I, 932, No. 240.
18 *Miracula Sancti Swithuni* II. 23-28 in *AASS*, 2 July, 297. There are several versions of this *Vita*; for the relationship between them, see Cyril Hart, "The Early Section of the *Worcester Chronicle*," *Journal of Medieval History* 9 (1983), 251-315, at p. 294. (I am grateful to Dr. Hart for an early offprint of his article.)
19 Margaret L. Faull, "The Semantic Development of Old English *Wealh*," *Leeds Studies in English* N.S. 8 (1975), 20-44; Kenneth Cameron, "The Meaning and Significance of Old English *walh* in English Place-Names," *English Place-Name Society Journal* 12 (1979-80), 1-46; Appendices 1 and 2 by Malcolm Todd, "The Archaeological Significance of Place-Names in *walh*," and John Insley, "The Continental Evidence: OHG *wal(a)h*, OSax *walh*," ibid., 47-53.

the reign of Athelstan.[20] The word thus displays exactly the same semantic shift as the English *slave* and French *esclave* and for the same reason. The latter two words are derived from the tribal designation "Slav," which started to be used in the legal sense of 'slave' from the tenth century on as a result of the conquests by the Germans on the eastern borders of their territory.[21]

Conquest was not, however, the only way in which people could become slaves. The laws show that persons could be enslaved for a number of criminal offences and for debt.[22] Furthermore, people could voluntarily enslave themselves and/or their children.[23] This might seem inconceivable—until we remember the uncertainties of life in the Middle Ages. An unusually dry winter could ruin the grain crop, as could an unexpected hail storm or the appearance of rust. The successive waves of pestilence that occurred throughout the Middle Ages could destroy the family as an economic unit and leave the survivors starving. Cattle disease, warfare, even physical and mental incapacity on the part of the breadwinners: all could reduce a family to destitution. As I shall show below, the servile state offered attractions to such unfortunates.

The consequences of these centuries of enslavement appear in Domesday Book, compiled in 1086 at the behest of William the Conqueror.[24] This great survey shows that in his reign slaves formed on average about ten per cent of the recorded population of England. The percentage varies from county to county, as might be expected. In Essex, highly developed agriculturally, but a victim of Viking incursions, slaves form some eleven per cent of the total recorded population. In Middlesex, the percentage drops to 5.2. In Cornwall, on the other hand, finally brought fully under Anglo-Saxon control only a century and a half before, no less than twenty-one per cent of the county's population were slaves.[25] With the exception of Cornwall, it may be assumed that by this time slaves were fully integrated into the Anglo-Saxon population, whatever their ethnic origin.

20 See William G. Hoskins, *The Westward Expansion of Wessex*, Leicester University, Department of English Local History, Occasional Papers 13 (Leicester, 1970), esp. 20-21.
21 Charles Verlinden, "L'Origine de *Sclavus* = Esclave," *Archivum Latinitatis Medii Aevi* 17 (1942), 97-128.
22 Ine 3.2, 7.1 (crime); Ine 62 (debt) in EHD I, 399-400, 406, No. 32. For other references, see David A. E. Pelteret, "Slavery in Late Anglo-Saxon England: an Interdisciplinary Approach to the Various Forms of Evidence" (Ph.D dissertation, University of Toronto, 1976), 494, s.v. *witeþeow*.
23 Robert Spindler (ed.), *Confessionale Pseudo-Egberti* 261-63, in *Das altenglische Bussbuch* (Leipzig, 1934), 176-94; cf. *Poenitentiale Theodori* II.13.1, in Haddan and Stubbs, *Councils* III, 173-204.
24 Abraham Farley (ed.), *Domesday Book*, Record Commission, 2 vols. (London, 1783).
25 See Pelteret, "Slavery," 301, Table 6.

What was it like for this not inconsiderable proportion of the population to be slaves? Because our slaves could not, in general, read and write (that was largely the preserve of the clergy)[26] and because they were an element in the society with little or no real power, we are dependent on scattered insights, and these from persons far removed from the needs and aspirations of the slaves mentioned by them. A touching exception is the picture of the ploughman that appears in a textbook called the *Colloquy*, compiled in ca. A.D. 1000 by the monk Ælfric for those learning Latin. Its purpose was primarily to expand a pupil's Latin vocabulary, but in the process provides a very sympathetic portrait of what it must have been like to be a slave:

> "What do you say, ploughman? How do you undertake your work?"
> "Oh my lord, I work excessively. I go out at day-break, badgering the oxen towards the field, and I join them to the plough: there is not a winter so harsh that I dare lurk at home for fear of my master. But after yoking the oxen and securing the ploughshare and coulter to the plough, the whole day I must plough a full acre or more."
> "Have you a companion?"
> "I have a boy spurring the oxen on with a whip, who even now is hoarse with the cold and with the shouting."
> "Do you do anything else during the day?"
> "Certainly I do more. I must fill the stall of the oxen with hay, and supply them with water, and carry their dung outside. Oh! Oh! it is a lot of work. Indeed, it is a lot of work because I am not free."[27]

In portraying the slave as an agrarian worker, and specifically a ploughman, the *Colloquy* was drawing on reality. Domesday Book, for instance, regularly associates the slave with the plough.[28] Another source, the tenth-century will of Æthelgifu, reveals that slaves were also shepherds and swineherds.[29] Women slaves, too, were employed in agricultural tasks, though some may also have been domestics. In the earliest Kentish laws, we read of female grinding-slaves: women whose function it was to grind corn, before medieval agrarian technology led to their being replaced by the much more efficient watermill;[30] and several sources mention slaves who were dairymaids.[31]

---

26 For a possible example of three slave-women who appear to have received some degree of education, see *The Will of Æthelgifu: A Tenth Century Anglo-Saxon Manuscript*, trans. and examined by Dorothy Whitelock, Roxburghe Club (Oxford, 1968), 13, lines 51-52, discussed on pp. 33-34.
27 See George N. Garmonsway (ed.), *Ælfric's Colloquy*, 2nd ed. (London, 1947), 20-21.
28 Pelteret, "Slavery," Ch. 7.II.2, pp. 305-17.
29 See Whitelock, *The Will of Æthelgifu*, 9, lines 25-26 and p. 15, line 56; cf. also pp. 35-36.
30 On mills, see Jean Gimpel, *The Medieval Machine: The Industrial Revolution of the Middle Ages* (New York, 1976), 1-28, and Philip Rahtz and Donald Bullough, "The Parts of an Anglo-Saxon Mill," *ASE* 6 (1977), 15-37; the latter study draws on evidence from an eighth-century mill excavated at Tamworth in Staffordshire.
31 On *daia* 'dairymaid,' see Pelteret, "Slavery," 172-73.

The harshness of the life of the ploughman-slave in the *Colloquy* is not, in itself, remarkable. Arable farming tends to impose a harsher regimen on its practitioners than a pastoral life does. The hard work and long hours that the ploughman had to suffer were probably not strikingly different from those that a poor free peasant was subject to; but it was not so much in the harshness of the labour that the ploughman made his lament. "It is a lot of work *because I am not free.*" It was in this lack of *freedom* that our author saw the harshness of the slave's position. As will be seen below, this was not a static concept in the Anglo-Saxon period any more than it is today; the way in which it changed is integral to an understanding of why slavery disappeared—but this is our third question, whose answer must be deferred to later. At this point it is useful to continue to follow our author by examining two elements that constituted an *absence* of freedom.

The first involved a set of very real legal disabilities. A freeman who had a wrong done against him had the support of the tribe's law. If he suffered an injury, he could claim a monetary compensation. If he was killed, his relatives were entitled to his wergeld, an assessment based on his social status and indicative of his economic value to the kin group.[32] A slave, however, was someone else's possession. Only his master, therefore, could claim for injuries done him. The slave himself had no recourse, nor did his kin. From a psychological point of view, this must have been a severe disability, since kinship was the strongest bond in Anglo-Saxon society.[33]

The slave also suffered another legal disability. If a freeman committed a wrong, he was, in general, allowed to compensate for that wrong by means of the monetary payments just mentioned. A slave, on the other hand, did not have any possessions in law—even if in practice this was not the case. Consequently, he could pay only with his hide. Thus, the characteristic punishment for a slave who committed a wrong was a lashing, and this marked him off from a freeman.

To this set of legal disabilities must be added a second element: the psychological dimension of the concept of freedom, which had an impact on both masters and slaves. A slave was a man with the lowest status in society, and a reflection of this is evident in the words given the ploughman. The text shows what an educated and privileged member of the ecclesiastical élite thought of slaves, and a few instances of legal actions initiated by some accused of not being "free" show that those at the lower end of the social spectrum shared these views.[34] It

---

32 On wergelds, see Hector M. Chadwick, *Studies on Anglo-Saxon Institutions* (Cambridge, 1905), 76-160.
33 On the nature of Anglo-Saxon kinship, see Lorraine Lancaster, "Kinship in Anglo-Saxon Society," *British Journal of Sociology* 9 (1958), 230-50, 359-77.
34 See Pelteret, "Slavery," 257-58. It has to be admitted that these records are late, and

would be too much to expect of human nature for us to believe that those in a position of power did not exploit and abuse persons suffering from such disabilities. For instance, the slave woman mentioned in the *Life of Saint Swithun* fled to the sanctuary of the saint's tomb because her new owner was a "very bad mistress" (*pessima domina*).[35] On the other hand, the slave's life does not seem to have differed from the rest of the peasantry's in some important areas of existence. The tenth-century manumission-documents, which record the freeing of slaves, mention wives and children, so family life was not proscribed—indeed, a couple of references in legal sources show that even unions between slave and free were sanctioned.[36] The slaves seem to have lived, like other poor peasants, in tofts, which consisted of a primitive dwelling, probably of thatch, wattle, and daub, and a small plot of land surrounding it in which produce could be grown and perhaps a few animals and chickens kept. Thus an early eleventh-century will declares: "And all my men are to be free, and each is to have his toft and his cow and his corn for food."[37] This implies that the slaves here were already occupying tofts even if they did not have legal ownership of them. They were not, therefore, herded together in compounds and so were in certain respects in a better state than some so-called "free" persons of today, such as the black goldminers in contemporary Johannesburg. Nor is there evidence of the harsh impersonality of the gangs of labourers found in the nineteenth-century plantations in the American south. In consequence, it was possible for personal relationships to form between owner and slave. This is implied in Æthelgifu's will, for instance, where a number of her slaves are mentioned by name as being entitled to freedom on her death and, in some instances, to receive property as well.[38]

The *Life of Saint Swithun* provides us with an instructive illustration of the contradictory realities of the slave's position in society. A slave belonging to a wealthy trader called Flodoald had been arrested and condemned by a reeve to the ordeal of hot iron. This was over the objections of his master, who not merely offered the reeve his slave instead, but also offered a pound of silver, in itself the purchase price of a man. The reeve rejected Flodoald's overtures, yet through the intervention of the saint was unable to see the slave's burns when, after the statutory period of time, the bandages were removed.[39] All who have

it may well be that these are actions initiated by those accused of being serfs. However, see also the attempt of one Putrael to avoid enslavement discussed in ibid., 257.
35 *AASS*, 2 July, 297, ll. 23-28.
36 For a discussion of this, see Pelteret, "Slavery," 374-76.
37 Dorothy Whitelock (ed. and trans.), *Anglo-Saxon Wills* (Cambridge, 1930), 68, lines 3-4 (text); p. 69 (translation).
38 See, for example, Whitelock, *The Will of Æthelgifu*, 7, 9, lines 6, 8, 15-16.
39 *AASS*, 2 July, 298, ll. 35-37.

lived in societies which exhibit wide social and legal disparities will feel that the essence of this story rings true. Here is the close personal bond between master and servant, where the master will seek to protect his underling even at cost to himself. But this personal bond is undercut by the slave's legal position; however genuinely felt by master and slave, it is essentially a paternalistic relationship since the slave does not possess any legal protection, as the actions of the reeve show.

In spite of its disadvantages, slavery could have some very real attractions. One must not prejudice the examination of slavery in early societies by the distaste felt today for American slavery and the modern relics of an institution that the Anti-Slavery Society of London reminds us still exists in various parts of the world. The uncertainty of life in the early Middle Ages has already been mentioned. Starvation was an ever-present possibility and not infrequently a reality. To the hungry man, slavery must have seemed an enviable state. Several Anglo-Saxon sources explain why. The prose *Solomon and Saturn* declares that "in twelve months you shall give your slaves seven hundred and twenty loaves, besides morning meals and noon meals."[40] Also, an eleventh-century custumal called the *Rectitudines singularum personarum* ('The Customary Obligations of Various Statuses') lays down that "all slaves belonging to the estate ought to have food at Christmas and Easter, a strip of land for ploughing and a harvest-handful besides their dues."[41] That some took advantage of this protection is evident from a tenth-century manumission-document from Durham in the north of England: "(Geatflæd) gave freedom for the love of God and for the need of her soul, namely, to Eckehard the smith and Ælfstan and his wife and all their progeny, born and unborn, and Arnkell and Cola and Ecgfrith, Æthelhun's daughter, and all those persons whose heads she took in exchange for their food in those evil days."[42] (The taking of heads obviously refers to an act of commendation, but unfortunately the document does not specify what the evil was that provoked this voluntary act of servitude.)

Finally, we arrive at the third question. How did slavery come to an end? It is the most complex of the questions to answer. Like all great historical changes, the factors that had a bearing on it were manifold—and like many other such changes it was not perceived by contemporaries, which does not make our task any easier. It will be necessary to start with a number of different themes and weave them together before we shall be able to discern a pattern emerging.

40 John M. Kemble (ed. and trans.), *The Dialogue of Salomon and Saturnus*, Ælfric Society (London, 1848), 192-93.
41 *Rectitudines* 9.1 in Liebermann, *Gesetze* I, 450 (text); EHD II, 877, No. 172 (translation).
42 Benjamin Thorpe (ed. and trans.), *Diplomatarium Anglicum Ævi Saxonici* (London, 1865), 621.

Let us start with the structure of early Anglo-Saxon society. Some of what I shall have to say about this will not gain the assent of all historians working in this area, but I believe that the sources support my viewpoint.[43] Early Anglo-Saxon society was, first and foremost, tribal in nature.[44] Tribes differ in kind; some are loosely organized, others have a strong central authority under the leadership of a powerful chief. The latter have a tendency to absorb the former through peaceful amalgamation or through conquest. This happened in Anglo-Saxon England, where, however, the leaders were called "kings" rather than "chiefs."[45]

Under the kings, I discern two main levels of tribesmen, who were all by definition "freemen," unlike the slaves, who were not members of the tribe and so fell outside the protection of the tribal law. The lower level of freemen occupied land sufficient for the kin group, in return for which they were expected to provide produce, and possibly services, for the king or his supporters. The latter were warriors whose primary function was to defend and enlarge the tribe's territory. Their

43 My debt to Eric John and Marc Bloch should be acknowledged, though much of the synthesis that follows is my own. See Eric John, "English Feudalism and the Structure of Anglo-Saxon Society," *Orbis Britanniae*, Studies in Early English History 4 (Leicester, 1966), 128-53; and Bloch, *Slavery and Serfdom in the Middle Ages*, 1-31. The portrayal of Anglo-Saxon society that follows is naturally a very simplified generalization of what must have been a very complicated set of developments.

44 In describing Anglo-Saxon society here, I have used "tribe" rather than "chiefdom" so as to avoid getting into a discussion of terminology. I recognize that "tribe" is a rather imprecise term, as has been pointed out by Aidan W. Southall in "The Illusion of Tribe," *Journal of Asian and African Studies* 5 (1970), 28-50; without committing myself to an evolutionary point of view, I feel that "chiefdom," as used by Elman R. Service, *Primitive Social Organization: An Evolutionary Perspective*, 2nd ed. (New York, 1971), is more appropriate in the context of Anglo-Saxon society. For a discussion of one of the primary sources that needs to be taken into account by anyone wishing to describe early Anglo-Saxon society, see Wendy Davies and Hayo Vierck, "The Contexts of Tribal Hidage: Social Aggregates and Settlement Patterns," *Frühmittelalterliche Studien* 8 (1974), 223-93.

45 This is a considerable—some might call it a gross—simplification of a complex institution. I have described kingship in these terms in order to emphasize the need to employ anthropological perspectives in examining this topic. Recent treatments of Anglo-Saxon kingship include William A. Chaney, *The Cult of Kingship in Anglo-Saxon England: The Transition from Paganism to Christianity* (Berkeley and Los Angeles, 1970); John Michael Wallace-Hadrill, *Early Germanic Kingship in England and on the Continent* (Oxford, 1971); and Hannah Vollrath-Reichelt, *Königsgedanke und Königtum bei den Angelsachsen bis zur Mitte des 9. Jahrhunderts*, Kölner Historische Abhandlungen 19 (Cologne and Vienna, 1971). Archaeological evidence now supplements the documentary material. Rupert L. S. Bruce-Mitford (ed.), *The Sutton Hoo Ship-Burial*, 3 vols. in 4 (London, 1975-83), and Brian Hope-Taylor, *Yeavering: An Anglo-British Centre of Early Northumbria*, Department of the Environment, Archaeological Report 7 (London, 1977), provide material from but two of a number of English royal sites; Continental evidence may also prove relevant—see, for example, Karl H. Krüger, *Königsgrabkirchen der Franken, Angelsachsen und Langobarden bis zur Mitte des 8. Jahrhunderts: ein historischer Katalog*, Münstersche Mittelalterschriften 4 (Munich, 1971).

reward, apart from war booty distributed by the king, was lordship over lands worked by the lower rank of tribesmen, lordship which entitled them to a proportion of the fruits of the land. Such lordship was at first only temporary; it was dependent on service and support for the king, and did not constitute ownership of the land.

We must now examine the role of the Church in this society. The ecclesiastical organization set up by Augustine and his successors for the propagation of the faith was based primarily on the monastery. To enable the monks to spend much of their day saying the Divine offices, to keep them clothed, to supply such necessities as skins for vellum onto which the scriptures could be copied, the monasteries needed land which could produce a surplus. Since, short of Divine intervention, their corporate existence would last longer than man's allotted three score years and ten, the traditional form of land grant was clearly unsatisfactory. And so, some time in the seventh century—possibly even with Augustine's arrival, if we are to accept Pierre Chaplais's suggestion[46]—the Roman land charter was introduced. This document attested the permanent alienation of land out of the power of the king and the tribe. The warrior class was, of course, quick to see the advantages of such a legal device. Already at the beginning of the eighth century, Bede was complaining about how they were establishing "monasteries" to further the interests of their own families.[47] His complaint, however, had no impact. By the reign of Offa, late in the eighth century, land was regularly being alienated from the tribe and made over into the hands of what had become an aristocracy.

This process was interrupted in the ninth century by the Viking incursions. By the beginning of the tenth century, power had shifted into the hands of the West Saxon tribe, whose kings steadily during that century established their control over the whole country. From this time on, the land charters grew in number. In this process, both the secular aristocracy and church institutions benefited.

I thus see the tenth century as being a key period when two decisive changes that had gradually been taking place in Anglo-Saxon society made themselves fully evident. The first was the accumulation of land into larger agrarian units, which could be inherited (in the case of secular overlords) or were inalienable (in the case of ecclesiastical institutions). The second was the unification of the country, with a concomitant diminution in the significance of the tribes and their laws.

Before we can understand the relevance of all this to the institution of slavery, it is necessary to introduce another theme into our picture:

---

46 Pierre Chaplais, "Who Introduced Charters into England? The Case for Augustine," *Journal of the Society of Archivists* 3 (1965-69), 526-42.
47 On Bede's Epistle to Egbert, see Eric John, *Land Tenure in Early England*, Studies in Early English History 1 (Leicester, 1960), 44-45.

the position of the ordinary freeman. From early in the settlement of the country, he will have been used to the idea of producing for an overlord outside the kin group. As land started to come under more stable control, it was inevitable that certain of his practices would harden into custom, such as how much and when he should hand over produce to his lord, or when and how long he should help the overlord on his own land, the demesne. In day-to-day terms, custom was likely to loom larger in such a man's mind than the provisions of the tribe's law, and from a lord's point of view, those occupying the land under his control would tend to become "his" men. He would have some justification for thinking this, since there were inevitably those who, for one reason or another, did not possess any family land or have the necessary means to work it. These he would have provided with land already sown with seed, together with implements and livestock—goods he would feel entitled to claim back on the death of the recipient. Others would have commended themselves and their property to his control and protection because of threats arising out of invasion or because of rapacious neighbours. A couple of sources show that ties over those defined in tribal law as "freemen" already existed in the time of Alfred (who died in 899).[48] From the middle of the tenth century, there are a few documents extant that show that some of the peasants called "boors" were having to make a payment in order to leave their land and go where they wanted. In many respects, these are just like the manumission-documents recording the release of slaves. For instance, one from Great Bedwyn in Wiltshire, dating from ca. 955, states: "Here is made known that Eadwine granted Wynsige and Æthelnoth, his man, that they may free for ever Beorhtgyth from the boorland for ten mancuses, free to travel to any place" (færfreoh).[49] Note here the right that is given: to be færfreoh. Whatever status Beorhtgyth may have possessed in tribal law, she did not have the freedom to extricate herself from the obligations of custom imposed on her through the land that she occupied. In other words, persons such as Beorhtgyth were what we today would term "serfs."[50] Their status was derived from the land rather than from their tribal ties. It is significant that in the tenth century we read more and more often in the charters and wills that when property is alienated or bequeathed by a lord it is to be handed over *mid mete and mid mannum*, 'with provisions and with persons.'[51] There is no specification as to what the status of these persons was. From the point of view of the lord who was alienating the property,

48 For the texts and a discussion of them, see David A. E. Pelteret, "The *Coliberti* of Domesday Book," *Studies in Medieval Culture* 12 (1978), 43-54.
49 Ed. by Herbert Meritt, "Old English Entries in a Manuscript at Bern," *Journal of English and Germanic Philology* 33 (1934), 346; cf. 350-51.
50 An account of the use of the word "serf" in historiography remains to be written.
51 See Whitelock, *Anglo-Saxon Wills*, Index rerum, s.v. *Mete 7 mid mannum, mid*.

their precise rights and obligations were unimportant; what mattered was that possession of the property carried with it certain rights in the labour of those occupying it.

Now perhaps the relevance of the preceding discussion can be seen. The concept of freedom was, by the tenth century, starting to change. In origin a term referring to a person's status *vis à vis* the tribe, by the tenth century it was shifting towards defining his status in terms of the land.

Throughout the Anglo-Saxon period, however, freedom in the old sense still survived as a relevant concept. In fact, from the tenth century on, this older sense is particularly common in certain sources. In this century manumission-documents start appearing, and from the latter part of the same century more and more wills free some or all of the persons belonging to the testator.[52] This growth in manumission continues well into the eleventh century, as is clearly evident in a number of counties in Domesday Book, where the population in 1066 (the year of Edward the Confessor's death) and 1086 is given. In Essex, for instance, there was a twenty-five per cent decline in the number of slaves between 1066 and 1086.[53]

How are we to account for this? If we were naïve, we would say that it was a change motivated by piety, since the extant records frequently mention that a person is being freed for the good of the former owner's soul. Now piety must not be discounted—but why was manumission felt to be a particularly suitable form of piety in England only from the tenth century on? After all, the Church had been encouraging the freeing of slaves by laymen since the days of Constantine, when a special form of manumission—*manumissio in ecclesia*, i.e., church manumission—had been introduced into Roman law.[54] The Roman Church had been in Britain since 597, and *manumissio in ecclesia* had existed in Anglo-Saxon law since at least 695.[55] Pious generosity thus does not seem to be an adequate explanation. Furthermore, the average person does not generally engage in acts involving great generosity unless his deeds have some social sanction, a sanction that frequently has an economic basis. To seek an answer to the problem, let us try to imagine the world as seen through the eyes of a layman who was lord over lands on which there were many slaves.[56] In all probability he possessed a body of men who had constantly to be supervised. Even if

52 See Pelteret, "Slavery," 197, Table 4.
53 Ibid., 321-26, Table 10, and p. 327.
54 C. G. Mor, "La 'Manumissio in Ecclesia'," *Rivista di storia del diritto italiano* 1 (1928), 80-150; Fabrizio Fabbrini, *La Manumissio in Ecclesia*, Pubblicazioni dell'istituto di diritto romano e dei diritti dell'oriente mediterraneo 40 (Milan, 1964).
55 Wihtred 8 in EHD I, 397, No. 31.
56 This is, of course, an imagined reconstruction based on Anglo-Saxon sources and other societies having analogous social institutions.

there was a crop failure, he was still obliged to feed them. Without a direct interest in the land, they probably lacked spirit and showed little initiative. Meanwhile, he would have acquired more efficient ploughs than his forefathers possessed and perhaps even a couple of watermills to grind corn and perform other useful tasks.[57] From an economic perspective, it made more sense to release these men. Some would be surplus to his needs and could be released at the crossroads to take the four roads to freedom and go where they would.[58] To others, he could grant the status of freeman and give them some land of their own to work. The new status would hold little significance for him, but if he was canny and well-informed, he would appreciate how it was valued by the peasants in their village.[59] *Plus ça change, plus c'est la même chose*. By "freeing" his slaves, the lord did not lose ultimate control of his land nor most of his former slaves; but no longer did he have the tedious obligation to supply them with their daily food and supervise their activities. As a bonus he also received the acclaim of the Church and the promise of spiritual rewards in the world to come.

You will note that I described the lord as a layman. Though the Church encouraged the freeing of slaves by laymen as a pious act, discouraged the harsh treatment of slaves as the *Life of Saint Swithun* shows, and strongly opposed the sale of men out of the country to heathens,[60] it could not actively free its own slaves since canon law prohibited the alienation of Church property. This explains why, for instance, in 1086 the four abbeys with major estates in Worcestershire—Pershore, Evesham, Westminster and Worcester—owned forty per cent of the slaves recorded in this county.[61] At no time in the Middle Ages did the Church condemn the institution of slavery.[62] We should not be surprised at this; it never occurred to men of the Middle Ages that slavery posed a problem—any more than the presence today of lands where millions go to bed hungry poses a problem to many who live in wealthier, more economically-developed countries.

57 See Gimpel, *The Medieval Machine*, 13-14 (the various functions of watermills), 40-43 (the plough).
58 On manumission at the crossroads, see Pelteret, "Slavery," 220-23.
59 Cf. n. 34 above.
60 On ecclesiastical opposition to the sale of slaves abroad, see, for instance, William of Malmesbury, *Vita Wulfstani* II.20, ed. by Reginald R. Darlington, Camden Society, 3rd Series, 40 (London, 1928), 43 (text); James H. F. Peile (trans.), *Life of St. Wulstan, Bishop of Worcester* (Oxford, 1934), 64-65 (translation). For other references and a discussion of them, see Pelteret, "Slavery," 104-105, 124-26.
61 See Pelteret, "Slavery," 337-45, esp. 340, and Tables 15 and 16.
62 David B. Davis, *The Problem of Slavery in Western Culture* (New York, 1966), 83-106. A. W. Rupprecht takes issue with some of Davis's interpretations in "Attitudes on Slavery among the Church Fathers," in Richard N. Longenecker and Merrill C. Tenney (eds.), *New Dimensions in New Testament Study* (Grand Rapids, Michigan, 1974), 261-77. See also Rayford W. Logan, "The Attitude of the Church toward Slavery prior to 1500," *Journal of Negro History* 17 (1932), 466-80.

By 1066, slavery had evidently started to decline considerably. It does not necessarily follow, however, that it would have disappeared completely, even if the Anglo-Saxons had remained in control of England. As long as the old tribal laws remained with the separate status they accorded to slaves, it is possible that the conservatism of what was a settled society would have preserved the institution. There were, after all, still ten per cent of the population who were slaves in 1086, a small but significant proportion. Yet within a hundred years of the Conquest, slaves vanish from the records. So completely did the institution disappear from English history that the standard Old English word for a slave, *theow*, ceased to remain in the language in any form.[63] The explanation for this that best accords with the evidence has been put forward by Professor J. A. Raftis: he has suggested that a terminological change took place after the Norman Conquest.[64] In order to understand this, let us once more take the perspective of a manorial overlord, this time a Norman who had been granted a fief by the Conqueror. In trying to learn who the peasants were that occupied his lands, he would have been met with a multiplicity of vernacular words. Some would be described in terms of their economic status, such as the *cotsettas* or cottagers.[65] Others would be referred to by their occupational functions, such as the *radmen* or riding men, who travelled about on manorial duties.[66] Yet others would be called *ceorlas* 'churls' and *theowas*, terminology indicative of their status in Anglo-Saxon law. We should not be surprised if our Norman lord found it all rather perplexing. He might grant some had more possessions or some spent more time working for him than others—yet all were, in a sense, "his men." When he was presented with the wide range of questions that the Domesday Commissioners posed on behalf of the king,[67] he was forced to draw on estate documents left behind by the former Anglo-Saxon overlord or had to get local inhabitants to supply the information, especially when it came to social matters.[68] Both the specific questions asked by the Commissioners as to how many slaves there had been at three different times and the means used

---

63 The word was revived in the historical novels of Sir Walter Scott. See *Oxford English Dictionary*, s.v. *theow*.
64 James A. Raftis, "The Trends towards Serfdom in Medieval England," *Report of the Canadian Catholic Historical Association* 22 (1955), 15-25.
65 See the *Rectitudines* for some of the terminology employed (Liebermann, *Gesetze* I, 444-53 [text]; EHD II, 875-79, No. 172 [translation]).
66 On the *radmen* and the related *radchenistri*, see Henry Ellis, *A General Introduction to Domesday Book*, Record Commission (London, 1833), I, 72-74.
67 On the terms of reference of the Domesday Commissioners, see Vivian H. Galbraith, *The Making of Domesday Book* (Oxford, 1961), 59-66.
68 On the use of documentary, as well as oral, sources in the compiling of Domesday Book, see Sally Harvey, "Domesday Book and its Predecessors," *EHR* 86 (1971), 753-73.

to answer the questions explain why slaves are so widely recorded in Domesday Book.[69] However, to a Norman overlord, the status of slave must have seemed an anomalous one. So far as he was concerned he had rights in all the persons resident on his lands. None could betake themselves off without his permission. How they were viewed and what they were called within their own community was irrelevant to him—and in any case, the numbers of slaves on any one estate was in most instances too low for them to stand out as a group. Usually, he would refer to them all as his "men," or else would describe them in terms of their function on the estate such as *bubulcus* 'ploughman' or *molendarius* 'miller.' Thus, by the end of the first quarter of the twelfth century, the word "slave" has just about disappeared from our sources. Significantly, one of the last works to use the term is the Black Book of Peterborough, compiled about that time.[70] It was the product of a well-endowed ecclesiastical institution whose stable control from the Anglo-Saxon period encouraged the preservation of old ways and old terminology.

From our perspective, the disappearance of slavery as an institution from large areas of Europe in the Middle Ages marks a momentous change in Western man's perception of himself and society. In England the change took place unremarked—even unnoticed.

69 Slaves are recorded in all Domesday Book counties except Huntingdonshire, Lincolnshire, Rutlandshire, and Yorkshire.
70 *Liber Niger Monasterii Sancti Petri de Burgo*, in Thomas Stapleton (ed.), *Chronicon Petroburgense*, Camden Society, Publications 47 (London, 1849), 157-83. Another late example is the earliest survey of the English estates of the Abbey of Holy Trinity, Caen (Bibliothèque Nationale, MS lat. 5650), which dates from 1106x1131 (possibly before 1113). This has a few references to *ancillae* and *servi*: see Marjorie Chibnall (ed.), *Charters and Custumals of the Abbey of Holy Trinity Caen*, British Academy, Records of Social and Economic History, N.S. 5 (London, 1982), 33, 35, and 36.

10

Germanic Warrior Terms in Old Saxon[1]

J. Douglas Woods

The student who is reading Old Saxon poetry for the first time might be excused for having the impression that something is not quite right. The only major piece of literature in the language is a 6,000 line alliterative verse gospel harmony, and although we have come to think of the Gospels as the story of the life of Jesus—and therefore being about love, reconciliation, and forgiveness—we find that this gospel harmony, the *Heliand*, seems to be full of *warrior* terminology. Prior to the last few years, to confirm or refute such a hypothesis would have been a daunting task, but now, in the age of the

---

[1] I am grateful to Sheila Embleton and Rob Fink of York University in Downsview, Ontario, and Barron Brainerd of the University of Toronto for suggestions about my lexicostatistical analysis; to Wolf Ahrens, also of York University, for suggestions about the Old Saxon view of Christianity; to Michael J. Swanton of the University of Exeter for his evaluation of the basic notion which underlies this paper; and to Angus Cameron and his team of researchers at the Dictionary of Old English Project, University of Toronto, for assistance with the basic data for this work (cf. notes 8-10 below). Faults which remain are my own.

The reader who wants to know more about the history and location of the Old Saxons should see Ferdinand Holthausen, *Altsächsisches Elementarbuch* 2nd ed. (Heidelberg, 1921), 9-11.

computer, and with the revival of lexicostatistics, such testing of a hypothesis is relatively easy.

In ideal circumstances, the obvious way to proceed would be to look at Old Saxon gospel and warrior poetry and compare the relative prominence of warrior terminology in the two types of poetry. The problem is that, as mentioned above, the only major document in Old Saxon is the *Heliand*; there is no warrior poetry in the language. Prior to the revival and refinement of lexicostatistics,[2] and the advent of computer concordances,[3] a Germanic linguist would have spent weeks or months doing what now takes days or weeks. Now we can make comparative linguistic studies with relative ease, and that helps us to solve the problem of the paucity of data in Old Saxon; through historical and comparative studies, we know that Anglo-Saxon was very closely related to Old Saxon. Anglo-Saxon (though many think of its corpus as being very limited) has precisely the sort of poetry which Old Saxon is missing, and if we can establish that the two languages are closely enough related, then we can borrow information from the former to answer questions about the latter.

In order to establish exactly how close the relationship between Anglo-Saxon and Old Saxon was, we can perform a simple diagnostic test which is merely the first set of steps in a process known as glottochronology, and which aims to find the time depth between any two genetically related languages (i.e., how long ago they began separating

2 Early works on lexicostatistics include Robert B. Lees, "The Basis of Glottochronology," *Language* 29 (1953), 113-27, and Morris Swadesh, "Towards Greater Accuracy in Lexicostatistic Dating," *International Journal of American Linguistics* 21 (1955), 121-37. C. Douglas Chrétien, "The Mathematical Models of Glottochronology," *Language* 38 (1962), 11-37, is highly critical of glottochronology. The following works refute such criticism and carry the methodology even further: Annette J. Dobson, "Lexicostatistical Grouping," *Anthropological Linguistics* 11 (1969), 216-21; Sheila Embleton, "Incorporating Borrowing Rates in Lexicostatistical Tree Construction," talk delivered at Linguistic Society of America Winter Meeting (San Antonio, Texas, December 28, 1980); Sheila Embleton, "Incorporating Borrowing Rates in Lexicostatistical Tree Reconstruction," Ph.D. Dissertation, University of Toronto, 1981; Sheila Embleton, "Lexicostatistical Tree Reconstruction Incorporating Borrowing," talk delivered at Linguistic Association of Canada and the United States Summer Meeting (Toronto, August 11, 1981); Sheila Embleton, "Lexicostatistical Tree Reconstruction Incorporating Borrowing," *Toronto Working Papers in Linguistics* 2 (1981), 1-29; David Sankoff, "Reconstructing the History and Geography of an Evolutionary Tree," *American Mathematical Monthly* 79 (1972), 596-603; David Sankoff, "Mathematical Developments in Lexicostatistic Theory," in Thomas A. Sebeok (ed.), *Current Trends in Linguistics* 11 (The Hague, 1973), 93-113; and David Sankoff and Annette J. Dobson, "Word Replacement, Borrowing and the Phylogenetics of Language Families," unpublished paper, Centre de Recherches Mathématiques, Université de Montréal. For a general discussion of lexicostatistics, see: Theodora Bynon, *Historical Linguistics* (Cambridge, 1977), 266-72, and Winfred P. Lehmann, *Historical Linguistics*, 2nd ed. (New York, 1973), 104-09.

3 Richard L. Venezky and Antonette di Paolo Healey, *A Microfiche Concordance to Old English* (Toronto, 1980).

from one another). It is not necessary for us to establish the time depth, *per se*, between Anglo-Saxon and Old Saxon, but our degree of relationship test would be an ingredient in such a calculation.[4] This test simply compares the vocabularies of the two languages to see what percentage of their words have remained cognate over the years since separation. Several lists of words which are so universal that they would be expected to occur in virtually any language have been compiled,[5] covering such concepts as the body and its parts, family relationships, directions, sizes, and so on. One of the original lists was by Morris Swadesh, so such lists are commonly referred to as "Swadesh lists." The 200-word Swadesh list (plus seven additional words) appears in Winfred Lehmann's *Historical Linguistics: An Introduction* (2nd ed. [New York, 1973], 108).

The first step in the test involves finding the usual word in each of the languages which is being compared for each meaning given on the list. A good place to begin the search is C. D. Buck's *Dictionary of Selected Synonyms in the Principal Indo-European Languages* (Chicago, 1949). Though most of the 200 items can be found in this work, there are still some problems. One is that there are some gaps in the Buck *Dictionary*, so that the researcher is forced to find the necessary items elsewhere. In the case of Anglo-Saxon and Old Saxon, filling in the gaps is not difficult because of the ready availability of information in other sources (q.v. in the Bibliographical Essay). Another problem is that of determining which of several synonyms for a given meaning from the Swadesh list is the "usual" one. If it were left to impressionistic choice, no two scholars would necessarily agree, but fortunately, we have reliable concordances for both Anglo-Saxon and Old Saxon, so it is possible to settle any disputes relatively objectively by arbitrarily choosing the synonym which occurs most often. Yet another problem with the Buck *Dictionary* is that it does not actually list Old Saxon, although it does very often mention the Old Saxon lexical item for a given meaning in the discussion which follows each list; quite often, however, the researcher is forced to seek the necessary lexical items elsewhere (which, as mentioned above, is relatively simple for Old Saxon and Anglo-Saxon). Finally, although the Buck *Dictionary* may well list one or more lexical items of a language for a given meaning on the list, it does not necessarily list all which might be possible, so the researcher must supplement the list from his or her own knowledge of the language and through consultation with experts in the language. Despite all the above-mentioned objections, it is interesting that, for Old Saxon, Buck agrees with the other sources (con-

---

4 For a simple version of the time depth formula, see Lehmann, *Historical Linguistics*, 105, and for its early development, see Lees, "Basis."

5 See, for example, Sarah C. Gudschinsky, "The ABC's of Lexicostatistics (Glottochronology)," *Word* 12 (1956), 175-210.

cordances, experts, this writer) 97 per cent of the time, and for Anglo-Saxon, 96 per cent of the time.

Having found the usual lexical items for the meanings on the Swadesh list (which, for reasons of space, cannot be listed here), we find that a comparison of Old Saxon vocabulary with that of Anglo-Saxon shows 87 per cent cognates. However, by itself, this figure is meaningless. One way of placing it in perspective is to do similar comparisons with other related languages, including some from within the Germanic group (e.g., Old High German and Old Norse) and some which are more distantly related to Old Saxon (e.g., Old French, Old Irish, and Old Church Slavonic). The same objections apply here as above: 1) There are gaps in that Buck fails to mention some of the meanings from the Swadesh list; 2) Old French is not listed, though it is sometimes mentioned in the discussion of a given meaning; and 3) not all possible synonyms are mentioned. In the case of the Germanic languages, as mentioned above, this is not a significant problem because of the ready availability of sources to fill in any missing information. The remaining Indo-European languages were quite another matter, however; here, the advice of experts in the languages was crucial (for Old French, Dr. Roger Pensom; for Old Irish, Mr. John Symonds; and for Old Church Slavonic, Mr. Aidan Cahill, all of the University of Exeter). Comparison of Old Saxon vocabulary with that of the remaining five languages showed the following percentages of cognates: Old High German 84 per cent, Old Norse 71 per cent, Old French 25 per cent, Old Church Slavonic 20 per cent, and Old Irish 19 per cent. Clearly, within the Germanic group, there is a high rate of cognate retention, although Old Norse shows a decidedly lower level, but the rate drops off markedly outside the Germanic group. For the entire group of comparisons, the average rate of cognate retention was 51 per cent.[6] The question is, are such differences in cognate retention rate significant? We can answer the question by subjecting each set of results to a chi-square test, which will determine which variations from the expected norm (51 per cent) can be accounted for simply by chance (we expect a certain amount of random variation in any statistical sample). We will demonstrate with the data from the Old Saxon/Anglo-Saxon comparison. All things being equal, we would expect 102 (or 51 per cent) of the 200 items from the Swadesh list to show cognate retention, while the remaining 98 (49 per cent) would not. Actual figures showed 174 cases of retention and 26 of non-retention. In the case of both retention and non-retention, the observed data varied

6 The reader should note that if we had taken a more representative sample, i.e., to include data from Hellenic, Iranian, and Italic, the average rate of retention would have been even lower, adding even greater strength to our claims about the degree of relationship between the Germanic languages, especially between Anglo- and Old Saxon.

by seventy-two examples from the expected norm. We show this as follows:

	Observed	Expected	Variation	$\frac{(\text{Variation})^2}{\text{Expected}}$
Retention	174	102	72	50.82
Non-retention	26	98	−72	52.90
Total	200	200		103.72(chi-square)

Reference to a chi-square table (e.g., Z. W. Birnbaum, *Introduction to Probability and Mathematical Statistics*, 317) shows that the probability of accounting for such a variation by chance is less than 0.1 per cent; the variation in question is highly significant (i.e., Old Saxon and Anglo-Saxon bear a much closer relationship to one another than that which the norm predicts). The chi-square values for all the comparisons are listed below; the reader will find that the same probability of random variation obtains in all cases (less than 0.1 per cent), but in the last three cases, it is the *lack* of relationship with Old Saxon which is significant (cf. the rates of cognate retention above).

Comparison	Chi-square	Probability
Close Relationship		
Old Saxon/Old High German	87.16	less than 0.1%
Old Saxon/Old Norse	32.02	less than 0.1%
Distant Relationship		
Old Saxon/Old French	54.11	less than 0.1%
Old Saxon/Old Irish	79.41	less than 0.1%
Old Saxon/Old Church Slavonic	76.91	less than 0.1%

Another way of putting the 87 per cent cognate retention rate between Old Saxon and Anglo-Saxon in perspective is to look at the rate of vocabulary decay *within a single language*. Even within one language, certain vocabulary items are dropped, and others take their place, but (based on research mentioned in R. B. Lees, "The Basis of

Glottochronology," *Language* 29 [1953], 113-25) over the course of a millennium, the average language retains 81 per cent of the items on the 200-word Swadesh list. It is commonly accepted[7] that the beginning of the Angle, Saxon, and Jute migration to Britain began in about the middle of the fifth century, so the split between Old Saxon and Anglo-Saxon would have begun at about that time. The samples which we have taken of these two languages are from the mid-ninth century, so four-tenths of a millenium would have gone by since the beginning of the split. If the average rate of vocabulary decay within a language is 19 per cent per millenium (the converse of 81 per cent retention), then four-tenths of a millenium should see about an 8 per cent decay (or 92 per cent retention). At 87 per cent retention (the figure obtained when comparing Old Saxon with Anglo-Saxon, see above) and 13 per cent decay, there is some variation from the expected 92 per cent retention and 8 per cent decay within a language, but is this variation significant? Again, we use a chi-square test:

	Observed	Expected	Variation	$\frac{(\text{Variation})^2}{\text{Expected}}$
Retention	87%	92%	−5%	0.272
Decay	13%	8%	5%	3.125
Total	100	100		3.397 (chi-square)

The probability that this variation could be accounted for by chance is greater than 5 per cent. Normally, such a high probability (in fact, anything over 2 per cent) indicates that the variation is not significant; it is likely to be due to random variation. In other words, there is such a high rate of cognate retention between Old Saxon and Anglo-Saxon that they fall *within the limits for variation within a single language*. In

---

7 Albert C. Baugh and Thomas Cable, *A History of the English Language* 3rd ed. (Englewood Cliffs, New Jersey, 1978), 46; Oliver Farrar Emerson, *The History of the English Language* (New York, 1921), 40; and Morton W. Bloomfield and Leonard Newmark, *A Linguistic Introduction to the History of English* (New York, 1964), 134 all place the beginning of the Anglo-Saxon(-Jute) invasion of Britain in the middle of the fifth century—circa 450—based on Bede's *Ecclesiastical History* (more discussion elsewhere in this work). However, Bloomfield and Newmark caution us to remember that the migration lasted for more than a century, so the break between the Saxons who accompanied the Angles and the Jutes to Britain and the Saxons who stayed behind on the Continent was not a "clean" one. For a lengthy annotated bibliography of the discussion surrounding the dating of the *Heliand*, see Otto Behaghel (ed.), *Heliand und Genesis*, 8th ed., rev. by Walter Mitzka, Altdeutsche Textbibliothek 4 (Tübingen, 1965), XXVIII ff.

effect, they are so closely related, even after four hundred years' separation, that they could be treated as *dialects of the same language*; thus, we are clearly justified in making comparisons between the two.

There are many words which are used in the *Heliand* which evoke heroic/warrior life and values, and these words are, in turn, cognate with certain words in Anglo-Saxon. A list of some of these items appears below.

Old Saxon		Anglo-Saxon	
erl	'important, distinguished, noble man'	eorl	'noble warrior'
aðal/eðili-	'noble family; the nobility; noble'	æðel-	'nobility, royal lineage'
drôm	'earthly life; heavenly joy; joyful state in sleep; dream'	drēam	'noisy merriment, music; gaiety, happiness (esp. in the hall)'
seg	'warrior; man; husband'	secg	'warrior; man'
eggia	'(sword-)edge'	ecg	'(sword-)edge'
uualdand	'ruler'	wealdand	'ruler'
hêrro	'lord'	hearra	'lord, master'
garu	'ready, armed; decorated'	gearu	'ready (e.g., for battle), prepared, complete'
êr	'messenger'	ār	'messenger (esp. one sent to bear a message in a battle)'
mâri	'shining, bright, splendid; famous, well-known, memorable; infamous'	mǣre	'illustrious, noble, splendid'
kuning	'king'	cyning	'king'
cunni	'race, tribe, family, folk'	cynn	'kind, quality, species; generation, race, people, family; etiquette, propriety'
rîki	'power, rule, might; land, empire; folk; rulers; palace, residence'	rīce	'dominion, realm'
man	'servant, vassal; (hu)man; man, husband; young man, youth, child; people'	mann	'man, human being'
drohtin	'lord'	dryhten	'lord, ruler'

uuard	'attendant, keeper, guardian, protector'	weard	'guardian, warden, protector, possessor; lord, king'
thegan	'boy, man, follower, retainer, servant'	þegn	'servant, retainer, disciple; royal officer, minister, thane; man, warrior'
ârundi	'mission, business'	ærende	'message, errand'

If a concept is important to the speakers of a language, they will talk about it, and it will occur relatively often in their speech (or texts). Conversely, if a concept is not important, it will occur relatively seldom in their speech. The occasion for surprise which we mentioned above was the impression that warrior-related concepts seemed to be so important in Old Saxon culture that they even turned up in Christian gospel poetry, although, given the subject matter of the Gospels, that is the last thing we would expect.

Before we begin our comparison of Old Saxon gospel poetry with that of Anglo-Saxon, we must ascertain certain things about the latter's literature. For one thing, is there a significant difference in the levels of warrior terminology in warrior poetry versus canonical gospel prose? The latter should serve as a good control because it is a relatively faithful representation of the basic notions expressed in the models from which it is translated. Another question is, is there a significant difference in the levels of warrior terminology in gospel prose versus gospel poetry? This may tell us something about the use of poetry or prose to create certain atmospheres. Finally, is there a significant difference in the levels of warrior terminology in gospel poetry versus warrior poetry? A high correlation between the two would constitute confirmation of our hypothesis that there is an unexpectedly high level of warrior terminology in gospel poetry. Obviously, the final question to be answered is whether the level of warrior terminology in Old Saxon gospel poetry is as high as it is in the same genre in Anglo-Saxon. In order to perform our analyses we must know:

(1) the total of all words which appear in: a) gospel prose texts, b) gospel poetic texts, and c) warrior poetic texts; and

(2) the total of the warrior terms from the list given above which appear in: a) gospel prose texts, b) gospel poetic texts, and c) warrior poetic texts.

To find these totals, we can use two concordances. For Anglo-Saxon, we now have a concordance for every word of the language which was known to exist as of 1980: the Venezky/Healey *Concordance*. For Old Saxon, we have E. H. Sehrt's *Heliand-Wörterbuch*. In Anglo-Saxon gospel prose, there are 2,892 occurrences of the words from our list in texts which total 223,069 words;[8] in Anglo-Saxon warrior poetry, there are 62 occurrences of the words from the list in texts which total 2,928 words.[9] The total number of words in texts of both types is 225,997, so the prose words account for 99 per cent, and the poetry for 1 per cent, of the total. All things being equal, we would expect 99 per cent of the occurrences of words from our list to be in gospel prose, and 1 per cent to be in the warrior poetry. However, there is a discrepancy, as shown below:

	Observed	Expected	Variation
Gospel Prose (GoPr)	2,892	2,924.46	−32.46
Warrior Poetry (WaPo)	62	29.54	32.46
Total	2,954	2,954.00	

8 The following gospel prose texts were used:

Name	Cameron Number	Total Words in Text
Mark 1: 27-31, 39-42 Yale University, MS. 578	B 8.4.1	164
Cambridge, Corpus Christi College, MS. 140: Skeat 1871-87	B 8.4.3	69,384
John London, British Library, MS. Cotton Vespasian D. XIV: Warner, 1917, 77	B 8.4.6	253
John Oxford, Bodleian Library, MS. Eng. Bib. C. 2: Napier 1891, 257-61	B 8.4.9	2,016
Lindisfarne Gospels (Marginalia): Skeat 1871-87	B 27.3.15	54
Rushworth Gospels (Marginalia): Skeat 1871-87	B 27.3.43	19
Lindisfarne Gospels (including Arguments): Skeat 1871-87	C 8.1	85,904
Rushworth Gospels: Skeat 1871-87	C 8.2	65,275

9

Name	Cameron Number	Total Words in Text
The Battle of Finnsburgh Dobbie 1942, 3-4	A 7	288
The Battle of Maldon Dobbie 1942, 7-16	A 9	2,275
The Battle of Brunanburgh Dobbie 1942, 16-20	A 10.1	365

It might be that the discrepancy could be accounted for by chance. As we did above, we will check the variation by a chi-square test, to see the likelihood that any variations could be accounted for by chance.

	Observed	Expected	Variation	$\dfrac{(\text{Variation})^2}{\text{Expected}}$
GoPr	2,892	2,924.46	−32.46	0.36
WaPo	62	29.54	32.46	35.67
Total	2,954	2,954.00		36.03 (chi-square)

Reference to the chi-square table shows us that the possibility that the discrepancy shown above could be accounted for by chance is less than one tenth of one per cent; the relatively high number of occurrences of warrior words in warrior poetry as against gospel prose confirms what the reader might have expected all along: gospel prose—because it is not about warrior notions—does not have, relatively, as many warrior terms as warrior poetry does. However, this merely sets up a standard; the reader will remember that the original impression was of a high percentage of occurrences in gospel *poetry*, the *Heliand*. To confirm this, we do a similar count of Anglo-Saxon gospel poetry. There were 494 occurrences of the warrior terms in texts totalling 17,359 words.[10]

10 Note that this comparison is a particularly good one because the poetry of both the *Heliand* and the Anglo-Saxon gospel poems (q.v. below) is alliterative verse.

Name	Cameron Number	Total Words in Text
Christ and Satan Krapp 1931, 135-58	A 1.4	4,374
Dream of the Rood Krapp 1932, 61-65	A 2.5	1,014
Christ Krapp and Dobbie 1936, 3-49	A 3.1	9,984
The Descent into Hell Krapp and Dobbie 1936, 219-23	A 3.26	822
The Lord's Prayer I Krapp and Dobbie 1936, 223-24	A 3.29	73
The Lord's Prayer II Dobbie 1942, 70-74	A 20	812
The Lord's Prayer III Dobbie 1942, 77-78	A 22	207
Ruthwell Cross Dickins and Ross 1934, 25-29; corrections by Elliott 1959a	E 39	73

The following is a chi-square determination for the comparison of gospel prose with gospel poetry.

	Observed	Expected	Variation	$\dfrac{(\text{Variation})^2}{\text{Expected}}$
GoPr	2,892	3,141.53	−249.53	19.82
Gospel Poetry (GoPo)	494	244.47	249.53	254.69
Total	3,386	3,386.00		274.51 (chi-square)

The evidence here is even more compelling. The likelihood that such large discrepancies could be accounted for by chance is *well under* one tenth of one per cent. Apparently, the authors of the gospel poems *intended* that there should be a high percentage of warrior terminology in their poems. Now, it could be objected at this point that the high percentage which we have shown is not so much due to the intentions of the authors as to the poetic vehicle itself. That is, alliterative verse is, traditionally, the verse of warrior poetry, so any poem cast in this type of verse would naturally sound warrior-like. We could test this by comparing gospel poetry with warrior poetry.

	Observed	Expected	Variation	$\dfrac{(\text{Variation})^2}{\text{Expected}}$
GoPo	494	475.75	18.25	0.70
WaPo	62	80.25	−18.25	4.15
Total	556	556.00		4.85 (chi-square)

The chi-square table shows us that the likelihood that such discrepancies between observed and expected occurrences could be accounted for by chance is greater than 5 per cent; in other words, there is a high correlation between the two types—gospel and warrior poetry are very similar in Anglo-Saxon. However, the conclusion from the objection stated above—that the type of poetry (alliterative verse) predestines it to come out a certain way—is not the only possible conclusion; it suggests, in fact, that the author has no control over how he writes. On the contrary, it could be more convincingly argued that the author chose the alliterative verse genre—and warrior terminology—because it was a good vehicle for what he wanted to say. When all is said and done, we must still establish that there is a good correlation between Anglo-Saxon and Old Saxon gospel poetry as regards the occurrence of warrior terminology. We do this by means of a chi-square determination for the comparison between the two. The figures for the count of warrior terms and the total word count in Anglo-Saxon gospel poetry are given above. In the Old Saxon of the *Heliand* there are 1,336 of the chosen warrior terms in a total corpus of 45,530 words.

	Observed	Expected	Variation	$\frac{(\text{Variation})^2}{\text{Expected}}$
Old Saxon	1,336	1,324.9	11.1	0.093
Anglo-Saxon	494	505.1	−11.1	0.244
Total	1,830	1,830.0		0.337 (chi-square)

For this value of chi-square, the probability that such small discrepancies between observed and expected values could be accounted for by chance is greater than 30 per cent. In other words, the levels of warrior terminology in Old Saxon and Anglo-Saxon gospel poetry show a high degree of correlation; they are highly comparable. The question remains; why would the authors of the various religious poems want their works to sound warrior-like? We will concentrate on the *Heliand* and its Old Saxon audience.

A look at well known facts of history tells us that the conversion of the Old Saxons was one of the hardest tasks which Christian missionaries of the time had to face. Years of efforts by, and on behalf of, Charlemagne to christianize these people were met with one setback after another. Nothing even approaching success occurred until after Charlemagne's death, and even during the reign of Louis the Pious, missionaries were still having to work very hard to achieve any sort of positive result. A reading of the *Heliand* with an eye toward content, as well as form, tells us that the poem was aimed at a people who were still very much attached to Germanic heroic views, and the author of the *Heliand* was at great pains to accommodate the heroic world with that of Christianity; but the use of warrior terminology to help create the necessary effect is only part of a greater constellation. To understand this, we must look at how the Germanic warrior viewed the gods (and, ultimately, God) and his fellow man.[11]

11 Very interesting in this regard are works by Hulda Göhler, "Das Christusbild in Otfrids Evangelienbuch und im Heliand," *Zeitschrift für deutsche Philologie* 59 (1934/5), 1ff., W. Baetke, "Die Aufnahme des Christentums durch die Germanen," in

First of all, for the Teuton, religion was man's relationship with his god(s), and morality was his set of values for a proper relationship with his fellow; when Christian missionaries told him that love for God is reflected in love for one's neighbour and for oneself, that the ultimate model for the relationship between self and neighbour is the relationship between self and God, and that one cannot love one without loving all three, the warrior's natural reaction was to reject such teaching.

Another major stumbling block was Christian humility. The idea that a warrior should be forbidden to avenge an injury to his honour or pride was completely unacceptable; the idea of turning the other cheek was foreign to him. A further clash occurred between the Christian notion of free will and the Germanic notion of fate; free will makes one responsible for one's actions (and this is a main ingredient in the notion of sin), whereas it is possible to disclaim at least a certain amount of the responsibility for one's actions if they can be assigned to the impersonal power of fate. One thing about Christianity which did impress the Germanic warrior was the idea that all power was concentrated in the hands of one god, rather than divided among many.[12]

How did the Teuton view God? In order to be accepted, certain aspects of his character would have to be emphasized:

(1) The powerful king and father. The author uses such terms as *waldand* 'the ruler,' *mahtig* 'mighty,' *rîki* 'rich, powerful,' *craftag* 'mighty, powerful'; *drohtin* 'lord,' *hêrro* 'lord,' *frâho* 'lord,' *heɓancuning* 'king of Heaven'; *mundboro* 'protector,' *râdgeɓo* 'counsellor,' and *sigidrohtin* 'lord of victory.'

(2) The creator. *aðalordfrumo* 'noble creator' and *the thar al giscôp, weroldi endi wunnea* 'he who created everything, world and joy.'

(3) The worker of signs and wonders; see, for example, discussion of the healing of Bartimaeus below.

(4) The generous giver. The term *mildi* 'generous' is commonly used to refer to God.

(5) The wise teacher.

(6) The stronghearted sufferer. See discussion of the Passion story below.

The author makes no attempt to play down other aspects of Christ's character which the Teuton found difficult to accept; rather he tries to show how they are logical extensions of existing Germanic ideals, e.g., mercy and love as extensions of generosity.

Vom Geist und Erbe Thules (Göttingen, 1944), and Elisabeth Grosch, "Das Gottes- und Menschenbild im Heliand," *Beiträge zur Geschichte der deutschen Sprache und Literatur* 72 (1951), 90-120.

12 Cf. Grosch, "Gottes- und Menschenbild," 93: "The awareness of serving the mightiest, most splendid god, and of sharing his might was able to counterbalance many things which the Teutons found strange." This translation is mine, as are all of those which follow.

As mentioned above, such a strong element as fate cannot be ignored either. Sometimes it is present as a force which appears (whether consciously or subconsciously) as independent of God: *wurd* 'fate,' *metod* 'fate,' and *giscapu* '(the judgment of) fate.' At other times, the notions of fate and God coexist: *that si thiu berhtun giscapu,/ Mariun gimanodun endi maht godes* 'that bright fate and the power of God told them, told Mary' (line 367 f.). And at other times, fate is clearly subordinated to God:

> Thiu wurd is at handun,
> that it sô gigangan scal, sô it god fader
> gimarcode mahtig.

> [F]ate is at hand,
> so that it will happen as God the Father
> mightily intended.
>
> (lines 4778 ff.)

The Teuton's view of man is well expressed in the story of the healing of the blind man, Bartimaeus, on the road outside of Jericho. Such miracles as the healing of the blind, deaf, dumb, or lame were taken as signs of great power. The notion of blindness vs. light (i.e., our spiritual blindness vs. the ability to see clearly) was not exclusively Old Saxon, however; it was a quite common ecclesiastical concept at the time (cf., e.g., Bede's commentary on Luke 18:35[13]). The author of the *Heliand* took every opportunity to speak against (heroic) pride, and to extend the more positive virtues, by suggesting that man constantly needs God's help against the Devil, that the only way to have true wisdom is to have good will and a pure heart, that the Germanic virtue of strongheartedness is reflected in faith, and that the continued struggle toward Heaven is even more important than loyalty to one's family:

> [B]etera is imu...
> that he...
> míde thes mâges endi ni hebbea thar êniga minnea tô,
> that he môti êno up gestîgan
> hô himilríki.

> [I]t is better for him...
> that he...
> reject his family and not have any love for them,
> so that he might climb up alone
> to the high Kingdom of Heaven.
>
> (lines 1496 ff.)

The author is able to say, in effect, "If you find all of these foreign notions difficult to accept, just think of the reward."

---

13 Ibid., 105.

[F]iriho barn   antfâhen scoldin,
lioht endi listi   endi lîf êuuig,
hôh heƀenriki   endi huldi godes.

[T]he children of men   should receive
light and wisdom   and eternal life,
the high Kingdom of Heaven   and God's grace.

(lines 3923 ff.)

Looking back, it seems that there is little about the nature of God—apart from the "disgrace" of the Crucifixion—which the Germanic hero would reject, but rather that his relationships with other people would be radically changed if he were to give up his pride, and in a way, this follows the clear line of division in the Germanic mind between the world of religion and that of morals. In Christianity, the two worlds are held together in the person of Jesus, who is both God and man. As long as the Germanic warrior looked at only one of these aspects of Jesus at a time (which would, of course, be heretical), there was no problem, but the Passion story forced him to view both together, and there the tension between the Germanic heroic world and that of Christianity was at its highest. Although the disciples had disgraced themselves by "disobeying their orders" and falling asleep in the Garden of Gethsemene, they might be forgiven on the grounds that the full realization of what was about to happen was so staggering that they were totally grief-stricken and therefore unable to do anything but sleep:

[F]and sie that barn godes
slâpan sorgandie.

[T]he child of God
found them grieving in sleep.

(lines 4770 f.)

The disciples' betrayal of Jesus as he was taken captive is not cowardice; it is predicted (predestined?) by the word of the prophets:

[N]i uuas it thoh be ênigaru blôđi,   that sie that barn godes
lioƀen farlêtun.   ac it uuas sô lango biforan
uuârsagono uuord,   that it scoldi giuuerđen sô.

[I]t was not by any cowardice   that they deserted
the beloved child of God;   rather it was the word of the prophets,
long before,   that it should happen like this.

(lines 4933 ff.)

The betrayal of Jesus by Peter, after earlier protestations of unshakeable loyalty, is justified by saying that God wanted to show Peter how little power there is in human courage without the power of God:

[L]êt ina gekunnon,   huilike craft haƀet
the mennisca môd   âno the maht godes.

> [He] let him know what kind of strength
> human courage has without the might of God.
>
> (lines 5031 f.)

The author of the *Heliand* (or his hearer) experiences difficulty here only if he is unwilling to see the disciples as they were: human. The difficulty comes only if the disciples are being set up as some sort of Germanic heroic ideals, whose honour may bear no blemish. As for the "disgrace" of the Crucifixion, the author can take advantage of several of the heroic ideals:

(1) it is a sign of heroic strength, not weakness (Jesus "awaits it as something powerful and splendid, as the Hero awaits his fate, when he knows that he is to pass his test"[14]);

(2) it is a sign of loyalty to his followers, but, more than that, it is a matter of grace (or favour)—*huldi*—and love—*minnea*; and

(3) it is a form of generosity, but the gift which is given this time is *himself*. So Jesus endures dishonour for a higher goal. He could withdraw by using his power, but that would endanger the work of redemption, which entails dying for mankind. He fails to emphasize that he is the Son of God because he is unwilling to do anything which might interfere with the ultimate act of redemption—his death on the cross. And finally, by his death, he defeats the Devil, and anything which could stand in the way of this, regardless of how well-intentioned (e.g., the dream of Pilate's wife), is viewed as the work of the Devil, thwarted by Jesus.

Seen in this larger context, the high frequency of occurrence of warrior terms in the *Heliand* is no surprise; it is merely a tool which the author uses to help him get his point across. He uses it to set up a comparison between the warrior ethic and that of Christianity, and then to suggest that the transition from the former to the latter would not be difficult.

14 Ibid., 98.

Bibliographical Essay

David A. E. Pelteret

This bibliography is designed to assist those who are not specialists in the areas covered by the essays in this volume. It aims at providing references to primary and secondary sources in the general field of the papers (e.g., literature, law), as well as to the specific topics examined. It does not in any way intend to be comprehensive. Many of the references are to recent publications that contain citations from, and bibliographies of, earlier scholarship.

Introduction: Catalogues, Bibliographies, and Basic Reference Works

Helmut Gneuss, "A Preliminary List of Manuscripts Written or Owned in England up to 1100," *ASE* 9 (1981 for 1980), 1-60, provides a list of Latin manuscripts known to have been in England in the Anglo-Saxon period. This should be used in association with Jack D. A. Ogilvy, *Books Known to the English, 597-1066*, Medieval Academy of America Publication No. 76 (Cambridge, Mass., 1967). Neil R. Ker, *Catalogue of Manuscripts Containing Anglo-Saxon* (Oxford, 1957) lists most manuscripts in which Old English is to be found with the exception of some legal texts. Vernacular texts cited according to their subject matter are recorded by Angus Cameron, "A List of Old English Texts," in Roberta Frank and Angus Cameron (eds.), *A Plan for the Dictionary of Old English*, TOES 2 (Toronto, 1973), 25-306. Most legal documents (with the exception of the laws themselves, manumissions, and some administrative texts) are listed by Peter H. Sawyer in *Anglo-Saxon Charters: An Annotated List and Bibliography*, Royal Historical Society Guides and Handbooks 8 (London, 1968).

Charles W. Phillips (ed.), *Britain in the Dark Ages*, 2nd ed., Ordnance Survey (Southampton, 1966) and *Britain before the Norman Conquest*, Ordnance Survey (Southampton, 1973) presents reasonably large-scale maps of England in the Anglo-Saxon period. Detailed maps incorporating the most recent archaeological discoveries are to be found in David Hill, *An Atlas of Anglo-Saxon England* (Toronto, Buffalo, and London, 1981).

The primary historical texts of the period are discussed by Antonia Gransden in *Historical Writing in England c. 550 to c. 1307* (London, 1974). For editions of the historical sources and discussions of them up to 1953, see Wilfrid Bonser, *An Anglo-Saxon and Celtic Bibliography (450-1087)*, 2 vols. (Oxford, 1957). More recent is Edgar B. Graves (ed.), *A Bibliography of English History to 1485* (Oxford, 1975). Many primary texts have been translated in Dorothy Whitelock (ed.), *English Historical Documents c. 500-1042*, 2nd ed., EHD I (London and New York, 1979) and David C. Douglas and George W. Greenaway (eds.), *English Historical Documents 1042-1189*, 2nd ed., EHD II (London and New York, 1981). The standard historical study of the period is by Frank M. Stenton, *Anglo-Saxon England*, 3rd ed., Oxford History of England 2 (Oxford, 1971). James Campbell (ed.), *The Anglo-Saxons* (Oxford and Ithaca, N.Y., 1982) is a lavishly illustrated general survey that takes much recent scholarship into account.

Whitney F. Bolton, *A History of Anglo-Latin Literature 597-1066*, I, *597-740* (Princeton, 1967) surveys the Latin literature of the early Anglo-Saxon period. See also the first two volumes of Max Manitius, *Geschichte der lateinischen Literatur des Mittelalters*, 3 vols. (Munich, 1911-31).

The standard work in English on the vernacular language of the Anglo-Saxons is Alistair Campbell, *Old English Grammar* (Oxford, 1959). General studies of Old English literature include Stanley B. Greenfield, *A Critical History of Old English Literature* (New York, 1965, and London, 1966) and Charles L. Wrenn, *A Study of Old English Literature* (London, 1967); these are both subject to limitations discussed by Angus Cameron in Chapter 2 above. These and other works are surveyed by Daniel G. Calder in "Histories and Surveys of Old English Literature: A Chronological Review," *ASE* 10 (1982), 201-44. To these should now be added Angus Cameron's study, "Anglo-Saxon Literature" in Joseph R. Strayer (ed.), *Dictionary of the Middle Ages* (New York, 1982-), I, 274-88. For editions of the texts and discussions of them, see Stanley B. Greenfield and Fred C. Robinson (eds.), *A Bibliography of Publications on Old English Literature to the End of 1972*, using the collections of E. E. Ericson (Toronto and Buffalo, 1980). A supplement to this work is now in preparation. Robert K. Gordon, *Anglo-Saxon Poetry*, new ed. (London, 1954) translates the poetic texts into modern English prose.

Current studies in fields relating to the Anglo-Saxons, in general, are recorded annually in Peter Clemoes (ed.), *Anglo-Saxon England* 1- (1972-). Archaeological excavations are constantly adding to our knowledge of the period. To remain *au courant*, the reader should consult the annual journal *Medieval Archaeology* 1- (1957-) and *British Archaeological Abstracts* 1- (1967-). Numismatics is also providing new historical and linguistic information. The Sylloge of Coins of the British Isles 1- (London, 1958-) is a series that is steadily cataloguing Anglo-Saxon coins in collections round the world. *Neuphilologische Mitteilungen* each year lists both work that is in progress and unpublished completed work of Anglo-Saxonists, especially in Old English language and literature. The *Old English Newsletter* 1- (1967-) records recent publications, publishes a review of the previous year's work in Anglo-Saxon studies, and frequently reports current research.

Chapter 1: The Bayeux Tapestry: History or Propaganda?

The fundamental reference work on the Tapestry is Frank M. Stenton (ed.), *The Bayeux Tapestry: A Comprehensive Survey*, 2nd ed. (London, 1965). Charles H. Gibbs-Smith, *The Bayeux Tapestry* (London, 1973) should also be consulted. The literary references in the work are examined by Hélène Chefneux, "Les Fables dans la Tapisserie de Bayeux," *Romania* 60 (1934), 1-35 and 153-94; Léon Herrman, *Les Fables antique et la Broderie de Bayeux*, Collection Latomus 69 (Brussels, 1964); Charles R. Dodwell, "The Bayeux Tapestry and the French Secular Epic," *Burlington Magazine* 108 (1966), 549-60; and Shirley A. Brown, "The Bayeux Tapestry and the *Song of Roland*," *Olifant* 6 (1978-79), 339-50. On the value of the Tapestry for political purposes, see Otto K. Werckmeister, "The Political Ideology of the Bayeux Tapestry," *Studi Medievali*, 3rd ser., 17 (2) (1976), 535-95 (with an extensive critical bibliography); Nicholas P. Brooks and

H. E. Walker, "The Authority and Interpretation of the Bayeux Tapestry," *Proceedings of the Battle Conference on Anglo-Norman Studies I—1978*, ed. by R. Allen Brown (Woodbridge, Suffolk, and Totowa, N.J., 1979), 1-34; and Richard D. Wissolik, "The Saxon Statement: Code in the Bayeux Tapestry," *Annuale Mediaevale* 19 (1979), 69-97. Other papers dealing with specific aspects of the Tapestry are listed by Werckmeister and in EHD II, 100-101, to which should be added P. E. Bennett, "Encore Turold dans la Tapisserie de Bayeux," *Annales de Normandie* 30 (1980), 3-13, and J. Bard McNulty, "The Lady Aelfgyva in the Bayeux Tapestry," *Speculum* 55 (1980), 659-68; Richard D. Wissolik, "Duke William's Messengers: an 'Insoluble, Reverse-Order' Scene of the Bayeux Tapestry," *Medium Ævum* 51 (1982), 102-107; and David Bernstein, "The Blinding of Harold and the Meaning of the Bayeux Tapestry," *Anglo-Norman Studies* 5 (1983), 40-64, an important paper with a postscript note on a physical examination of the Tapestry.

An exhaustive biography of William I has been written by David C. Douglas, *William the Conqueror: The Norman Impact upon England* (Berkeley and Los Angeles, 1964), which should be consulted for the primary and secondary works relevant to the period. Frank Barlow's biography, *William Rufus* (Berkeley and Los Angeles, 1983), contains much that relates to the Conqueror's reign, notably on the latter's family and on Domesday Book. David Bates provides a history of the Normans antecedent to the conquest of England in *Normandy before 1066* (London and New York, 1982). The nine-hundredth anniversary of the Battle of Hastings stimulated a commemorative volume by Dorothy Whitelock and others under the aegis of the Battle and District Historical Society entitled *The Norman Conquest: Its Setting and Impact* (London, 1966); included in it is an analysis by Charles H. Lemmon of the 1066 campaign. The annual *Proceedings of the Battle Conference on Anglo-Norman Studies* 1- (1979 for 1978-), now called *Anglo-Norman Studies*, should be consulted for current work on the Conquest period.

Chapter 2: The Boundaries of Old English Literature

For catalogues of vernacular texts, see Ker, *Catalogue* and Cameron, "A List"; for editions of primary texts and for secondary studies, see Greenfield and Robinson (eds.), *A Bibliography of Publications*; and for literary histories, see Greenfield, *A Critical History*, Wrenn, *A Study*, and Cameron, "Anglo-Saxon Literature," all cited in the Bibliography to the "Introduction" above.

Chapter 3: Beowulf, Bede, and St. Oswine: The Hero's Pride in Old English Hagiography

The implications for the dating of *Beowulf* of Colin Chase's examination of saints' lives are discussed by him in his paper "Saints' Lives, Royal Lives, and the Date of *Beowulf*" in Colin Chase (ed.), *The Dating of Beowulf*, TOES 6 (Toronto, 1981), 161-71. The standard edition of *Beowulf* remains that by Frederick Klaeber, 3rd ed. (Boston, 1950). The translation by Michael Alexander, *Beowulf: A Verse Translation*, Penguin Classics (Harmondsworth, 1973) is readily available.

The best edition of Bede's *Historia Ecclesiastica* is now that by Bertram Colgrave and Roger A. B. Mynors, *Bede's Ecclesiastical History of the English People*, Oxford Medieval Texts (Oxford, 1969) (with a facing English translation), though Charles Plummer's edition (Oxford, 1896) remains valuable for its notes; it also contains the additional Bedan texts, *Historia Abbatum* and *Epistola ad Ecgberctum*, and the anonymous *Historia Abbatum* (see below, Bibliography to Chapter 5).

The *Vita Oswini* is edited by James Raine in *Miscellanea biographica*, Publications of the Surtees Society 8 (London and Edinburgh, 1838), 1-17.

The largest single collection of saints' lives is the series that has been issued by the Bollandist Fathers over several centuries, the *Acta Sanctorum*, new ed. by Joannes Carnandet, 69 vols. (Paris, Brussels, and Rome, 1863). The journal *Analecta Bollandiana* 1- (1882-) is devoted to editions of lives and hagiographical studies. Two useful introductions to the genre are Hippolyte Delehaye, *The Legends of the Saints*, trans. by V. M. Crawford (London, 1907; rptd. with intro. by Richard J. Schoeck, Notre Dame, Ind., 1961), and René Aigrain, *L'Hagiographie—ses Sources, ses Méthodes, son Histoire* (Paris, 1953). The twelve-volume *Bibliotheca Sanctorum* (Rome, 1961-69; Index, 1970) (in Italian) contains brief discussions of saints with individual bibliographies. On English saints' lives, in general, in the Anglo-Saxon and Anglo-Norman periods, see Gransden, *Historical Writing in England* (cited above, Bibliography to the "Introduction"), 67-91 and 105-35. Professor Gransden does not discuss the *Vita Oswini*.

Chapter 4: Domestic Peace and Public Order in Anglo-Saxon Law

The basic edition of the Anglo-Saxon laws is by Felix Liebermann, *Die Gesetze der Angelsachsen*, 3 vols. (Halle, 1903-16). Editions with

English translations are *The Laws of the Earliest English Kings*, ed. and trans. by Frederick L. Attenborough (Cambridge, 1922); *The Laws of the Kings of England from Edmund to Henry I*, ed. and trans. by Agnes J. Robertson (Cambridge, 1925); and *Leges Henrici Primi*, ed. and trans. by L. J. Downer (Oxford, 1972). It must not be forgotten that much Anglo-Saxon law is embedded in charters and wills. All the charters are being newly edited in a series published under the aegis of the British Academy. The two that have appeared so far are Alistair Campbell (ed.), *Charters of Rochester*, and Peter H. Sawyer (ed.), *Charters of Burton Abbey*, Anglo-Saxon Charters 1 and 2 (London, 1973; Oxford, 1979). Many of the charters in Old English have been edited and translated by Agnes J. Robertson in *Anglo-Saxon Charters*, Cambridge Studies in English Legal History, 2nd ed. (Cambridge, 1956), and most of the vernacular wills by Dorothy Whitelock in *Anglo-Saxon Wills*, Cambridge Studies in English Legal History (Cambridge, 1930; rptd. New York, 1973). EHD I should also be consulted for translations of many of these documents. Other editions of legal documents in Latin and Old English are listed in Sawyer, *Anglo-Saxon Charters* (cited above, Bibliography to the "Introduction").

Many of the Germanic legal codes are edited in the folio and quarto volumes of the series Monumenta Germaniae historica, Leges 1-5 (Hanover, 1835-89) and 1- (Hanover, 1902-). The main manuscripts of the Icelandic code known as Grágás were edited in 1852, 1879, and 1883 and conveniently reprinted in three volumes by Odense University Press in 1974. A number of the codes have been translated into English: see *The Earliest Norwegian Laws: Being the Gulathing Law and the Frostathing Law*, trans. by Laurence M. Larson, Columbia University, Records of Civilization, Sources and Studies 20 (New York, 1935); *The Burgundian Code: Book of Constitutions or Law of Gundobad; Additional Enactments*, trans. by Katherine F. Drew (Philadelphia, 1949); *The Lombard Laws*, trans. with intro. by Katherine F. Drew (Philadelphia, 1973); *Laws of the Alamans and Bavarians*, trans. with intro. by Theodore J. Rivers (Philadelphia, 1977); and *Laws of Early Iceland: Grágás; The Codex Regius of Grágás with Material from Other Manuscripts*, trans. by Andrew Dennis, Peter Foote, and Richard Perkins, Vol. I, University of Manitoba Icelandic Studies 3 (Winnipeg, 1980).

Heinrich Brunner, *Deutsche Rechtsgeschichte*, 2 vols., 2nd ed. of Vol. I (Leipzig, 1906), and Vol. II by Claudius Freiherr von Schwerin (Leipzig, 1928) is a comparative study of Germanic law that has never been superseded. Anglo-Saxon law is placed in the context of the early law of other societies by Arthur S. Diamond, *Primitive Law, Past and Present* (London, 1971). On the role of law within Anglo-Saxon society, see Julius Goebel, *Felony and Misdemeanor: A Study in the History of*

English Criminal Procedure, Vol. 1, Commonwealth Fund (New York, 1937; rptd. with intro. by Edward Peters, Philadelphia, 1976).

There have been considerable advances in recent decades in knowledge about the authorship and historical contexts of the later Anglo-Saxon codes, many of which have been shown to be associated with Archbishop Wulfstan of York. Notable here is the work of Dorothy Whitelock: "Wulfstan and the So-Called Laws of Edward and Guthrum," *EHR* 56 (1941), 1-21; "Archbishop Wulfstan, Homilist and Statesman," *Transactions of the Royal Historical Society*, 4th ser., 24 (1942), 25-45; "Two Notes on Ælfric and Wulfstan," *Modern Language Review* 38 (1943), 122-26; "Wulfstan and the Laws of Cnut," *EHR* 63 (1948), 433-52; "Wulfstan's Authorship of Cnut's Laws," *EHR* 70 (1955), 72-85; "Wulfstan *Cantor* and Anglo-Saxon Law," *Nordica et Anglica: Studies in Honor of Stefán Einarsson*, ed. by Allan H. Orrick (The Hague, 1968), 83-92; see also Dorothy Bethurum, "Six Anonymous Old English Codes," *Journal of English and Germanic Philology* 49 (1950), 449-63, and A. G. Kennedy, "Cnut's Law Code of 1018," *ASE* 11 (1983), 57-81.

Thomas P. Oakley, *English Penitential Discipline and Anglo-Saxon Law in Their Joint Influence*, Studies in History, Economics and Public Law, edited by the Faculty of Political Science of Columbia University 107, No. 2 (New York, 1923) underlined the importance of the Anglo-Saxon penitentials for an understanding of Anglo-Saxon law. Allen J. Frantzen has made several contributions to the study of penitentials that are now essential reading: "The Tradition of Penitentials in Anglo-Saxon England," *ASE* 11 (1983), 23-56; "The Penitentials Attributed to Bede," *Speculum* 58 (1983), 573-95; and *The Literature of Penance in Anglo-Saxon England* (New Brunswick, N.J., 1983). Good modern editions of the Latin penitentials along the lines of Ludwig Bieler's *The Irish Penitentials*, Scriptores Latini Hiberniae 5 (Dublin, 1963) are needed to replace *Die Bussordnungen der abendländischen Kirche nebst einer rechtsgeschichtlichen Einleitung*, ed. by Friedrich W. H. Wasserschleben (Halle, 1851), in order to encourage further research. For English translations of some of the penitentials, see John T. McNeill and Helena M. Gamer, *Medieval Handbooks of Penance: A Translation of the Principal Libri Poenitentiales and Selections from Related Documents*, Columbia University, Records of Civilization, Sources and Studies 29 (New York, 1938).

Chapter 5: Two Early Anglo-Saxon Holy Men: Oswald and Cuthbert

Primary texts on the period A.D. 400-600 are exiguous, so there are few controls that can be placed on material derived from other sources. Three relevant texts are now conveniently available in the series Arthurian Period Sources, edited by John Morris: Gildas, *Ruin of Britain and Other Works*, ed. and trans. by Michael Winterbottom; Nennius, *British History and the Welsh Annals*, ed. and trans. by John Morris; and St. Patrick, *His Writings and Muirchu's Life*, ed. and trans. by Allan B. E. Hood, Arthurian Period Sources 7-9 (Chichester and London, 1978, 1980, and 1978).

Place-name evidence can supplement conventional written sources for the "Dark Age" period of English history, but its interpretation is complex and treacherous. The best guide to current studies in English place-names is the *Journal of the English Place-Name Society* 1- (1968/69-) and recent county volumes of the English Place-Name Society. See also *Place-Name Evidence for the Anglo-Saxon Invasion and Scandinavian Settlements: Eight Studies*, ed. by Kenneth Cameron, intro. by Margaret Gelling (Chichester and London, 1975), and Margaret Gelling, *Signposts to the Past: Place-Names and the History of England* (London, 1978).

Archaeological excavation is the main means whereby our knowledge of this period has expanded over the past half century. The archaeological evidence on Late Roman and Sub-Roman Britain is accumulating so rapidly that reassessments are likely to be needed every few years. Formulations of little more than a decade ago are proving to be inadequate or invalid. The journal *Medieval Archaeology* and *British Archaeological Abstracts* (cited above, Bibliography to the "Introduction") will enable the reader to keep abreast of the latest excavations and publications. A number of studies relevant to the period have appeared in British Archaeological Reports, notably Trevor Rowley (ed.), *Anglo-Saxon Settlement and the Landscape, Papers presented to a Symposium, Oxford 1973*, BAR 6 (Oxford, 1974); Lloyd Laing (ed.), *Studies in Celtic Survival*, BAR 37 (Oxford, 1977); and P. J. Casey (ed.), *The End of Roman Britain: Papers arising from a Conference, Durham 1978*, BAR 71 (Oxford, 1979). See also Richard Reece, "Town and Country: The End of Roman Britain," *World Archaeology* 12 (1980), 77-92. David M. Wilson (ed.), *The Archaeology of Anglo-Saxon England* (London, 1976; rptd. Cambridge, 1981) provides a general introduction to the archaeology of the whole Anglo-Saxon era.

For general histories of the period A.D. 400-600, see Robin G. Collingwood and John N. L. Myres, *Roman Britain and the English Settlements*, 2nd ed., Oxford History of England 1 (Oxford, 1937), which will remain a classic, but now should be supplemented by Peter Salway, *Roman Britain*, Oxford History of England 1A (Oxford, 1981); John Morris, *The Age of Arthur: A History of the British Isles from 350 to 650* (London, 1973; rptd. with corrections, in 3 vols., Chichester,

1977); Leslie Alcock, *Arthur's Britain: History and Archaeology, AD 367-634* (London, 1971); and Stephen Johnson, *Later Roman Britain*, Britain before the Conquest (London and Henley, 1980) (with useful maps and illustrations). None of these works would command general assent in matters of detail. (Morris's book, in particular, should be treated with circumspection.) They are useful for drawing attention to the primary written sources. On the difficulty of handling these, see David N. Dumville, "Sub-Roman Britain: History and Legend," *History* 62 (1977), 173-92. On the role of the Church in Roman and Sub-Roman Britain, see Charles Thomas, *Christianity in Roman Britain to AD 500* (London, 1981). This work has a very extensive bibliography and draws on the latest archaeological discoveries. Thomas's other book, *The Early Christian Archaeology of North Britain*, The Hunter Marshall Lectures (London, 1971), covering a slightly later period and having a narrower geographic focus, contains much valuable information, though Thomas himself has acknowledged that this presentation now needs revision. See also Maurice W. Barley and Richard P. C. Hanson (eds.), *Christianity in Britain, 300-700* (Leicester, 1968) and Susan M. Pearce (ed.), *The Early Church in Western Britain and Ireland: Studies presented to C. A. Ralegh Radford*, BAR 102 (Oxford, 1982).

Frederick R. Hoare (ed. and trans.), *The Western Fathers: Being the Lives of SS. Martin of Tours, Ambrose, Augustine of Hippo, Honoratus of Arles, and Germanus of Auxerre* (New York, 1954), and Athanasius, *Vita S. Antonia* in Roy J. Deferrari (ed.), *Early Christian Biographies*, The Fathers of the Church 15 (New York, 1952), 125-216 provide translations of some of the earliest saints' lives. For the text of Sulpicius Severus's *Life of Saint Martin*, see Sulpicius Severus, *Vie de Saint Martin*, ed. and trans. by Jacques Fontaine, 3 vols., Sources chrétiennes 131-35, Série des textes monastiques d'Occident 22-24 (Paris, 1967-69). The others are to be found in Jacques P. Migne (ed.), *Patrologiae cursus completus*, Series Latina, 221 vols. (Paris, 1844-80).

For the anonymous *Life of Saint Cuthbert* and Bede's prose *Life*, see Bertram Colgrave (ed. and trans.), *Two Lives of St. Cuthbert* (Cambridge, 1940); for Bede's metrical version, see Werner Jaager (ed.), *Bedas metrische Vita sancti Cuthberti*, Palaestra 198 (Leipzig, 1935). For other editions and translations of early Anglo-Saxon saints' lives, see the following: Bertram Colgrave (ed. and trans.), *The Earliest Life of Gregory the Great by an Anonymous Monk of Whitby* (Lawrence, Kansas, 1968); Bertram Colgrave (ed. and trans.), *The Life of Bishop Wilfrid by Eddius Stephanus* (Cambridge, 1927); *The Life of Ceolfrith*, by an anonymous monk of Monkwearmouth-Jarrow, in Charles Plummer (ed.), *Venerabilis Baedae Opera Historica* (Oxford, 1896), I, 388-404 (text) and II, 371-77 (notes), translated by Dorothy

Whitelock, in EHD I, 758-70; Bede's *The Lives of the Holy Abbots of Wearmouth and Jarrow*, in Plummer (ed.), *Venerabilis Baedae Opera Historica* I, 364-87 (text) and II, 355-70 (notes), translated by David H. Farmer in *The Age of Bede*, ed. by David H. Farmer, Penguin Classics, rptd. with revisions (Harmondsworth, 1983), 185-208; Bertram Colgrave (ed. and trans.), *Felix's Life of Saint Guthlac* (Cambridge, 1956); Æthelwulf, *De Abbatibus*, ed. and trans. by Alistair Campbell (Oxford, 1967); Charles W. Jones, *Saints' Lives and Chronicles in Early England: Together with the First English Translations of* The Oldest Life of Pope St. Gregory the Great *by a Monk of Whitby, and* The Life of St. Guthlac of Crowland *by Felix* (Ithaca, 1947); and Clinton Albertson, *Anglo-Saxon Saints and Heroes* (New York, 1967). Bertram Colgrave, "The Earliest Saints' Lives Written in England," *PBA* 44 (1958), 35-60, provides an introduction to these works in a brief compass.

Of Peter Brown's writings, perhaps the most important in the context of this essay are his collected papers of the last ten years published under the title *Society and the Holy in Late Antiquity* (Berkeley and Los Angeles, 1982); *The Making of Late Antiquity*, Carl Newell Jackson Lectures (Cambridge, Mass. and London, 1978); and *The Cult of Saints: Its Rise and Function in Late Christianity*, The Haskell Lectures on History of Religions, N.S. 2 (Chicago, 1981) (with a wide-ranging bibliography).

Chapter 6: The Celtic Church in Anglo-Saxon Times

A bibliography of material relevant to Celtic Britain is provided by Bonser, *An Anglo-Saxon and Celtic Bibliography* (cited above, Bibliography to the "Introduction"). Rachel Bromwich's *Medieval Celtic Literature: A Select Bibliography*, Toronto Medieval Bibliographies 5 (Toronto, 1974) also contains much useful material and is more up-to-date than Bonser. For introductions to the Irish sources, see James F. Kenney, *The Sources for the Early History of Ireland I: Ecclesiastical*, Columbia University Records of Civilization, Sources and Studies 11 (New York, 1929; rptd. Shannon, Ireland, 1968) and Kathleen Hughes, *Early Christian Ireland: Introduction to the Sources*, The Sources of History: Studies in the Uses of Historical Evidence (London, 1972); sources for Scotland are provided, with a commentary, by Alan Orr Anderson, *Early Sources of Scottish History A.D. 500 to 1286*, 2 vols. (London, 1922); for a discussion of the Welsh sources, see R. Ian Jack, *Medieval Wales*, The Sources of History: Studies in the Uses of Historical Evidence (London, 1972); for a survey of the sources and a history of early Brittany that draws on French scholarship, see Léon Fleuriot, *Les origines de la Bretagne* (Paris, 1980). Histories of various parts of the Celtic world include Gearóid MacNiocaill, *Ireland before the Vikings*, and Donncha Ó Corráin, *Ireland before the Normans*, The Gill History of Ireland 1 and 2 (London and Dublin, 1972); Wendy Davies, *Wales in the Early Middle Ages*, Studies in the Early History of Britain 1 (Leicester, 1982) and John E. Lloyd, *A History of Wales from the Earliest Times to the Edwardian Conquest*, 3rd ed., 2 vols. (London, 1939), which is somewhat dated but remains valuable; Nora K. Chadwick, "The Colonization of Brittany from Celtic Britain," *PBA* 51 (1965), 235-99, and *Early Brittany* (Cardiff, 1969). Kenneth Jackson moves beyond the analysis of Welsh, Cornish, and Breton phonology to make some important historical observations in his *Language and History in Early Britain* (Edinburgh, 1953). Edward A. Thompson, "Britonia," in Barley and Hanson (eds.), *Christianity in Britain*, 201-205 (cited above, Bibliography to Chapter 5), draws attention to Celtic colonization of northern Spain.

Pre-Christian Celtic religion is examined by Marie Louise Sjoestedt[-Jonval], *Gods and Heroes of the Celts*, trans. by Myles Dillon (London, 1949); Jan de Vries, *Keltische Religion*, Die Religionen der Menscheit 18 (Stuttgart, 1961), trans. by L. Jospin, *La Religion des Celtes* (Paris, 1963); Joseph Vendryès, "La Religion des Celtes," in "Mana": Introduction à l'Histoire des religions—2: *Les Religions de l'Europe ancienne* III (Paris, 1948), 239-320; Anne Ross, *Pagan Celtic Britain: Studies in Iconography and Tradition* (London, 1967); and Stuart Piggott, *The Druids* (London, 1968).

General studies of Celtic Christianity include Louis Gougaud, *Christianity in Celtic Lands: A History of the Churches of the Celts, Their Origin, Their Development, Influence and Mutual Relations*, trans. by Maud Joynt (London, 1932); Olivier Loyer, *Les Chrétientés celtiques*, Mythes et Religions (Paris, 1956); and John T. McNeill, *The Celtic Churches: A History A.D. 200 to 1200* (Chicago and London, 1974). On more specific topics, though covering a wide geographic area, is Nora K. Chadwick, et al., *Studies in the Early British Church* (Cambridge, 1958). Studies limited to specific areas are, for Britain, Leslie Hardinge, *The Celtic Church in Britain*, Church Historical Society Series 91 (London, 1972) (with a copious bibliography); for Ireland, Kathleen Hughes, *The Church in Early Irish Society* (London, 1966), Kathleen Hughes and Ann Hamlin, *The Modern Traveller to the Early Irish Church* (London, 1977), which describes the extant archaeological remains, and Denis L. T. Bethell, "The Originality of the Early Irish Church," *PRSAI* 111 (1981), 36-49; for Wales, Victor E. NashWilliams, *The Early Christian Monuments of Wales* (Cardiff, 1950) and Siân Victory, *The Celtic Church in Wales* (London, 1977); for Scotland, William Douglas Simpson, *The Celtic Church in Scotland: A*

Study of its Penetration Lines and Art Relationships, Aberdeen University Studies 111 (Aberdeen, 1935), a work that is dated in a number of respects and should be read in conjunction with Thomas's two books, *The Early Christian Archaeology of North Britain* and *Christianity in Roman Britain* (cited above, Bibliography to Chapter 5); and for Brittany, René Largillière, *Les Saints et l'Organisation chrétienne primitive dans l'Armorique bretonne* (Rennes, 1925). A provocative essay in the context of the preceding works is Kathleen Hughes, "The Celtic Church: Is This a Valid Concept?" *Cambridge Medieval Celtic Studies* 1 (1981), 1-20. Relations between the Celtic and Anglo-Saxon Church are discussed by Henry Mayr-Harting, *The Coming of Christianity to Anglo-Saxon England* (London, 1972).

For links between the Celtic world and Gaul, see Mayr-Harting, *The Coming of Christianity*, whose viewpoint has been adopted by Edward James, "Ireland and Western Gaul in the Merovingian Period," in *Ireland in Early Medieval Europe: Studies in Memory of Kathleen Hughes*, ed. by Dorothy Whitelock, Rosamond McKitterick and David Dumville (Cambridge, 1982), 362-86. They argue against the view that Ireland had intellectual links with Spain, propounded by Jocelyn N. Hillgarth in "The East, Visigothic Spain and the Irish," *Studia Patristica* 4, ed. by Frank L. Cross, Texte und Untersuchungen zur Geschichte der altchristlichen Literatur 79 (1961), 442-56, and "Visigothic Spain and Early Christian Ireland," *PRIA* 62 C (1961-62), 167-94 and 1 plate. Charles Thomas, "Imported Late-Roman Mediterranean Pottery in Ireland and Western Britain: Chronologies and Implications," *PRIA* 76 C (1976), 245-55, deals with the evidence of material links between Ireland and the Mediterranean. On early Eastern monasticism, see Derwas J. Chitty, *The Desert a City: An Introduction to the Study of Egyptian and Palestinian Monasticism under the Christian Empire* (Oxford, 1966). For Tintagel, see Courtenay A. Ralegh Radford, "Tintagel: The Castle and Celtic Monastery: Interim Report," *Antiquaries Journal* 15 (1935), 401-19, though one should be aware of the doubts expressed by Ian C. G. Burrow, "Tintagel—Some Problems," *Scottish Archaeological Forum* 5 (1973), 99-103, and Charles Thomas, "East and West: Tintagel, Mediterranean Imports and the Early Insular Church" in Pearce (ed.), *The Early Church in Western Britain and Ireland*, 17-34. Giles Constable provides a guide to publications in the field of monasticism in *Medieval Monasticism: A Select Bibliography*, Toronto Medieval Bibliographies 6 (Toronto, 1976). For monasticism in Ireland, see John Ryan, *Irish Monasticism: Origins and Early Development*, rptd. with new intro. and bibl. (Shannon, Ireland, 1972). On the phenomenon of *peregrinatio*, see Kathleen Hughes, "The Changing Theory and Practice of Irish Pilgrimage," *Journal of Ecclesiastical History* 11 (1960), 143-51. Collections of Penitentials are to be found in McNeill and Gamer, *Medieval Handbooks of Penance* and *The Irish Penitentials*, ed. by Bieler, and Frantzen discusses the Irish evidence in *The Literature of Penance* (all cited above, Bibliography to Chapter 4). Penance is put in its historical context by Robert C. Mortimer, *Origins of Private Penance in the Western Church* (Oxford, 1939). For Irish monastic learning, see especially Bernard Bischoff, "Turning Points in the History of Latin Exegesis in the Early Irish Church: A.D. 650-800," in Martin McNamara (ed.), *Biblical Studies: The Medieval Irish Contribution*, Proceedings of the Irish Biblical Association 1 (Dublin, 1976), 74-160. For the diffusion of Celtic learning on the Continent, see Max L. W. Laistner, *Thought and Letters in Western Europe A.D. 500 to 900*, rev. ed. (London, 1957).

Editions of Celtic saints' lives (as opposed to Romano-British saints such as Ninian and Patrick) include Arthur W. Wade-Evans (ed. and trans.), *Vitae Sanctorum Britanniae et Genealogiae*, University of Wales, Board of Celtic Studies, History and Law Series 9 (Cardiff, 1944); Charles Plummer (ed.), *Vitae Sanctorum Hiberniae*, 2 vols. (Oxford, 1910) (in Latin only); Henry Osborn Taylor (ed. and trans.), *The Life of St. Samson of Dol* (London, 1925); and Alan O. and Marjorie O. Anderson (eds. and trans.), *Adomnan's Life of St. Columba* (London, 1961). Canon Gilbert H. Doble published numerous studies of Cornish and Welsh saints, which included substantial translations from the *Vitae*; most of these have now been collected together as Donald Attwater (ed.), *The Saints of Cornwall*, 5 parts to date (Truro, 1960-), and Daniel S. Evans (ed.), *Lives of the Welsh Saints* (Cardiff, 1971).

A general study of the migration of the early saints is to be found in Nora K. Chadwick's Riddell Lectures, *The Age of the Saints in the Early Celtic Church* (London, 1961). For studies employing a topographical approach, see, in addition to the works by Doble cited above, the three books by Emrys G. Bowen, *The Settlements of the Celtic Saints in Wales*, 2nd ed. (Cardiff, 1956), *Saints, Seaways and Settlements in the Celtic Lands* (Cardiff, 1969), and *Britain and the Western Seaways*, Ancient Peoples and Places 80 (London, 1972); see also Joseph Loth, *Les Noms des Saints bretons* (Paris, 1910). A published detailed treatment of the place-names of Cornwall would promote further studies of this kind.

The basic primary texts on the Easter controversy are in *Bede's Ecclesiastical History* (cited above, Bibliography to Chapter 3) and the *Life of Wilfrid* (cited above, Bibliography to Chapter 5). For the earlier history of the controversy, see Paul Grosjean, "Recherches sur les débuts de la controverse Pascale chez les Celtes," *Analecta Bollandiana* 64 (1946), 200-44. On the different methods of chronological computation, see D. J. O'Connell, "Easter Cycles in the Early Irish

Church," *PRSAI* 66 (1936), 67-106 and 311 and cf. H. Morris, ibid., 67 (1937), 131-32, and Kenneth Harrison, *The Framework of Anglo-Saxon History to A.D. 900* (Cambridge, 1976), Chap. 3. More general treatments of the Synod of Whitby itself are to be found in Hardinge, *The Celtic Church*; Mayr-Harting, *The Coming of Christianity*; and Richard Abel, "The Council of Whitby: A Study in Early Anglo-Saxon Politics," *Journal of British Studies* 23 (1983), 1-25.

Chapter 7: Anglo-Saxon Use of the Apocryphal Gospel

Edgar Hennecke, *New Testament Apocrypha*, ed. by Wilhelm Schneemelcher, English translation ed. by Robert McL. Wilson, 2 vols. (Philadelphia, 1963-65) is the best collection in English of apocryphal texts, though Montague R. James's somewhat dated volume, *The Apocryphal New Testament* (Oxford, 1924), is still serviceable. For apocryphal texts in Old English, see Cameron, "A Plan," Section 8.5, 118-19 (cited above, Bibliography to the "Introduction"). Antonette di P. Healey has recently edited an Anglo-Saxon vernacular version of the *Visio Pauli* and provides references to studies of the Latin versions in *The Old English Vision of St. Paul*, Speculum Anniversary Monographs 2 (Cambridge, Mass., 1978). H. Kim (ed.), *The Gospel of Nicodemus*, Toronto Medieval Latin Texts 2 (Toronto, 1973) is a convenient edition of this Latin apocryphon. David Dumville has edited an Anglo-Saxon Harrowing of Hell text in Latin in an article that has wide-ranging implications for a number of fields of scholarship, "Liturgical Drama and Panegyric Responsory from the Eighth Century? A Re-examination of the Origin and Contents of the Ninth-Century Section of the Book of Cerne," *Journal of Theological Studies*, N.S. 23 (1972), 374-406. Some instances of the use of apocryphal texts in homiletic material are discussed by Milton McC. Gatch, "Two Uses of Apocrypha in Old English Homilies," *Church History* 33 (1964), 379-91. On the Old English homily, see Milton McC. Gatch, *Preaching and Theology in Anglo-Saxon England: Ælfric and Wulfstan* (Toronto and Buffalo, 1977) (with an extensive bibliography) and *The Old English Homily and Its Backgrounds*, ed. with intro. by Paul E. Szarmach and Bernard F. Huppé (Albany, N. Y., 1978).

In studying the apocryphal texts in England, one should also be aware of the Irish evidence. For a catalogue of these texts, see Martin McNamara, *The Apocrypha in the Irish Church* (Dublin, 1975), and for a discussion of them with many useful references, see David N. Dumville, "Biblical Apocrypha and the Early Irish: A Preliminary Investigation," *PRIA* 73 C (1973), 299-338.

The appearance of James H. Charlesworth (ed.), *The Old Testament Pseudigrapha*, Vol. 1: *Apocalyptic Literature and Testaments*

(Garden City, N.Y., 1983) should promote the re-examination of Old English homiletic and poetic material, especially for the influence of IV Ezra (Esdras), on which see Michael E. Stone, "The Metamorphosis of Ezra: Jewish Apocalypse and Medieval Vision," *Journal of Theological Studies*, N.S. 33 (1982), 1-18.

Chapter 8: The Image of the Worm: Some Literary Implications of Serpentine Decoration

The most comprehensive reference work on Anglo-Saxon art is Gerard Baldwin Brown, *The Arts in Early England*, 6 vols. in 7 (London, 1903-37). Charles R. Dodwell, *Anglo-Saxon Art: A New Perspective* (Ithaca, N.Y., 1982) discusses the literary evidence. The origins of interlace in art are treated by Nils F. Åborg in *The Occident and the Orient in the Art of the Seventh Century, Part 1, The British Isles*, Kungliga Vitterhets Historie och Antikvitets Akademiens Handlingar, Del 56.1 (Stockholm, 1943) and Rupert L. S. Bruce-Mitford in *Codex Lindisfarnensis*, ed. by Thomas D. Kendrick, et al. (Olten and Lausanne, 1956-60), II, 197-260. See also George Speake, *Anglo-Saxon Animal Art and Its Germanic Background* (Oxford, 1980); this work contains a number of detailed line drawings. For interlace in metalwork, see David M. Wilson, *Anglo-Saxon Ornamental Metalwork 700-1100*, Catalogue of Antiquities of the Later Saxon Period 1 (London, 1964) and David A. Hinton, *A Catalogue of the Anglo-Saxon Ornamental Metalwork 700-1100 in the Department of Antiquities, Ashmolean Museum* (Oxford, 1974). The discoveries at Sutton Hoo included some fine examples of serpentine decoration: see Rupert L. S. Bruce-Mitford, et al., *The Sutton Hoo Ship-Burial*, 3 vols. in 4 (London, 1975-83) and the brief British Museum guide by the same author, *The Sutton Hoo Ship-Burial: A Handbook*, 3rd ed. (London, 1978). For ivories, see John Beckwith, *Ivory Carvings in Early Medieval England* (London, 1972). On manuscripts, see Jonathan J. G. Alexander, *Insular Manuscripts 6th to the 9th Century*, and Elżbieta Temple, *Anglo-Saxon Manuscripts 900-1066*, A Survey of Manuscripts Illuminated in the British Isles 1 and 2 (London, 1978, 1976). See also David Talbot Rice, *English Art 871-1100*, Oxford History of English Art 2 (Oxford, 1952). The art of Ireland and of Scandinavia should not be overlooked in the examination of serpentine decoration; see Françoise Henry's three books, *Irish Art in the Early Christian Period to AD 800* (London, 1965), *Irish Art during the Viking Invasions, 800-1200 AD* (London, 1967), and *Irish Art in the Romanesque Period, 1020-1170 AD* (London, 1970), and David M. Wilson and Ole Klindt-Jensen, *Viking Art*, 2nd ed. (London, 1980). For facsimiles of the Book of Kells and the Book of

Durrow, see Ernest H. Alton, et al. (eds.), *Evangeliorum Quattuor Codex Cenannensis*, 3 vols. (Berne, 1950-51); *The Book of Kells: Reproductions from the Manuscript in Trinity College Dublin*, with a Study of the Manuscript by Françoise Henry (London, 1974); and Arthur A. Luce, et al. (eds.), *Evangeliorum Quattuor Codex Durmachensis*, 2 vols. (Olten, Lausanne, and Freiburg i. Br., 1960).

The standard collected edition of Old English poetry is contained in the series Anglo-Saxon Poetic Records, ed. by George Krapp and Elliott van K. Dobbie, 6 vols. (New York, 1931-53). Norman F. Blake (ed.), *The Phoenix*, Old and Middle English Texts (Manchester, 1964) is one of many editions of individual poems and groups of poems that have appeared more recently. The text is available in facsimile in *The Exeter Book of Old English Poetry*, introductory chapters by Raymond W. Chambers, Max Förster, and Robin Flower (Bradford, 1933), fols. 55v-65v.

The poem on which *The Phoenix* was based has been edited and translated with an introduction and commentary by Mary C. Fitzpatrick, *Lactanti De Ave Phoenice* (Philadelphia, 1933).

As Andrew Patenall points out in his essay, Roy F. Leslie in his "Analysis of Stylistic Devices and Effects in Anglo-Saxon Literature," *Stil- und Formprobleme in der Literatur*, ed. by Paul Böckmann (Heidelberg, 1959) used the term "interlace" in describing Old English poetic syntax and structure, and the value of the "interlace" metaphor in the analysis of a major Old English poem was shown in detail by John Leyerle in "The Interlace Structure of *Beowulf*," *University of Toronto Quarterly* 37 (1967), 1-17. The metaphor has also been found to be of value in the analysis of musical troping written in continental Europe; see Gérard Le Coat, "Anglo-Saxon Interlace Structure, Rhetoric and Musical Troping," *Gazette des Beaux-Arts*, 6th ser., 87 (1976), 1-6. For those wishing to examine literature using the "interlace" approach, a valuable tool is Jess B. Bessinger, Jr., *A Concordance to the Anglo-Saxon Poetic Records*, with an Index of Compounds by Michael W. Twomey (Ithaca, N. Y. and London, 1978).

For secondary analysis of Old English poetry, in general, see Greenfield and Robinson (eds.), *A Bibliography* (cited above, Bibliography to "Introduction"), and for a selection of studies relevant to *The Phoenix*, see Blake's edition (cited above). Recent studies that employ a variety of approaches toward the poem include: James E. Cross, "The Conception of the Old English *Phoenix*," in Robert P. Creed (ed.), *Old English Poetry: Fifteen Essays* (Providence, R. I., 1967), 129-52, which should be read in association with Bruce Mitchell, "The 'fuglas scyne' of *The Phoenix*, Line 591," in Robert B. Burlin and Edward B. Irving, Jr. (eds.), *Old English Studies in Honour of John C. Pope* (Toronto, 1974), 255-61; Daniel G. Calder, "The Vision of

Paradise: A Symbolic Reading of the Old English *Phoenix*," *ASE* 1 (1972), 167-81; John Bugge, "The Virgin Phoenix," *Mediaeval Studies* 38 (1976), 332-50; Robert D. Stevick, "Mathematical Proportions and Symbolism in *The Phoenix*," *Viator* 11 (1980), 95-121; and Carol F. Heffernan, "The Old English *Phoenix*: A Reconsideration," *Neuphilologische Mitteilungen* 83 (1982), 239-54.

Chapter 9: Slavery in Anglo-Saxon England

References to slaves are widely scattered through Anglo-Saxon sources, especially in the laws (for references, see the Bibliography to Chapter 4 above), charters, wills, manumission-documents, and Domesday Book. The vernacular documents are frequently more useful than those in Latin. Many of the Old English charters are in Robertson (ed.), *Anglo-Saxon Charters*, and most of the wills in Whitelock (ed.), *Anglo-Saxon Wills* (cited above, Bibliography to Chapter 4), to which must be added Dorothy Whitelock's important edition *The Will of Æthelgifu: A Tenth Century Anglo-Saxon Manuscript*, The Roxburghe Club (Oxford, 1968). There is no single edition of the manumission-documents. A number are translated in EHD I, 607-11, Nos. 140-50, where references to editions of the texts are given. The Record Commission's diplomatic text of 1783 and a translation of Domesday Book are appearing, county by county, in a series formerly under the general editorship of the late John Morris. There are also translations of the entries for many of the counties in the relevant Victoria County History volumes. A complete facsimile and translation are scheduled to appear in 1986.

The largest single treatment of Anglo-Saxon slavery in print remains John M. Kemble's Chapter 8 in his *The Saxons in England*, new ed., rev. by Walter de G. Birch (London, 1876), I, 185-227. There are brief discussions of slavery in Domesday Book in a number of the Victoria County Histories, and maps based on information derived from Domesday Book appear in the volumes of the Domesday Geography of England, ed. by Henry C. Darby (Cambridge, 1952-57). Howard B. Clarke discusses the Domesday evidence on slavery briefly in his review article "Domesday Slavery (Adjusted for Slaves)," *Midland History* 1 (1972), 37-46. Evidence on the slave trade is examined by Erik I. Bromberg, "Wales and the Mediaeval Slave Trade," *Speculum* 17 (1942), 263-69, and David A. E. Pelteret, "Slave Raiding and Slave Trading in Early England," *ASE* 9 (1981), 99-114; the trade is placed in a wider economic and political context (without, however, any detailed reference to the Anglo-Saxon evidence) in Alexander Murray, *Reason and Society in the Middle Ages* (Oxford, 1978), 39-55. Slavery in medieval continental Europe is treated by Charles Verlinden,

L'Esclavage dans l'Europe médiévale I: Péninsule Ibérique-France, and II: Italie, Colonies italiennes du Levant, Levant latin, Empire byzantin, Universiteit te Gent, Werken uitgaven door de Faculteit van de Letteren en Wijsbegeerte 119 and 162 (Bruges, 1955 and Ghent, 1977); the third volume on the Germanic world has yet to appear. Reasons for the decline of slavery in western Europe are suggested by Marc Bloch, "How and Why Ancient Slavery Came to an End," in Marc Bloch, *Slavery and Serfdom in the Middle Ages: Selected Essays by Marc Bloch*, trans. by William R. Beer (Berkeley, Los Angeles, and London, 1975), 1-31. On the same topic but with more ideology than evidence is Pierre Dockès's *Medieval Slavery and Liberation*, trans. by Arthur Goldhamer (Chicago, 1982). David B. Davis provides a synoptic view of the phenomenon of slavery in *The Problem of Slavery in Western Culture* (New York, 1966). An ambitious survey examining slavery in world history is Orlando Patterson's *Slavery and Social Death: A Comparative Study* (Cambridge, Mass., 1982). Moses I. Finley, *Ancient Slavery and Modern Ideology* (New York, 1980) should be consulted for the historiography of slavery; for bibliographies on the subject, see Joseph C. Miller, *Slavery: A Comparative Teaching Bibliography* (Waltham, Mass., 1977), and his annual supplements in *Slavery and Abolition* 1- (1980-).

The study of slavery must take into consideration the structure of the rest of the society. Works that deal in general with the structure of Anglo-Saxon society at different periods and/or in various regions include Frederick Seebohm, *The English Village Community*, 4th ed. (London, 1890); Frederic W. Maitland, *Domesday Book and Beyond* (Cambridge, 1897; rptd. with new pagination, intro. by Edward Miller, London, 1960); Hector M. Chadwick, *Studies on Anglo-Saxon Institutions* (Cambridge, 1905; rptd. New York, 1963); Paul Vinogradoff, *English Society in the Eleventh Century: Essays in English Mediaeval History* (Oxford, 1908); Frank M. Stenton, *Types of Manorial Structure in the Northern Danelaw*, Oxford Studies in Social and Legal History 2 (Oxford, 1910), 3-96; David C. Douglas, *The Social Structure of Medieval East Anglia*, Oxford Studies in Social and Legal History 9 (Oxford, 1927); Eric John, "English Feudalism and the Structure of Anglo-Saxon Society," in *Orbis Britanniae and Other Studies*, Studies in Early English History 4 (Leicester, 1966), 128-53; Herbert P. R. Finberg, "Anglo-Saxon England to 1042," in Herbert P. R. Finberg (ed.), *The Agrarian History of England and Wales I. ii: AD 43-1042* (Cambridge, 1972), 383-525; and G. Tugène, "Remarques sur les classes sociales en Angleterre du 7e au 11e siècle," *Littérature et Politique: Actes du Congrès de la Société des Anglicistes de l'Enseignement Supérieur 1974* (Paris, 1977), 15-46.

Works on specific social classes include: Frank M. Stenton, "The Free Peasantry of the Northern Danelaw," *Bulletin de la Société royale des Lettres de Lund* (1925-26), 73-185 (rptd. separately, Oxford, 1969); Reginald Lennard, "The Economic Position of the Domesday *Villani*," *Economic Journal* 56 (1946), 244-64; Reginald Lennard, "The Economic Position of the Domesday Sokemen," ibid. 57 (1947), 179-95; Reginald Lennard, "The Economic Position of the Bordars and Cottars of Domesday Book," ibid. 61 (1951), 342-71; K. P. Witney, "The Economic Position of Husbandmen at the Time of Domesday Book: A Kentish Perspective," *Economic History Review*, 2nd ser., 37 (1984), 23-34; Henry R. Loyn, "Gesiths and Thegns in Anglo-Saxon England from the Seventh to the Tenth Century," *EHR* 70 (1955), 529-49; Frank M. Stenton, "The Thriving of the Anglo-Saxon Ceorl," in Doris M. Stenton (ed.), *Preparatory to Anglo-Saxon England: Being the Collected Papers of Frank Merry Stenton* (Oxford, 1970), 383-93; Anne K. G. Kristensen, "Danelaw Institutions and Danish Society in the Viking Age: *Sochemanni, Liberi Homines* and *Königsfreie*," *Medieval Scandinavia* 8 (1975), 27-85; Peter H. Sawyer and Ian N. Wood (eds.), *Early Medieval Kingship* (Leeds, 1977) (with an extensive bibliography); David A. E. Pelteret, "The *Coliberti* of Domesday Book," *Studies in Medieval Culture* 12 (1978), 43-54; David N. Dumville, "The Ætheling: A Study in Anglo-Saxon Constitutional History," *ASE* 8 (1979), 1-33; Pauline Stafford, "The King's Wife in Wessex 800-1066," *Past and Present* 91 (May 1981), 3-27; and Pauline Stafford, *Queens, Concubines, and Dowagers: The King's Wife in the Early Middle Ages* (Athens, Ga., 1983).

Chapter 10: Germanic Warrior Terms in Old Saxon

Lexicostatistics is a fairly new branch of linguistic study. For brief introductions to the subject, see Winfred P. Lehmann, *Historical Linguistics: An Introduction*, 2nd ed. (New York, 1973), 104-09; Raimo Anttila, *An Introduction to Historical and Comparative Linguistics* (New York and London, 1972), 395-98; Theodora Bynon, *Historical Linguistics* (Cambridge, London, New York, Melbourne, 1977), 266-72, and in more detail, Charles Muller, *Principes et Méthodes de Statistique lexicale* (Paris, 1977). Illustrating the principles of lexicostatistics in practice are the papers delivered at two conferences devoted to the subject: Isidore Dyen (ed.), *Lexicostatistics in Genetic Linguistics: Proceedings of the Yale Conference, Yale University, April 3-4, 1971*, Janua Linguarum, Series Maior 69 (The Hague and Paris, 1973) and Isidore Dyen and Guy Jucquois (eds.), *Lexicostatistics in Genetic Linguistics II: Proceedings of the Montreal Conference, Centre de Recherches Mathématiques, Université de Montréal, May 19-20, 1973*, Cahiers de l'Institut de Linguistique de Louvain 3, 5-6

(1975-76); see also Isidore Dyen, *Linguistic Subgrouping and Lexicostatistics* (The Hague and Paris, 1975), a collection of papers drawing mainly on the Austronesian languages, but also containing some theoretical discussions. The methodology is not without its critics: see, for example, the books by Lehmann and Anttila cited above and Hendrik Birnbaum, *Linguistic Reconstruction: Its Potentials and Limitations in New Perspective*, Journal of Indo-European Studies, Monograph 2 (Washington, D.C., n.d. [1977]), 17 and n. 13. For refutation of the criticisms, see the works cited in the Notes to Chapter 10 in this volume.

Indispensable for any statistical analysis of Old English is Richard L. Venezky and Antonette di P. Healey, *A Microfiche Concordance to Old English*, Dictionary of Old English Project (University of Toronto and University of Delaware, 1980). Until the Toronto Dictionary of Old English is published the standard dictionary will remain Joseph Bosworth, *An Anglo-Saxon Dictionary*, ed. by Thomas Northcote Toller (Oxford, 1898) with a *Supplement* by Thomas Northcote Toller (Oxford, 1921) and *Enlarged Addenda and Corrigenda to the Supplement* by Alistair Campbell (Oxford, 1972).

Old Saxon is likely to be known to far fewer readers of this book than Old English. For an introduction to the language and the few pieces of literature that are extant, see Thomas L. Markey, *A North Sea Germanic Reader* (Munich, 1976). The only major surviving monument in Old Saxon is the *Heliand*; for an edition, see *Heliand und Genesis*, ed. by Otto Behaghel, 8th ed., rev. by Walther Mitzka, Altdeutsche Textbibliothek 4 (Tübingen, 1965). For other texts, see Johan H. Gallée, *Altsächsische Sprachdenkmäler* (Leiden, 1894). For lexicostatistical purposes, one should consult Edward H. Sehrt, *Vollständiges Wörterbuch zum Heliand und zur altsächsischen Genesis*, 2nd ed., Hesperia, Schriften zur germanischen Philologie 14 (Göttingen, 1966), supplemented by Ferdinand Holthausen, *Altsächsisches Wörterbuch*, 2nd ed., Niederdeutsche Studien 1 (Cologne and Graz, 1967) and Samuel Berr, *An Etymological Glossary to the Old Saxon Heliand*, European University Papers, Series I, German Language and Literature 33 (Berne and Frankfurt, 1971).

Index

abbaye-évêché, 79-80
Abbo of St. Germain-des-Prés, 6 n. 20
Acta Silvestri, 65
Acts of Pilate, 95
Adamnán, abbot of Iona, 89
Advent Lyrics, 34
Ældred, archbishop of York, 21
Ælfric, *Colloquy*, 123, 124
Ælfric, abbot of Eynsham, 30, 33, 34, 93-94, 100, 102, 104
Æthelgifu, tenth-century testatrix, 123, 125
Æthelwine, reeve of Oswy, 38
Aesop's Fables, 2, 25
Aetius, 71
Agilbert, bishop of Wessex, 88
Aidan, bishop of Lindisfarne, 39, 45, 67, 68, 72, 90-91
Ailbe of Emly (Imlech), 80
Alban, St., 63, 64
Albertson, Clinton, 66
Alcuin of York, 28, 44 n. 11, 92
Aldhelm, abbot of Malmesbury, 89, 93
Alexander's Letter to Aristotle, Old English, 34
Alfred, king of Wessex, 30-35 *passim*, 129
Alfrith, king of Deira and son of Oswy, king of Bernicia, 88
alliterative verse, 145
Ambrosius Aurelianus, 71
Anatolius of Laodicaea, bishop, 86, 88

Anderson, George K., 29, 31, 32
Anglians, 120
Anglo-Saxon Chronicle, 15, 29, 30, 34, 40
anmchara, 81, 92
Annales Cambriae, 89
Anselm, archbishop of Canterbury, 90
Apocalypse of St. John, 94
Apocalypse of Thomas, 94, 100, 104
Apostles' Creed, 95, 96
archaeology, 78, 158
Ardagh Chalice, 91
art, Anglo-Saxon, 106-107, 114-15, 165; Irish, 165-66; Scandinavian, 165
Arthur, legendary king of Britain, 35, 79
Athelstan, king of Wessex, 89, 122
Augustine of Canterbury, St., 5, 72, 87, 120, 128

Badon Hill, battle of, 71
Baduthegn, 69-70, 71
Bangor, Ireland, 87
baptism, 86
Bardney, Abbey of, 68
Bartimaeus, 147, 148
Bateson, Mary, 54
Battle of Maldon, The, 30, 34, 41
Bayeux, Normandy, 20 pl. 3 and n. 23; cathedral, 14 n. 11; Tapestry, 2, 7, 11-25 *passim*, 153-54
Bede, 5, 30, 33, 39, 40, 42, 43, 64 and n. 4, 73, 75, 91, 128; *Commentary*

on *St. Luke's Gospel*, 148; *Ecclesiastical History*, 37, 38, 39, 41, 67-71 *passim*, 73, 99, 120, 155; Leningrad and Moore MSS of *Ecclesiastical History*, 32; *Lives of Saint Cuthbert* (prose and verse), 66, 67, 70; *Martyrologium*, 73
Benedict of Nursia, St., 78, 79, 80
Benedict X, Pope, 21 n. 25
Benedictine monastic reform, 32, 35
Benedictine Rule, 90
Beowulf, 1, 3, 29, 31, 33, 34, 38, 40-48 *passim*, 65, 106, 155
Bernicia, 37, 67, 88
Bertha, wife of King Æthelberht of Kent, 72
Bible, 36
biblical translations, Old English, 34, 36
bibliography, Anglo-Saxon, 152, 153; Celtic Britain, 160
Black Book of Peterborough, 133
Blackstone, Sir William, 54
Blake, Norman F., 108, 112
Blickling Homily 7, 100-101
Bobbio, monastery of, 92
Boethius, Old English, 30
Bonneville-sur-Touques, 19-20
Book of Cerne, 92, 96
Book of Durrow, 91, 106-107, 108, 112
Book of Kells, 91, 107, 111, 112
boors, 129
Bosham, Sussex, 2, 17
Bothelm, 67
bounds, Old English, 34
Bracton, 50, 52, 54, 61
Brioc, St., 84
Bristol Cathedral, 102, 104
Britain, Celtic, 160; A.D. 400-600, 71, 73, 77, 118-19, 140 n. 7, 157-59; Roman, 39, 118
Brittany, 6, 17, 78, 82, 84, 85, 86, 89-90, 91, 160-61
Britton, 52, 60
Brown, Peter, 5, 65 n. 6, 66 n. 8, 75, 160
Brunner, Heinrich, 50, 52, 59
Buck, C. D., *Dictionary of Selected Synonyms* . . . , 137-38
Budoc, St., 84-85
burgbryce, 58
butsecarl, 8 n. 31
Byrhtnoth, 40
Byrhtwold, 40

Cadoc, St., 84
Cædmon MS, 30
Cædmon's Hymn, 32, 33
Cædwalla, king of Wessex, 41, 67, 73
Canterbury, 72, 73; Cathedral of Sts. Peter and Paul, 72; St. Martin's Church, 64 n. 4, 72, 73 n. 21
Carannog, St., 84
Carthach of Lismore, 80
Catterick, 38
Celts, 5, 121
Ceolfrith, abbot of Wearmouth, 86
ceorl, 8 n. 31
Cerne Abbas, Dorset, monastery of, 92
chanson-de-geste, 25
Chaplais, Pierre, 128
Charlemagne, emperor and king of the Franks, 92, 146
charms, Old English, 34, 36, 94, 103-104
charters, 128, 129; Anglo-Saxon, 34, 156, 157; Old English, 34
Chichester, Sussex, 17
Chi-Rho, 107
chi-square table and test, 139, 140, 144, 145, 146
Christ and Satan, 101, 104
Christ II, 101, 104
Christianity, Celtic, 161-62; Roman, 78; Romano-British, 5
Church, Anglo-Saxon, 6, 63, 64, 93, 128; British, 64, 71, 90; Celtic, 5-6, 64, 73, 77-92 *passim*; Columban, 87; Roman, 78, 79, 85-86, 87, 130, 159; Romano-British, 64 n. 4, 73, 159; Welsh, 71
Cicero, Marcus Tullius, 54
Clonmacnois, Offaly, monastery of, 91
Colgrave, Bertram, 65, 66
Colman, bishop of Lindisfarne, 88-89
Columba of Iona, St., 80, 88, 89
Columban, St., 81, 90, 91
Comgall of Bangor, St., 80
computus, Old English, 34
Conan, duke of Brittany, 13, 16, 17, 18 pl. 1, 19 pl. 2
confession, 81, 92
Constantine the Great, emperor of Rome, 57, 130
Cornwall, 6, 77, 78, 82, 84, 85, 89, 121, 122
Couesnon River, Normandy, 17

Index 173

Culdees, 80, 90
Cumbran, 40
Cuthbert, St., 64-75 *passim*
Cyneheard, brother of Sygebryht, king of Wessex, 40
Cynewulf, 101
Cynewulf, king of Wessex, 40

Dalbey, Marcia, 100
David, St., 80, 87
dedications, Old English, 34
Deira, 37, 88
demography, 8 and n. 29
Denisesburn, 67
Denmark, 118
Descent into Hell, 101, 104
Devon, 89
dictionaries, Old English, 170
Dictionary of Old English, Toronto, 27
Dinan, Brittany, 18, 19 pl. 2
Diocletian, emperor of Rome, 39
discþegn, 8 n. 31
Dismas, legendary name of thief crucified with Christ, 97
Dol, Brittany, 17-18 and pl. 1
Domesday Book, 8 n. 27, 122, 123, 130, 132-33, 167
Dover, 20 n. 22
dragons, 42, 44, 47
drama, liturgical, 96
Dream of the Rood, The, 34, 102, 104, 115
dreng, 8 n. 31
Dumézil, Georges, 3-4, 45
Durham, England, 126
Durham Hymnal, 95-96

Eadmer, *Historia Novorum in Anglia*, 12 n. 4, 14, 16
Ealdwine of Winchcombe, 41
Eanflæd, wife of Oswy, king of Bernicia, and daughter of Edwin, king of Deira, 87, 88
Eanfrith, uncle of King Oswine, 39
East Anglia, 71 and n. 15, 90
East Saxons, 39
Easter controversy, 85-86, 87-90, 163-64
Echternach Gospels, 111
Eddius Stephanus, 88
Edith, wife of Edward the Confessor, 15
Edward the Confessor, king of England, 13, 14, 16, 17, 19 n. 22, 21, 22 pl. 5, 33
Edwin, king of Northumbria, 37, 67
Egbert, a monk, 89
Egbert, king of Wessex, 89
Elfodd, bishop of Gwynedd, 89
Elmet, 77
enslavement, 119-22, 126
epic, Old English, 41
episcopacy, 79-80
Essex, 122, 130
Ethelfrid, brother-in-law of Edwin, king of Northumbria, and father of Oswald, king of Northumbria, 67
Eu, castle of, 17
Eustace II, count of Boulogne, 13, 24
Evagrius, *Life of St. Antony*, 65
Evesham, abbey of, 131
Exeter Book, 34, 101, 106, 108, 115

færfreoh, 129
Farne, Isle of, 69
Felix of Burgundy, St., 90
Finn, 40
Finnian of Clonard, 81
Flodoald, a trader, 125
Florence of Worcester, 21
France, 118
Franks, 72
Franks Casket, 7 n. 24
freedom, 130-31
freemen, 127, 129-30
Fursa, founder of monastery at Yarmouth, 90

Gaius, 58 n. 19
Gallican rite, 87
Gaul, 5, 66, 78, 79, 88, 162
Geoffrey of Anjou, 18
George, St., 42
Geraint, king of Cornwall, 89
Germanic languages, 138 and n. 6
Germanus of Auxerre, St., 64, 71
Germany, 118
Gestas, legendary name of thief crucified with Christ, 97
Gildas, 71, 73; *De excidio Britanniae*, 119, 121
Gilling, Deira, 38, 39, 87
glosses and glossaries, Old English, 32
glottochronology, 136-37
Godwin, earl of Wessex, 17, 21 n. 25
Goldsmith, Margaret, 46

Gospel of Nicodemus, 94-102 *passim*
Gospel of Pseudo-Matthew, 6 n. 19, 94, 102-103
gospel poetry, Old English, 144-45, 146; Old Saxon, 142, 144, 146
gospel prose, Old English, 142-43, 144, 145
gospels, 135, 142; West-Saxon, 30, 98
Great Bedwyn, Wiltshire, 129
Greenfield, Stanley B., 27-28, 31, 35
Gregory I, the Great, Pope, 79, 87, 120; *Dialogues*, 65, 66; *Pastoral Care*, Old English, 31
Gregory of Tours, bishop, 66 n. 8, 68 n. 9, 69, 70, 72 and n. 17, 73, 74, 75
grith, 58
Guthlac, St., 55
Guthlac poems, 115
Guy of Amiens, 15 n. 15, 24; *Carmen de Hastingae proelio*, 14 n. 11, 15, 16, 19, 23, 24
Guy of Ponthieu, 17
Gyrth, earl of East Anglia, son of Earl Godwine, 13

Hæthcyn, 40
hairstyles, 23 n. 27
Hakon, hostage of William, duke of Normandy, 17
hamsocn, 4-5, 50-61 *passim*; see also *Heimsuchung*, *hemsoken*, *husfrithbrøthe*
haraidum, 52
Harold II, king of England, son of Earl Godwine, 2, 12-24 *passim*
Harrowing of Hell, 6, 95-104 *passim*
Hart, H. L. A., 57
Hastings, 13, 23; battle of, 12, 13, 15, 29, 154
Hatfield Chase, Yorkshire, 67
Hefenfelth, 67
Heimsuchung, 50 n. 1, 51, 55, 58-59; see also *hamsocn*, *hemsoken*, *husfrithbrøthe*
Heliand, 135, 136, 141, 144, 146, 148, 150
hemsoken, 50 n. 1; see also *hamsocn*, *Heimsuchung*, *husfrithbrøthe*
Hengest and Horsa, 32
here, 56
Heremod, 47
Hexham, 67
Hild, abbess of Whitby, 38

historical texts, Anglo-Saxon, 152
hloth, 56
Hnæf, 40
Holdsworth, William S., 50-51, 54, 60
Holland, 118
holy men, 5, 63-75 *passim*
homilies, Old English, 34, 36, 96, 99-101, 104, 164
Hrothgar, 46, 47
Humber River, 71 n. 15
Hunwald, thane of Tondhere, 38, 39
husbryce, 56, 59
husfrithbrøthe, 50 n. 1, 52; see also *hamsocn*, *Heimsuchung*, *hemsoken*
hymns, Old English, 34

Iceland, 81 n. 26
Illtud, abbot of Llantwit Major, St., 85, 91
Imma, Mercian thegn, 120
Indo-European languages, 138 and n. 6
Ine, king of Wessex, 56
Ingeld, 28, 35, 40
Ingulph of Croyland, 21
Innisbofin, Ireland, monastery of, 89
interlace, 106-16 *passim*, 165, 166
Iona, Scotland, 81, 88, 89, 91
Ireland, 68, 77, 78, 80, 85, 90, 91, 92, 160, 161, 165-66
Italy, 78, 88

Jesus Christ, passion and crucifixion of, 147, 149-50
John, St., 88
John, king of England, 52
John the Baptist, 97, 101
Joseph of Arimathea, 97, 98
journals, Anglo-Saxon, 153

Karinus, 97
Ker, Neil R., 32; *Catalogue of Manuscripts Containing Anglo-Saxon*, 31
kingship, concept of, 127 and n. 45

Lactantius, *De ave phoenice*, 108, 111, 112
Lanfranc, archbishop of Canterbury, 21 n. 25, 90
language, Old English, 152
lapidary, Old English, 34
Latin, 35
laws, Alemannic, 56, 58 n. 19; Anglo-

Index 175

Saxon, 3, 4, 30, 36, 130, 155-57; Anglo-Warnian, 59; Bavarian, 52 55, 59; *Code Concerning the Blood Feud*, 51, 56; Danish, 52, 55; *De Institutis Lundonie*, 51; *Edictus Rothari*, 61; Frankish, 55; Frisian, 59; Germanic, 156; *Grant Lai*, 52; Kentish, 123; Laws of Alfred, 51, 56, 58 n. 18; Laws of Cnut, 51, 56, 59; Laws of Edmund, 51, 59; Laws of Ine, 56, 57; *Leges Henrici Primi*, 51, 52, 59; *Lex Julia de vi publica*, 57; *Lex Ribuaria*, 52, 56; *Lex Salica*, 55, 56, 57; Lombard, 52, 55; Old English, 34; Roman, 57, 130; Salic, 56, 57; Scottish, 53, 60; Spanish, 58 n. 18; tribal, 124, 127, 128, 132, 133; *Weistümer*, 54 n. 13; West-Saxon, 120

legal documents, Anglo-Saxon, 152
Legation of Nathan the Jew, 103
Legend of St. Veronica, 103, 104
Leofwine, 13
Leslie, Roy, 105-106
Leuticus (Leucius), 97
lexicostatistics, 9, 136 and n. 2, 169-70
Leyerle, John, 43, 45, 46, 47, 106
Liebermann, Felix, 51, 52
Life of St. Martin, 65, 73
Life of St. Swithun, 121, 125, 131
Lincolnshire, 71 and n. 15
Lindisfarne, 65; monastery of, 67, 69, 88, 89, 91
Lindisfarne Gospels, 7 n. 23, 91, 107, 112
literature, Anglo-Latin, 35, 152; apocryphal, 3, 6, 93-104, 164-65; Hiberno-Latin, 3; homiletic, 3 n. 7; Old English, 27-35 *passim*, 152-53, 154, 166-67; patristic, 3; runic, 29
liturgical poems, Old English, 34
liturgy, 86-87
Lives of St. Cuthbert, 65, 67
Longinus, 97
Louis the Pious, Emperor, and king of the Franks, 89, 146
Luxeuil, Burgundy, monastery of, 81, 92

Magh Lene, Synod of, 87
Magoun, Francis Peabody, Jr., 33
Maildubh, founder of Malmesbury, 90
Maine, Sir Henry, 50, 60
Maitland, Frederic W., 50, 52

Malmesbury, Wiltshire, 90
manumissio in ecclesia, 130
manumission and manumission-documents, 125, 126, 129, 130, 131
manuscripts, Anglo-Saxon, 165; Latin, 151; Old English, 31-32, 152; texts: Cambridge: Corpus Christi College (CCC) 41, 99, 100; CCC 303, 100; CCC 367, 102; University Library Ii. 2. 11, 96, 98, 99, 103; London, BL: Cotton Julius A.x, 41 and n. 5; Cotton Vespasian D.xiv, 98-99, 103; Cotton Vitellius A.xv, Part I, 44, 96-97; Oxford, Bodleian Library: Bodley 343, 102; Hatton 114, 102; Junius 11, 101; Junius 121, 101
maps, 152
Marseilles, 120
Martin of Tours, St., 64 n. 4, 66, 70-75 *passim*; feast of, 73
Mathilde, wife of William I, 15 n. 15
Matmonoc, abbot of Landévennec, 89
maxims, Old English, 34, 36
medical texts, Old English, 34, 36
medicine, Anglo-Saxon, 94, 103-104
Mellitus, bishop of London, 39
Melrose Abbey, 69
Mercians, 68
metre, 33
Metres of Boethius, 34
Meugan, St., 84
Middle English, 29
Middlesex, 122
Mirror of Justices, 52
mnemonics, Old English, 34
monasticism, monasteries and monks, Anglo-Saxon, 128, 131; Benedictine, 79; Celtic, 78-92 *passim*, 162; Coptic, 79; Egyptian, 87; Irish, 79
Monkwearmouth and Jarrow, monasteries of, 41
Mont-Saint-Michel, 17, 18
mundbryce, 51

Nathan the Jew, 103
Nechtan IV, king of Picts, 89
Nicaea, Council of, 86
Nicene Creed, 92
Ninian, St., 64 n. 4, 71 and n. 16, 78
Norman Conquest, 28, 35, 41, 49, 77, 132
Normandy, 13, 16, 17, 19, 23, 25

Normans, 154
North Africa, 79
Northumbria, 65, 69, 71, 90
notes, Old English, 35
numismatics, Anglo-Saxon, 153

Odo, bishop of Bayeux, 13, 14 n. 11, 18, 20 and n. 23, 23
Offa, king of Mercia, 128
Old Church Slavonic, 138, 139
Old English language and literature, 9, 136-45 *passim*, 152-53
Old French, 138, 139
Old High German, 138, 139
Old Irish, 138, 139
Old Norse, 138, 139
Old Saxon language and literature, 9, 135-50 *passim*, 170
Old Testament, Old English translations of, 30
Ongentheow, 40
oral traditions, 33
Ordericus Vitalis, 14, 15 n. 16
ordination, clerical, 86
Orosius, Old English translation of, 30
Osric, father of King Oswine, 37, 39, 41
Oswald, king of Northumbria, 66-75 *passim*, 90
Oswestry, Shropshire, 68
Oswine, king of Deira, 37, 39-46 *passim*
Oswy, king of Northumbria, 37, 39, 42, 45, 87, 88

Parker, Matthew, archbishop of Canterbury, 30
Patrick, St., 78
patrocinium, 74-75, cf. 70-71
Paul Aurelian, St., 84
Pedrog, St., 84
Pelagius, 63, 71
penance and penitentials, 80-81, 92, 162-63; Anglo-Saxon, 157; Old English, 34
Penda, king of the Mercians, 40, 67, 68
peregrinatio and *peregrini*, 81, 162
Pershore, abbey of, 131
Peter, St., 86, 88
Pevensey, Sussex, 13, 23
Phoenix, The, 8, 107-16 *passim*, 166-67

Picts, 64, 67, 71, 78
Pilate, Pontius, 95, 96-97, 98
place-names, 158; derived from saints' names, 81-85, 163
Ponthieu, county of, 13
poetry, Old English, 101, 104, 115, 166
Possidius, 65
pottery, 79
Procula, legendary wife of Pontius Pilate, 97
prognostics, Old English, 34
prose, Old English, 34
Psalter, Old English, 30

Rectitudines singularum personarum, 126
Reinfrid, Norman knight and subsequently monk, 41
relics, 69
religion, Celtic, 161; Germanic, 147-49
Rennes, county of, 18
riddles, Old English, 34, 106
Riwallon, lord of Dol, 17, 18
Robert de Torigny, 15 n. 16
Robert fitzWimarch, 16, 24
Robert of Jumièges, archbishop of Canterbury, 21 n. 25
Romano-British, 77
Rome and the Roman Empire, 5, 6, 38, 63-64, 78, 79, 117, 118
Rouen, Normandy, 17
rules for monks and canons, Old English, 34, 35
runes, 29, 32
Ruthwell Cross, 7 n. 24, 103, 104

saints' lives, 3, 34, 42, 66, 155, 159-60; Celtic, 163
Saint-Vigor, Bayeux, abbey of, 18
Samson, St., 85, 91
Saxons, 64
Scellig Michael, Ireland, 79
Scotland, 51, 54, 60, 72, 77, 78, 160, 161-62
Scots, 64, 67
scriptoria, 32, 35
Seafarer, The, 115
Sehrt, E. H., *Heliand-Wörterbuch*, 142
serfs, 129
Severn River, 87
Sigemund, 47
Sigurd, 42
Simon Magus, 86

Index

Sisam, Kenneth, 29
slave, etymology of the word, 122
slave trade, 120-21
slavery, 8, 117-33 *passim*, 167-68; Anglo-Saxon, 167
social structure, Anglo-Saxon, 8, 168-69
social terminology, 8, 132-33
Soliloquies of St. Augustine, 33
Solomon and Saturn, Prose, 126
Spain, 92, 118, 162
Stamford Bridge, Lincolnshire, battle of, 24
Stigand, archbishop of Canterbury, 2, 13, 16, 21 and n. 25
Stowe Missal, 92
Streonæshealh, 87
Sulpicius Severus, *Dialogues*, 73; *Life of St. Martin*, 65, 72 n. 17, 73
Sutton Hoo, 1, 165
Swadesh list, 137, 138-40
Sweet, Henry, 31; *Anglo-Saxon Reader*, 29
Sygebryht, king of Wessex, 40
syntax, Old English, 105-106, 114-15

theow, 132
Thomas Aquinas, St., 44
Tintagel, Cornwall, 79 and n. 13, 162
Titus, king of Libya, 103
Todd, Malcolm, 57
Tondhere, soldier of Oswine, king of Deira, 38
tonsure, monastic, 86, 90
Tostig, earl of Northumbria, son of Earl Godwine, 41
Tours, 71
Transvaal, South Africa, 57
Tréguier, Brittany, 79
tribe, concept of, 127 and n. 44

Venezky, Richard, and Healey, Antonette, *Concordance*, 142
Vercelli Book, 102-103
Veronica, St., 97, 103-104
Vespasianus, 103
Vikings, 77, 121, 122, 128
Vindicta Salvatoris, 94, 103
Virtutes, 68 n. 10

Vision of St. Paul, 93, 94
Vita Aedwardi regis, 15, 24
Vita Oswini, 3, 41, 42, 44, 45, 46, 155
Vortigern, 64

Wace, Robert, 14
Wales, 77, 78, 80, 81, 82, 84, 89, 91, 160, 161
Wanderer, The, 106, 115
warrior poetry, Old English, 142, 143, 144, 145
warrior terminology, 9, 135-50 *passim*
wealh, 121
wergeld, 56, 124
West Saxons, 90, 128
Westminster Abbey, 13, 131
Whitby, Northumbria, 87; Synod of, 6, 40, 77, 87-89, 92, 164
Whithorn, Galloway, 64 n. 4, 71, 73, 78
Widsith, 33
Wiglaf, 44, 47
Wilda, Wilhelm E., 49, 51, 55
Wilfaresdun, 37, 42
Wilfrid, bishop of Ripon, 88
William I, king of England and duke of Normandy, 12-24 *passim*, 29, 122, 154
William of Jumièges, *Gesta Normannorum Ducum*, 15, 16, 17, 21, 23, 24
William of Malmesbury, 14
William of Poitiers, *Gesta Guillelmi*, 12 n. 4, 15-19 *passim*, 21, 23, 24
wills, Anglo-Saxon, 123, 125, 129, 130, 156; Old English, 36
Winchester, Hampshire, 121
Winchester School of Illumination, 7 n. 26
Worcester, abbey of, 131
Wormald, Patrick, 40
Wrenn, C. L., 28-29, 31
writs, Anglo-Saxon, 33
Wulfnoth, hostage of William, duke of Normandy, 17
Wulfstan II, archbishop of York, 6 n. 20, 33, 34, 92, 121, 157

York, Anonymous Chronicler of, 21